Italian for Travelers

Fodor's LIVING LANGUAGE®

Italian
for
Travelers

Fodor's Travel Publications New York, Toronto, London, Sydney, Auckland

AUSTRIA

SWITZERLAND

TRENTINO-ALTO ADIGE

FRIULI-VENEZIA GIULIA

SLOV

Lake Maggiore

Lake Como

Lake Garda

THE DOLOMITES

VENICE

Trieste

Mt. Blanc

VALLE D'AOSTA

ALPI

Milan

Padua

Adige

Venice

Golfo di Venezia

Turin

Po

LOMBARDY

PIEMONTE

ALPI

LIGURIA

Parma

Po

Bologna

Ravenna

Rimini

FRANCE

Genoa

EMILIA-ROMAGNA

Florence

SAN MARINO

San Remo

MONACO

Pisa

Arno

Livorno

TUSCANY

Siena

THE MARCHES

Ancona

Ligurian Sea

Perugia

Assisi

UMBRIA

Pes

Elba

ABRUZZI

Corsica

Tiber

Rome

LAZIO

M

Olbia

Naples

Sassari

Sorrento

Capri

A

SARDINIA

Tyrrhenian Sea

Cagliari

Mediterranean Sea

Palermo

Trapani

SICILY

ALGERIA

TUNISIA

Tunis

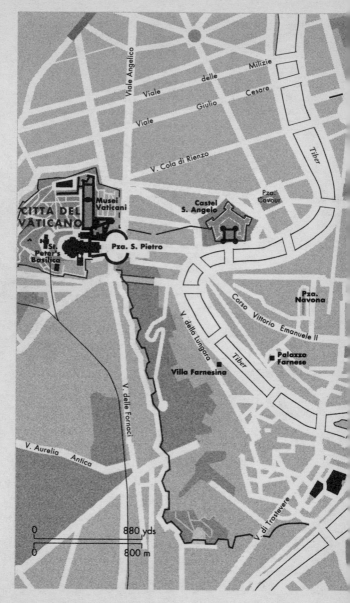

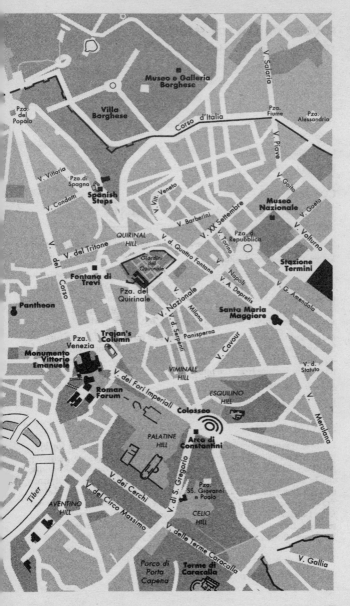

FODOR'S ITALIAN FOR TRAVELERS

EDITORS: Emmanuelle Morgen, Christopher Warnasch

Contributors: Patricia Rucidlo, George Semler, and Joseph Sofia.

Editorial Production: Marina Padakis

Maps: David Lindroth, *cartographer;* Rebecca Baer and Robert P. Blake, *map editors*

Design: Guido Caroti, *cover and interior designer;* Jolie Novak, Melanie Marin, *photo editors;* Kayley LeFaiver, *graphics*

Cover Photo: Bob Krist

Production/Manufacturing: Pat Ehresmann

SPECIAL SALES

Fodor's Travel Publications are available at special discounts for bulk purchases for sales promotions or premiums. Special editions, including personalized covers, excerpts of existing guides, and corporate imprints, can be created in large quantities for special needs. For more information, contact your local bookseller or write to Special Markets, Fodor's Travel Publications, 1745 Broadway, New York, NY 10019. Inquiries from Canada should be directed to your local Canadian bookseller or sent to Random House of Canada, Ltd., Marketing Department, 2775 Matheson Boulevard East, Mississauga, Ontario L4W 4P7. Inquiries from the United Kingdom should be sent to Fodor's Travel Publications, 20 Vauxhall Bridge Road, London SW1V 2SA, England.

PRINTED IN THE UNITED STATES OF AMERICA

10 9 8 7 6 5

CONTENTS

PREFACE

You don't need to know Italian to get along in the Italian-speaking world. The hundreds of Italian phrases in this guide will see you through almost every situation you encounter as a tourist, from asking for directions at the start of your trip to conversing in a bar at the end. To make yourself understood, all you have to do is read the phonetics that appear after each expression, just as you would any English sentence. You'll come closer to approximating Italian sounds if you study the pronunciation guide at the beginning of the book, and you can really polish your speech with *Fodor's Italian for Travelers* cassette or CD, on which native speakers pronounce the guide's key Italian dialogues. The boldfaced words and phrases in this book are those that are recorded on the audio supplement. The recordings also contain other key words and phrases that appear in bold. You will hear most of these expressions first in English, then in Italian. If you are more likely to encounter an expression in Italian first—an item on a menu, or questions such as "Are you here on vacation?"—you will hear the expression first in Italian, then in English.

If you want to understand the structure of the language and begin to learn it on your own, check out the grammar chapter, Chapter 16. Additionally, a two-way 1,600-word dictionary at the end references all the key words in the book.

To help you get the most out of your trip, read the travel tips and cultural information about Italy interspersed throughout the chapters. You'll find, among other things, traditional Italian menu items, bank and store hours, metric conversion tables, and federal holidays, all gathered by Fodor's expert resident-writers.

Before you start chatting away, be sure to familiarize yourself with the table of contents on the previous pages, so that you know where to quickly find phrases and information when you need them.

Buon Viaggio! [bwohn VYAH-joh] Have a good trip!

ABOUT THE ITALIAN LANGUAGE

Italian, like French, Spanish, Portuguese, and Romanian, developed from the spoken Latin of the Roman Empire, and today it resembles Latin more than any other Romance language. Yet Italy was one of the latest European countries to adopt a national language.

For centuries after the collapse of the Roman Empire, the peninsula's independently governed city-states, each with its own distinct dialect, vied for power and dominance. The city-states' dialects differed so much that people from different regions could not understand each other. In written texts, respectable writers and scholars only used Latin, but by the 13th century only a very small minority could read and speak Latin. More and more influential thinkers, and especially those opposed to papal rule and literary dominance, began to call for the establishment of a national language that the greater population could both speak and read.

La questione della lingua, the question of language, evolved into a widespread political debate. There were the papists who believed in the purity and sanctity of Latin, the literary language, and there were the anti-papists, a minority, who believed in the clout and usefulness of the vulgar tongue. The latter group, which sought to select and codify a common language, was made up of intellectuals for the most part associated with universities throughout the country. These universities could not agree which dialect should predominate. And in any case, papal authority refused to recognize any works written in dialect or their authors.

One city-state, Tuscany, expanded its power and influence, and consequently the Tuscan dialect prevailed as well. In the early 14th century, the Tuscan city of Florence was an unchallenged cultural center, and it attracted many progressive thinkers and anti-papal imperialists. Once Dante (1265–1321), Petrarch (1304–1374), and Boccaccio (1313–1375) emerged with their influential works written in Tuscan, the dialect closest in morphology to the original Latin, the authority of the language became unquestionable. The groundwork for establishing a national language was complete.

1

Widespread recognition of the new language helped to glue the fractured country together. After the reunification of the Italian city-states in 1861, the government began an aggressive campaign to promote a nationwide system of education, where all classes were taught in the national language. Regional dialects remain strong in Italy, but 90% of the population or more can speak and understand what is considered proper Italian, the language which developed from Dante's Tuscan.

You'll find today's Italian relatively easy to speak and understand. Italian language teachers love to remind their students that the language is completely phonetic, meaning that you say it exactly the way it is spelled. You will likely hear the difference in accents from north to south, but ask an Italian to speak *piano, piano,* and he or she will most certainly slow down and enunciate so that you may better understand. Italians have another way of expressing themselves, too: with gestures. Through the careful use of eyes, hands, and even arms, whole conversations can be conducted without saying anything. So don't be afraid to sign out what you mean in a sort of charade when you need to get your point across. Remember, most of the people you meet will welcome even your most halting attempts to use their language.

PRONUNCIATION GUIDE

Each English word or phrase in this book is presented with an Italian translation. An easy-to-follow phonetic transcription guides you to the correct pronunciation of the Italian word. You do not need any previous knowledge of Italian. Just read the phonetics as you would read English and you will be speaking comprehensible Italian.

You may use this phrasebook by itself, but the *Italian for Travelers* cassettes or CDs will help you learn how to pronounce words more accurately. Just listen and repeat after the native speakers.

PRONUNCIATION CHART

The pronunciation chart below is your guide to the phonetic transcriptions used in this book. With practice, you will become more and more familiar with these sounds. Eventually, you will be able to read Italian words without the help of this guide. Three points should be emphasized about pronouncing Italian:

1. Italian spelling is more consistent than English spelling, and therefore it is easier to tell how a word should be pronounced, once you learn the sounds.

2. Pay special attention to the vowel sounds. They vary from English pronunciations. It is crucial to learn the Italian vowel pronunciations to make yourself understood.

3. Italian vowels are more flat than in English. The *o* sound, for instance, does not carry the *w* sound that usually accompanies it in English.

In this phonetic system, the stressed syllables are capitalized.

Vowels

Italian Spelling	Approximate Sound in English	Phonetic Symbol	Example (Phonetic Transcription)
a	father	ah	banana (bah-NAH-nah)
e	met	eh	breve (BREH-veh)
i	machine	ee	vino (VEE-noh)
o	hope	oh	moto (MOH-toh)
u	rule	oo	fumo (FOO-moh)

Vowel Combinations

Diphthongs A diphthong is a double vowel combination that produces a single sound. Here is a list of frequent diphthongs and their pronunciations:

Italian Spelling	Approximate Sound in English	Phonetic Symbol	Example (Phonetic Transcription)
ai	ripe	ahy	daino (DAHY-noh)
au	now	ow	auto (OW-toh)
ei	may	ay	sei (SAY)
eu	—	ehoo	neutro (NEHOO-troh)
ia	yarn	yah	italiano (ee-tahl-YAH-noh)
ie	yet	yeh	miele (MYEH-leh)
io	yodel	yoh	campione (kahm-PYOH-neh)
iu	you	yoo	fiume (FYOO-meh)
oi	soy	oy	poi (poy)
ua	wand	wah	quando (KWAHN-doh)
ue	wet	weh	questo (KWEH-stoh)
uo	war	woh	suono (SWOH-noh)
ui	sweet	wee	guido (GWEE-doh)

Words that begin, incorporate, or end in *cia, cie, cio, ciu, gia, gie, gio, giu, scia, scie, scio,* or *sciu* are pronounced as follows: if the *i* is stressed, the two vowels are pronounced separately as in *farmacia* (fahr-mah-CEE-ah), *bugia* (boo-GEE-ah), *scia* (SHEE-ah). If the *i* is not stressed, follow this chart for pronunciation:

Italian Spelling	Phonetic Symbol	Example (Phonetic Transcription)
cia	chah	ciambella (<u>chah</u>m-BEHL-lah)
cie	cheh	cielo (<u>CHEH</u>-loh)
cio	choh	cioccolata (<u>choh</u>-koh-LAH-tah)
ciu	choo	ciuffo (<u>CHOO</u>F-foh)
gia	jah	giacca (<u>JAH</u>K-kah)
gie	jeh	ciliegie (chee-LYEH-<u>jeh</u>)
gio	joh	giovane (<u>JOH</u>-vah-neh)
giu	joo	giusto (<u>JOO</u>-stoh)
scia	shah	fasciare (fah-<u>SHAH</u>-reh)
scie	sheh	scienza (<u>SHEHN</u>-tsah)
scio	shoh	sciopero (<u>SHOH</u>-peh-roh)
sciu	shoo	sciupare (<u>shoo</u>-PAH-reh)

Hiatus A hiatus is a double vowel combination whose sounds are pronounced separately, rather than elided.

Italian Spelling	Example (Phonetic Transcription)
ae	maestro (m<u>ah</u>-<u>EH</u>-stroh)
au	paura (p<u>ah</u>-<u>OO</u>-rah)
ea	reato (r<u>eh</u>-<u>AH</u>-toh)
ia	bugia (boo-<u>JEE</u>-<u>ah</u>)
oa	boato (b<u>oh</u>-<u>AH</u>-toh)
oe	poeta (p<u>oh</u>-<u>EH</u>-tah)
ue	bue (B<u>OO</u>-<u>eh</u>)

Identical Vowels Any same two vowels must be pronounced separately, with the stress on the first vowel:

Italian Spelling	Example (Phonetic Transcription)
ee	idee (ee-DEH-eh)
ii	addii (ahd-DEE-ee)
oo	zoo (DZOH-oh)

Triphthongs A triphthong is a combination of three vowels:

Italian Spelling	Example (Phonetic Transcription)
aia	baia (BAH-yah)
aio	saio (SAH-yoh)
iei	miei (mee-AY)
uio	buio (BOO-yoh)
uoi	buoi (boo-OY)

Consonants

Italian Spelling	Approximate Sound in English
b/d/f/k/l/m/n/p/q/t/v	similar to English

Italian Spelling	Approximate Sound in English	Phonetic Symbol	Example (Phonetic Transcription)
c (before e/i)	chin	ch	cena (CHEH-nah) cibo (CHEE-boh)
c (before a/o/u)	catch	k	caffè (kahf-FEH) conto (KOHN-toh) cupola (KOO-poh-lah)
ch (with e/i)	can	k	amiche (ah-MEE-keh) chilo (KEE-loh)
g (before e/i)	jelly	j	gente (JEHN-teh) gita (JEE-tah)
g (before a/o/u)	gold	g	gala (GAH-lah) gondola (GOHN-doh-lah) gusto (GOO-stoh)

gh	get	g	spaghetti (spah-GET-tee) ghiotto (GYOHT-toh)
	ghost	gh	funghi (FOON-ghee)
gl (plus vowel followed by consonant)	globe	gl	globo (GLOH-boh) negligente (neh-glee-JEHN-teh)
gli	scallion	lyee	gli (lyee)
glia		lyah	famiglia (fah-MEE-lyah)
glie		lyeh	moglie (MOH-lyeh)
glio		lyoh	aglio (AH-lyoh)
gn	canyon	ny	Bologna (Boh-LOH-nyah)
h	silent	—	hotel (oh-TEHL)
r	trilled	r	rumore (roo-MOH-reh)
s (generally)	set	s	pasta (PAH-stah)
s (between two vowels and before b/d/g/l/m/n/v/r)	zero	z	rosa (ROH-zah) sbaglio (ZBAH-lyoh)
sc (before e/i)	fish	sh	pesce (PEH-sheh) sci (shee)
sc (before a/o/u)	scout	sk	scala (SKAH-lah) disco (DEE-skoh)
sch (with e/i)	sky	sk	pesche (PEH-skeh) fischi (FEE-skee)
z (generally like ts)	pits	ts	zucchero (TSOOK-keh-roh) grazie (GRAH-tsyeh)
z (sometimes like dz)	toads	dz	zingaro (DZEEN-gah-roh) zanzara (dzahn-DZAH-ra-h)

7

Double Consonants

All consonants, except h, can be doubled. They have a much more forceful sound than single consonants. The sound is slightly prolonged. Note the difference in pronunciation between single and double consonants:

nono (NOH-<u>n</u>oh) and **nonno** (NOH<u>N</u>-noh)

fato (FAH-<u>t</u>oh) and **fatto** (FAH<u>T</u>-toh)

babbo (BAH<u>B</u>-<u>b</u>oh)

mamma (MAH<u>M</u>-<u>m</u>ah)

gatto (GAH<u>T</u>-toh)

ELISION

Certain words, especially articles and prepositions, drop the final vowel when the next sound begins with a vowel:

lo studente (loh stoo-DEHN-teh)

but **l'amico** (lah-MEE-koh)

una matita (OO-nah mah-TEE-tah)

but **un'amica** (oo-nah-MEE-kah)

di Francia (dee FRAHN-chah)

but **d'Italia** (dee-TAH-lyah)

Stress

Italian words are usually (but not always) stressed on the next-to-the-last syllable. An accent grave (`) is only used when the stress is on the final vowel of a word, such as *città* (cheet-TAH), *falò* (fah-LOH), *caffè* (kahf-FEH).

Capitals

Many words that are capitalized in English are not in Italian. Days, months, seasons, proper adjectives (except when used as plural nouns, e.g., the Italians) and titles such as Mr., Mrs., Miss, Dr., and Prof.:

Sunday	domenica (doh-MEH-nee-kah)
January	gennaio (jehn-NAH-yoh)
Spring	la primavera (lah pree-mah-VEH-rah)

| She is Italian. | È italiana. (eh ee-tah-LYAH-nah) |
| Prof. Rossi | Il prof. Rossi. (eel proh-fehs-SOHR ROHS-see) |

Italian Alphabet

The Italian alphabet has twenty-one letters plus five found in foreign words:

A ah	G jee	N EHN-neh	S EHS-seh
B bee	H AHK-kah	O oh	T tee
C chee	I ee	P pee	U oo
D dee	L EHL-leh	Q koo	V vee
E eh	M EHM-meh	R EHR-reh	Z DZEH-tah
F EHF-feh			

Foreign Letters

J ee LOON-gah	W DOHP-pyah voo	Y ee GREH-kah (or)
K KAHP-pah	X eeks	EEP-see-lohn

1 APPROACHING PEOPLE

COURTESY

Please.	Per piacere.	pehr pyah-CHEH-reh
	(or) Per favore.	pehr fah-VOH-reh
Thank you.	Grazie.	GRAH-tsyeh
You're welcome.	Prego.	PREH-goh
I'm sorry.	Mi dispiace.	mee dee-SPYAH-cheh
Sorry (excuse me).	Scusi.	SKOO-zee
Excuse me (may I get through?).	Permesso.	pehr-MEHS-soh
It doesn't matter.	Non importa.	nohn eem-POHR-tah
	(or) Di niente.	dee NYEHN-teh

GREETINGS

Good morning.	Buon giorno.	bwon JOHR-noh
Good afternoon (to a group.)	Buon pomeriggio.	bwon poh-meh-REE-joh
Good evening.	Buona sera.	bwoh-nah SEH-rah
Good night.	Buona notte.	bwoh-nah NOHT-teh
Good-bye (formal).	Arrivederci.*	ahr-ree-veh-DEHR-chee
Hello/Good-bye (informal).	Ciao.	chow
See you soon.	A presto.	ah PREH-stoh
See you later.	A più tardi.	ah pyoo TAHR-dee
See you tomorrow.	A domani.	ah doh-MAH-nee
Let's go!	Andiamo!	ahn-DYAH-moh!

*ArrivederLa should be used when addressing a single person formally.

QUESTION WORDS

Who?	Chi?	kee?
What?	Che cosa?	keh KOH-sah
Why?	Perché?	pehr-KEH?
When?	Quando?	KWAHN-doh?

Where?	Dove?	DOH-veh?
How?	Come?	KOH-meh?
How much?	Quanto?	KWAHN-toh?

ASKING FOR HELP

Excuse me,	Mi scusi,	mee SKOO-zee,
_Sir.	_signore.	_see-NYOH-reh
_Madam/Mrs.	_signora.	_see-NYOH-rah
_Miss/Ms.	_signorina.	_see-nyoh-REE-nah
Do you speak English?	Parla inglese?	PAHR-lah een-GLEH-zeh?
Do you understand English?	Capisce l'inglese?	kah-PEE-sheh leen-GLEH-zeh?
Yes./No.	Sì./No.	see/noh
I'm sorry.	Mi scusi. (or) Mi dispiace.	mee SKOO-zee mee dee-SPYAH-cheh
I am a tourist.	Sono turista.	SOH-noh too-REE-stah
I don't speak Italian.	Non parlo italiano.	nohn PAHR-loh ee-tah-LYAH-noh
I speak very little.	Lo parlo poco.	loh PAHR-loh POH-koh
I understand a little.	Capisco un po'.	kah-PEE-skoh oon poh
Please speak more slowly.	Per favore, parli più adagio.	pehr fah-VOH-reh, PAHR-lee pyoo ah-DAH-joh
Please repeat.	Per favore, ripeta.	pehr fah-VOH-reh, ree-PEH-tah

---

*In Italian, adjectives agree in gender and number with the nouns they modify. *Desolato* is the masculine form and *desolata* is the feminine form. Herein, the feminine endings will appear in parentheses.

**Although there are a few exceptions (*turista*, for example), in Italian most nouns and adjectives end in -o in the masculine singular and in -a in the feminine singular. There are also several nouns ending in -e that are either masculine or feminine singular. The gender has to be learned. In the plural, -o becomes -i, -a becomes -e, and -e becomes -i for both genders. See also Chapter 15, "Grammar in Brief," regarding the gender and number of nouns and adjectives.

May I ask a question?	Posso fare una domanda?	POHS-soh FAH-reh OO-nah doh-MAHN-dah?
Could you please help me?	Può aiutarmi, per favore?	pwoh ah-yoo-TAHR-mee, pehr fah-VOH-reh?
Okay./Sure.	D'accordo.	dahk-KOHR-doh
Of course.	Certamente.	cher-tah-MEHN-teh
Where is . . . ?	Dov'è . . . ?	doh-VEH?
Where is the bathroom?	Dov'è la toilette?***	doh-VEH lah twah-LEHT?
Thank you very much.	Molte grazie. (or) Mille grazie.	MOHL-teh GRAH-tsyeh (or) MEEL-leh GRAH-tsyeh

***Toilette, or *il gabinetto*, refers to public bathrooms. At someone's home, you would ask "*Dov'è il bagno?*" (doh-VEH eel BAH-nyoh?)

EMERGENCIES

Look!	Guardi!	GWAHR-dee!
Listen!	Ascolti! (or) Senta!	ah-SKOHL-tee! SEHN-tah!
Watch out!	Attenzione!	aht-tehn-TSYOH-neh!
Fire!	Al fuoco!	ahl FWOH-koh!
Help!	Aiuto!	ah-YOO-toh!
Stop!	Fermo! (or) Alt!	FEHR-moh! ahlt!
Stop him!	Fermatelo!	fehr-MAH-teh-loh!
Thief!	Al ladro!	ahl LAH-droh!
Call the police!	Chiami la polizia!	KYAH-mee lah poh-lee-TSEE-oh!
Call the fire department!	Chiami i pompieri!	KYAH-mee ee pohm-PYEH-ree!
I'm sick!	Sto male!	stoh MAH-leh!
Call a doctor!	Chiami un dottore!	KYAH-mee oon doht-TOH-reh!
It's an emergency!	È un'emergenza!	eh oo-neh-mehr-JEHN-tsah!

I'm lost!	Mi sono perso!	mee SOH-noh PEHR-soh!
Can you help me?	Mi può aiutare?	mee PWOH ah-yoo-TAH-reh?
Leave me alone!	Mi lasci in pace!	mee LAH-shee een PAH-cheh
Someone/They stole my . . .	Mi hanno rubato . . .	mee AHN-noh roo-BAH-to . . .
_camera.	_la macchina fotografica.	_lah MAHK-kee-nah foh-toh-GRAH-fee-kah
_handbag.	_la borsetta.	_lah bohr-SEHT-tah
_money.	_i soldi.	_ee SOHL-dee
_suitcase.	_la valigia.	_lah vah-LEE-jah
_wallet.	_il portafoglio.	_eel pohr-tah-FOH-lyoh
_watch.	_l'orologio.	_loh-roh-LOH-joh
I've lost my . . .	Ho perso . . .	oh PEHR-soh . . .
_car keys.	_le chiavi della macchina.	_leh KYAH-vee DEHL-lah MAHK-kee-nah
_credit cards.	_le carte di credito.	_leh KAHR-teh dee KREH-dee-toh

2 THE BASICS

COLORS

red	rosso	ROHS-soh
yellow	giallo	JAHL-loh
green	verde	VEHR-deh
blue	azzurro	ah-TSOO-roh
white	bianco	BYAHN-koh
brown	marrone	mah-ROH-neh
orange	arancione	ah-rahn-CHOH-neh
purple	viola	VYOH-lah
black	nero	NEH-roh
gold	dorato	doh-RAH-toh
silver	argento	ahrr-JEHN-toh

NUMBERS AND QUANTITIES

Take the time to learn how to count in Italian. You will find that knowing the numbers will make everything easier during your trip.

Cardinal Numbers

0	zero	DZEH-roh
1	uno	OO-noh
2	due	DOO-eh
3	tre	treh
4	quattro	KWAHT-troh
5	cinque	CHEEN-kweh
6	sei	SEH-ee
7	sette	SEHT-teh
8	otto	OHT-toh
9	nove	NOH-veh
10	dieci	DYEH-chee

11	undici	OON-dee-chee
12	dodici	DOH-dee-chee
13	tredici	TREH-dee-chee
14	quattordici	kwaht-TOHR-dee-chee
15	quindici	KWEEN-dee-chee
16	sedici	SEH-dee-chee
17	diciassette	dee-chahs-SEHT-teh
18	diciotto	dee-CHOHT-toh
19	diciannove	dee-chahn-NOH-veh
20	venti	VEHN-tee
21	ventuno	vehn-TOO-noh
22	ventidue	vehn-tee-DOO-eh
23	ventitrè	vehn-tee-TREH
24	ventiquattro	vehn-tee-QWAHT-troh
25	venticinque	vehn-tee-CHEEN-kweh
26	ventisei	vehn-tee-SAY
27	ventisette	vehn-tee-SEHT-teh
28	ventotto	vehn-TOHT-toh
29	ventinove	vehn-tee-NOH-veh
30	trenta	TREHN-tah
40	quaranta	kwah-RAHN-tah
50	cinquanta	cheen-KWAHN-tah
60	sessanta	sehs-SAHN-tah
70	settanta	seht-TAHN-tah
80	ottanta	oh-TAHN-tah
90	novanta	noh-VAHN-tah
100	cento	CHEHN-toh
101	centouno	chehn-toh-OO-noh
102	centodue	chehn-toh-DOO-eh
110	centodieci	chehn-toh-DYEH-chee
120	centoventi	chehn-toh-VEHN-tee
200	duecento	dweh-CHEHN-toh

300	trecento	treh-CHEHN-toh
400	quattrocento	kwaht-troh-CHEHN-toh
500	cinquecento	cheen-kweh-CHEHN-toh
600	seicento	say-CHEHN-toh
700	settecento	seht-teh-CHEHN-toh
800	ottocento	oh-toh-CHEHN-toh
900	novecento	noh-veh-CHEHN-toh
1,000 (1.000)*	**mille**	**MEEL-leh**
1,100	millecento	meel-leh-CHEHN-toh
1,200	milleduecento	meel-leh-dweh-CHEHN-toh
2,000	**duemila**	**dweh-MEE-lah**
3,000	tremila	treh-MEE-lah
10,000	diecimila	dyeh-chee-MEE-lah
50,000	cinquantamila	cheen-kwahn-tah-MEE-lah
100,000	centomila	chehn-toh-MEE-lah
1,000,000	un milione	oon mee-LYOH-neh
1,000,000,000	un miliardo	oon mee-LYAHR-doh

*The plural of *mille* is *mila*. In Italian, the use of commas and decimal points are the reverse of how they are used in English. For example, 10,000 would be written 10.000, and 5.4 would be written 5,4 and pronounced "CHEEN-kweh VEER-goh-lah KWAHT-troh."

Ordinal Numbers*

first	primo	PREE-moh
second	secondo	seh-KOHN-doh
third	terzo	TEHR-tsoh
fourth	quarto	KWAHR-toh
fifth	quinto	KWEEN-toh
sixth	sesto	SEH-stoh
seventh	settimo	seht-TEE-moh

*Ordinal numbers agree in gender with the nouns they modify. For example, *la Quinta Strada* (lah KWEEN-tah STRAH-dah), Fifth Avenue, and *le prime notizie* (leh PREE-meh noh-TEE-tsyeh), the first news.

eighth	ottavo	oht-TAH-voh
ninth	nono	NOH-noh
tenth	decimo	DEH-chee-moh
eleventh	undicesimo	oon-dee-CHEH-zee-moh
twentieth	ventesimo	vehn-TEH-zee-moh
hundredth	centesimo	chehn-TEH-zee-moh

Quantities

once	una volta	OO-nah VOHL-tah
twice	due volte	DOO-eh VOHL-teh
whole	intero	een-TEH-roh
half	mezzo	MEHD-dzoh
half of	metà di	meh-TAH dee
a half hour	mezz'ora	mehd-DZOH-rah
a third	un terzo	oon TEHR-tsoh
a quarter	un quarto	oon KWAHR-toh
two-thirds	due terzi	DOO-eh TEHR-tsee
percent	percento	pehr-CHEHN-toh
a lot of	molto	MOHL-toh
a little	poco	POH-koh
a little of	un po' di	oon POH dee
a few	alcuni	ahl-KOO-nee
half a kilo of	mezzo chilo di	MEHD-dzoh KEE-loh dee
enough	abbastanza	ahb-bah-STAHN-tsah
That's enough!	Basta!	BAH-stah
too much	troppo	TROHP-poh
too little	troppo poco	TROHP-poh POH-koh
a glass of	un bicchiere di	oon beek-KYEH-reh dee
a cup of	una tazza di	OO-nah TAHT-tsah dee
a dozen of	una dozzina di	OO-nah dohd-DZEE-nah dee

DAYS, MONTHS, AND SEASONS

Days of the Week	Giorni della settimana	JOHR-nee DEHL-lah seht-tee-MAH-nah
What day is it today?	Che giorno è oggi?	keh JOHR-noh eh OHD-jee?
Today is . . .	Oggi è . . .	OHD-jee eh . . .
_Monday.	_lunedì.	_loo-neh-DEE
_Tuesday.	_martedì.	_mahr-teh-DEE
_Wednesday.	_mercoledì.	_mehr-koh-leh-DEE
_Thursday.	_giovedì.	_joh-veh-DEE
_Friday.	_venerdì.	_veh-nehr-DEE
_Saturday.	_sabato.	_SAH-bah-toh
_Sunday.	_domenica.	_doh-MEH-nee-kah

Months of the Year	Mesi dell'anno	MEH-zee dehl-LAHN-noh
January	gennaio	jehn-NAH-yoh
February	febbraio	fehb-BRAH-yoh
March	marzo	MAHR-tsoh
April	aprile	ah-PREE-leh
May	maggio	MAHD-joh
June	giugno	JOO-nyoh
July	luglio	LOO-lyoh
August	agosto	ah-GOH-stoh
September	settembre	seht-TEHM-breh
October	ottobre	oht-TOH-breh
November	novembre	noh-VEHM-breh
December	dicembre	dee-CHEM-breh

Seasons	Le stagioni	leh stah-JOH-nee
spring	la primavera	lah pree-mah-VEH-rah
summer	l'estate	leh-STAH-teh
autumn	l'autunno	low-TOON-noh
winter	l'inverno	leen-VEHR-noh

THE DATE

What's today's date?	Quanti ne abbiamo oggi?	KWAHN-tee neh ahb-BYAH-moh OHD-jee?
Today is . . .	Oggi è . . .	OHD-jee eh . . .
_January 29, 2003.	_il ventinove gennaio duemila e tre.	_eel vehn-tee-NOH-veh jehn-NAH-yoh DOO-eh-MEE-la eh TREH
_Monday, April 1.	_lunedì, primo aprile.*	_loo-neh-DEE PREE-moh ah-PREE-leh

*The ordinal number *il primo* (the first) is used for the first day of each month. Otherwise, regular cardinal numbers are used for dates.

HOLIDAYS

The following are public holidays in Italy—they are either religious or national. Be aware that when a holiday falls on a Thursday or on a Tuesday, many businesses close for a four-day weekend. This practice of filling the gap is called *fare il ponte* (FAH-reh eel POHN-teh), literally, building the bridge. Keep holidays in mind when planning your trip, because stores, public offices, and banks will be closed on the following dates:

January 1	Capodanno (kah-poh-DAHN-noh)	New Year's Day
January 6	Epifania (eh-pee-fah-NEE-ah)	Epiphany
March/April	Pasqua (PAH-skwah)	Easter
March/April	Lunedì dell'Angelo/ Pasquetta (loo-neh-DEE dehl-LAHN-jeh-loh/pah-SKWEHT-tah)	Easter Monday
April 25	Anniversario della Liberazione (ahn-nee-vehr-SAH-ryoh DEHL-lah lee-beh-rah-TSYOH-neh)	Liberation Day
May 1	Giornata del Lavoro (johr-nah-tah dehl lah-VOH-roh)	Labor Day

June 2	Festa della Repubblica (FEH-stah DEH-lah reh-POO-blee-kah)	
August 15	Assunzione/ Ferragosto (ahs-soon-TSYOH-neh/fehr-rah-GOH-stoh)	Assumption Day
November 1	Ognissanti (oh-nyees-SAHN-tee)	All Saints Day
November 4	Festa della Vittoria (FEH-stah DEH-lah vee-TOH-ryah)	Victory Day (WWI)
December 8	Immacolata Concezione (eem-mah-koh-LAH-tah kohn-cheh-TSYOH-neh)	Immaculate Conception
December 25	Natale (nah-TAH-leh)	Christmas
December 26	Santo Stefano (SAHN-toh STEH-fa-no)	Saint Steven
Best wishes!	Auguri!	ow-GOO-ree!
Merry Christmas!	Buon Natale!	bwohn nah-TAH-leh!
Happy New Year!	Buon Anno!	bwohn AHN-noh!
Happy Easter!	Buona Pasqua!	BWOH-nah PAH-skwah!
Happy holidays!	Buone vacanze!	BWOH-neh vah-KAHN-tseh!
Happy birthday!	Buon compleanno!	bwohn kohm-pleh-AHN-noh!
Happy name day!	Buon onomastico!	bwohn oh-noh-MAH-stee-koh!
Happy anniversary!	Buon anniversario!	bwohn ahn-nee-vehr-SAH-ryoh!
Congratulations!	Congratulazioni!	kohn-grah-too-lah-TSYOH-nee!

AGE

How old are you?	Quanti anni ha?	KWAHN-tee AHN-nee ah?
I'm 27.	Ho ventisette anni.	oh vehn-tee-SEHT-teh AHN-nee
How old is he/she?	Quanti anni ha lui/lei?	KWAHN-tee AHN-nee ah LOO-ee/lay?
He/she is 30.	Ha trent'anni.	ah trehn-TAHN-nee
I was born in . . . (year)	Sono nato(-a) nel . . .	SOH-noh NAH-toh (-tah) nehl . . .
I'm younger/older than he/she is.	Sono più giovane/vecchio (-a) di lui/lei.	SOH-noh pyoo JOH-vah-neh/VEHK-kyoh (-kyah) dee LOO-ee/lay
His/her birthday is March 6.	Il suo compleanno è il sei marzo.	eel SOO-oh kohm-pleh-AHN-noh eh eel say MAHR-tsoh

TELLING TIME AND EXPRESSIONS OF TIME

What time is it?	Che ora è? (or) Che ore sono?	keh OH-rah eh? keh OH-reh SOH-noh?
It's . . .	È . . .	eh . . .
_one o'clock.	_l'una.	_LOO-nah
_noon.	_mezzogiorno.	_mehd-dzoh-JOHR-noh
_midnight.	_mezzanotte.	_mehd-zah-NOHT-teh
It's . . .	Sono . . .	SOH-noh . . .
_2:00.	_le due.	_leh DOO-eh
_2:15.	_le due e un quarto.	_leh DOO-eh eh oon KWAHR-toh
_2:30.	_le due e mezzo (-a).	_leh DOO-eh eh MEHD-zoh (-ah)
_2:45.	_le due e tre quarti. (or) le tre meno un quarto.	_leh DOO-eh eh treh KWAHR-tee _leh treh MEH-noh oon KWAHR-toh
_2:50.	_le tre meno dieci.	_leh treh MEH-noh DYEH-chee

21

_3:10.	_le tre e dieci.	_leh treh eh DYEH-chee
_4:00 sharp.	_le quattro in punto.	_leh KWAHT-troh een PUHN-toh
_5:00 in the morning.	_le cinque di mattina.	_leh CHEEN-kweh dee maht-TEE-nah
_5:00 in the afternoon.	_le cinque del pomeriggio.	_leh CHEEN-kweh dehl poh-meh-REED-joh
_9:00 in the evening.	_le nove di sera.	_leh NOH-veh dee SEH-rah
_1:00 at night.	_l'una di notte.	_LOO-nah dee NOHT-teh
five minutes ago	cinque minuti fa	CHEEN-kweh mee-NOO-tee fah
in a half-hour	fra mezz'ora	frah mehdz OH-rah
before 9:00 a.m.	prima delle nove di mattina	PREE-mah DEHL-leh NOH-veh dee maht-TEE-nah
after 8:00 p.m.	dopo le otto di sera	DOH-poh leh OHT-toh dee SEH-rah
since 3:00 p.m.	dalle tre del pomeriggio	DAHL-leh treh dehl poh-meh-REED-joh
When does it begin?	Quando comincia?	KWAHN-doh koh-MEEN-chah?
He came . . .	È arrivato . . .	eh ahr-ree-VAH-toh . . .
_on time.	_in orario.	_een oh-RAH-ryoh
_early.	_in anticipo.	_een ahn-TEE-cee-poh
_late.	_in ritardo.	_een ree-TAHR-doh

The 24-Hour Clock

In Italy, as in most European countries, the 24-hour system (used by the military in the United States) is generally used for transportation schedules and theater times. To convert the P.M. hours to the 24-hour system, just add 12 to the regular time. For example, 3 P.M. is 12 plus 3, or 15 hours. The show you are planning to see might start at 7:30 P.M. or 19:30. Midnight, or 24 hours, is also expressed as 00:00, and minutes past midnight are expressed as 00:01, and so forth, until 01:00. The following chart may be used for quick reference:

1 A.M.	01:00 l'una	LOO-nah
2 A.M.	02:00 le due	leh DOO-eh
3 A.M.	03:00 le tre	leh treh
4 A.M.	04:00 le quattro	leh KWAHT-troh
5 A.M.	05:00 le cinque	leh CHEEN-kweh
6 A.M.	06:00 le sei	leh SEH-ee
7 A.M.	07:00 le sette	leh SEHT-teh
8 A.M.	08:00 le otto	leh OHT-toh
9 A.M.	09:00 le nove	leh NOH-veh
10 A.M.	10:00 le dieci	leh DYEH-chee
11 A.M.	11:00 le undici	leh OON-dee-chee
12 noon	12:00 le dodici (mezzogiorno)	leh DOH-dee-chee (mehd-zoh-JOHR-noh)
1 P.M.	13:00 le tredici	leh TREH-dee-chee
2 P.M.	14:00 le quattordici	leh kwaht-TOHR-dee-chee
3 P.M.	15:00 le quindici	leh KWEEN-dee-chee
4 P.M.	16:00 le sedici	leh SEH-dee-chee
5 P.M.	17:00 le diciassette	leh dee-chahs-SEHT-teh
6 P.M.	18:00 le diciotto	leh dee-CHOHT-toh
7 P.M.	19:00 le diciannove	leh dee-chahn-NOH-veh
8 P.M.	20:00 le venti	leh VEHN-tee
9 P.M.	21:00 le ventuno	leh vehn-TOO-noh
10 P.M.	22:00 le ventidue	leh vehn-tee-DOO-eh
11 P.M.	23:00 le ventitre	leh vehn-tee-TREH
12 midnight	24:00 le ventiquattro (mezzanotte)	leh vehn-tee-KWAHT-troh (mehd-zah-NOH-teh)

Expressions of Time

now	ora/adesso	OH-rah/ah-DEHS-soh
earlier	più presto/prima	pyoo PREH-stoh/PREE-mah
later	più tardi/dopo	pyoo TAHR-dee/DOH-poh
before	prima	PREE-mah
after	dopo	DOH-poh
soon	presto	PREH-stoh
once	una volta	OO-nah VOHL-tah
in the morning	di mattina	dee maht-TEE-nah

23

at noon	a mezzogiorno	ah mehd-dzoh-JOHR-noh
in the afternoon	di pomeriggio	dee poh-meh-REED-joh
in the evening	di sera	dee SEH-rah
at night	di notte	dee NOHT-teh
at midnight	a mezzanotte	ah mehd-dzah-NOHT-teh
yesterday	ieri	YEH-ree
today	oggi	OHD-jee
tomorrow	domani	doh-MAH-nee
the day before yesterday	l'altro ieri	LAHL-troh YEH-ree
the day after tomorrow	dopodomani	doh-poh-doh-MAH-nee
this week	questa settimana	KWEH-stah seht-tee-MAH-nah
next week	la settimana prossima	lah seht-tee-MAH-nah PROHS-see-mah
last week	la settimana scorsa	lah seht-tee-MAH-nah SKOHR-sah
every week	ogni settimana	OH-nyee seht-tee-MAH-nah
in a week (from now)	fra una settimana	frah OO-nah seht-tee-MAH-nah
in a week (actual time)	in una settimana	een OO-nah seht-tee-MAH-nah
every day	ogni giorno	OH-nyee JOHR-noh
in three days	fra tre giorni	frah treh JOHR-nee
two days ago	due giorni fa	DOO-eh JOHR-nee fah
on Saturday	sabato	SAH-bah-toh
on Saturdays	**il sabato**	**eel SAH-bah-toh**
on weekends	il fine settimana (or) il weekend	eel FEE-neh seht-tee-MAH-nah eel wee-KEHND

on weekdays	durante la settimana	doo-RAHN-teh lah seht-tee-MAH-nah
a working day	un giorno feriale	oon JOHR-noh feh-RYAH-leh
a day off (from work)	un giorno di permesso	oon JOHR-noh dee pehr-MEHS-soh
a day off (a free day)	un giorno libero	oon JOHR-noh LEE-beh-roh
in January	in gennaio	een jehn-NAH-yoh
last January	gennaio scorso	jehn-NAH-yoh SKOHR-soh
next January	gennaio prossimo	jehn-NAH-yoh PROHS-see-moh
each month	**ogni mese**	**OH-nyee MEH-zeh**
every month	tutti i mesi	TOOT-tee ee MEH-zee
since August	**da agosto**	**dah ah-GOH-stoh**
in summer	in estate	een eh-STAH-teh
this month	questo mese	KWEH-stoh MEH-zeh
last month	il mese scorso	eel MEH-zeh SKOHR-soh
next year	**l'anno prossimo**	**LAHN-noh PROHS-see-moh**
every year	ogni anno	OH-nyee AHN-noh
In what year . . .	In che anno . . .	een keh AHN-noh . . .
In 1990 . . .	Nel milleno-vecentono-vanta . . .	nehl MEEL-leh-noh-veh-CHEHN-toh-noh-VAHN-tah . . .
In the nineteenth century . . .	Nel diciannovesimo secolo . . .	nehl dee-chahn-noh-VEH-zee-moh SEH-koh-loh . . .
In the sixties . . .	Negli anni sessanta . . .	NEH-lyee AHN-nee sehs-SAHN-tah . . .

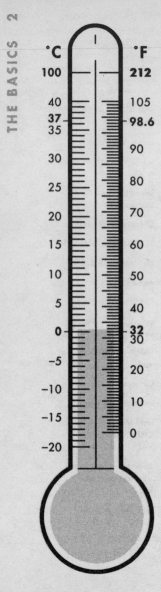

TEMPERATURE CONVERSIONS

In Italy, temperature is measured in degrees Celsius, or centigrade. To convert degrees Celsius into degrees Fahrenheit, use this formula:

To convert centigrade to Fahrenheit

$$\left(\frac{9}{5}\right)C° + 32 = F°$$

1. Divide by 5
2. Multiply by 9
3. Add 32

To convert Fahrenheit to centigrade

$$(F° - 32)\frac{5}{9} = C°$$

1. Subtract 32
2. Divide by 9
3. Multiply by 5

WEATHER

The protection provided by the Alps against the cold northern winds and the influence of Mediterranean and Adriatic seas moderate the harshness of winter and bless Italy with fairly mild climate. However, the weather varies a great deal according to the location. Around the Ligurian Riviera, the southern coasts, and Sicily, winter temperatures range from 50°F to 60°F (10°C to 15.5°C), whereas it is cold in northern Italy, especially in the Alps. In the Po Valley and the Apennines, winters are humid and foggy. Summers are hot and humid almost everywhere, but a pleasant breeze at the seaside mitigates the temperature there, while in the mountains the weather is pleasant and cool.

What's the weather today?	Che tempo fa oggi?	keh TEHM-poh fah OHD-jee?
It's a nice day.	Fa bel tempo.	fah behl TEHM-poh
It's a nasty day.	Fa brutto tempo. (or) . . . cattivo . . .	fah BROOT-toh TEHM-poh . . . kaht-TEE-voh . . .
It's raining.	Piove.	PYOH-veh
It's pouring.	Piove a catinelle.	PYOH-veh ah kah-tee-NEHL-leh
It's snowing.	Nevica.	NEH-vee-kah
It's . . .	Fa . . .	fah . . .
_cold.	_freddo.	_FREHD-doh
_cool.	_fresco.	_FREH-skoh
_hot.	_caldo.	_KAHL-doh
It's cloudy.	È nuvoloso.	eh-noo-voh-LOH-zoh
It's . . .	C'è . . .	cheh . . .
_foggy.	_nebbia.	_NEHB-byah
_sunny.	_il sole.	_eel SOH-leh
It's windy.	Tira vento.	TEE-rah VEHN-toh
What's the forecast for tomorrow?	Quali sono le previsioni del tempo di domani?	KWAH-lee SOH-noh leh preh-vee-ZYOH-nee dehl TEHM-poh dee doh-MAH-nee?
Is it going to rain?	Pioverà?	pyoh-veh-RAH?

27

3 AT THE AIRPORT

As a tourist, you should proceed through customs, *dogana* [doh-GAH-nah], as smoothly and quickly as airport security and the number of arriving passengers will allow. Most personal belongings are duty-free, however, tobacco products and alcohol over certain amounts are taxed.

When you're ready to leave Italy, remember that no products containing meat derivatives are allowed back into the United States. This means all those delicious cured meats you sampled must remain a wonderful culinary memory. No fresh fruits or vegetables are allowed either, and the only cheeses that are permitted entry are the hard ones such as parmesan and pecorino. If you're 21 and older, you may bring back $400 worth of souvenirs, including 1 liter of alcohol, duty-free. Residents of the United Kingdom don't pass through customs when returning from a trip spent wholly in the European Union. Canadian residents who have been out of Canada for more than seven days may return with C$500 worth of goods duty-free, or C$200 if they've been away less than 7 days (but more than 48 hours). Australian residents 18 and older may bring home A$400 worth of souvenirs, and New Zealand residents 17 and older may bring home NZ$700 worth of souvenirs.

DIALOGUE
Customs and Immigration (Controllo dei Passaporti)

Doganiere:	Buon giorno. Il passaporto, per favore.	bwohn JOHR-noh, eel pahs-sah-POHR-toh, pehr fah-VOH-reh
Turista:	Ecco il passaporto.	EHK-koh eel pahs-sah-POHR-toh
Doganiere:	È americana?	eh ah-meh-ree-KAH-nah?
Turista:	Sì, sono americana.	see, SOH-noh ah-meh-ree-KAH-nah
Doganiere:	Quanto tempo si trattiene?	KWAHN-toh TEHM-poh see traht-TYEH-neh?
Turista:	Resterò tre settimane.	reh-steh-ROH treh seht-tee-MAH-neh

Doganiere:	**Buona permanenza!**	BWOH-nah pehr-mah-NEHN-tsah!
Officer:	Good morning. May I see your passport, please?	
Tourist:	Here's my passport.	
Officer:	Are you American?	
Tourist:	Yes, I am American.	
Officer:	How long will you stay?	
Tourist:	I'll be here for three weeks.	
Officer:	Have a nice stay!	

CLEARING CUSTOMS

What is your nationality?	Di che nazionalità è?	dee keh nah-tsyoh-nah-lee-TAH eh?
I am American.	Sono americano (-a).	SOH-noh ah-meh-ree-KAH-noh(-nah)
What's your name?	**Come si chiama?**	KOH-meh see KYAH-mah?
My name is . . .	Mi chiamo . . .	mee KYAH-moh . . .
Where are you staying?	Dove alloggia?	DOH-veh ahl-LOHD-jah?
I am staying at the . . . Hotel.	Alloggio all'hotel . . .	ahl-LOHD-joh ahl-loh-TEHL . . .
Are you here on vacation?	È qui in vacanza?	eh kwee een vah-KAHN-tsah?
Yes, I am on vacation.	Sì, sono in vacanza.	see, SOH-noh een vah-KAHN-tsah
No, I am passing through.	No, sono di passaggio.	noh, SOH-noh dee pahs-SAHD-joh
I'm here on a business trip.	Sono in viaggio d'affari.	SOH-noh een VYAHD-joh dahf-FAH-ree
I'll be here . . .	Rimarrò . . .	ree-mahr-ROH . . .
_a few days.	_alcuni giorni.	_ahl-KOO-nee JOHR-nee

29

_a week.	_una settimana.	_OO-nah seht-tee-MAH-nah
_several weeks.	_parecchie settimane.	_pah-REHK-kyeh seht-tee-MAH-neh
_a month.	_un mese.	_oon MEH-zeh
Do you have anything to declare?	Ha qualcosa da dichiarare?	ah kwahl-KOH-zah dah dee-kyah-RAH-reh?
I have nothing to declare.	**Non ho niente da dichiarare.**	nohn oh NYEHN-teh dah dee-kyah-RAH-reh
Can you open your bag, please?	Può aprire la valigia, per cortesia?	pwoh ah-PREE-reh lah vah-LEE-jah, pehr kohr-teh-ZEE-ah?
Certainly.	Certamente.	chehr-tah-MEHN-teh
They are my personal effects.	Sono effetti personali.	SOH-noh ehf-FEHT-tee pehr-soh-NAH-lee
They are gifts.	Sono regali.	SOH-noh reh-GAH-lee
Do I have to pay duty?	**Devo pagare la dogana?**	**DEH-voh pah-GAH-reh lah doh-GAH-nah?**
Yes./No.	Sì./No.	see/noh
Have a nice stay!	Buona permanenza!	BWOH-nah pehr-mah-NEHN-tsah

LUGGAGE AND PORTERS

Porters are available at major airports and train stations. Baggage carts may be found at airports, however, they are rare at train stations. Porters charge a standard fee for each piece of baggage and expect a 50¢ tip or so.

I need . . .	**Ho bisogno di . . .**	oh bee-ZOH-nyoh dee . . .
_a porter.	_un portabagagli (*or*) un facchino.	_oon pohr-tah-bah-GAH-lyee oon fahk-KEE-noh
_a baggage cart.	_un carrello.	_oon kahr-REHL-loh
Here's my luggage.	Ecco il mio bagaglio.	EHK-koh eel MEE-oh bah-GAH-lyoh

Take my bags . . .	Porti le valigie . . .	POHR-tee leh vah-LEE-jeh . . .
_to the taxi.	_al taxi.	_ahl TAHK-see
_to the bus stop.	_alla fermata dell'autobus.	_AHL-lah fehr-MAH-tah dehl-OW-toh-boos
_to the luggage checkroom.	_al deposito bagagli.	_ahl deh-POH-zee-toh bah-GAH-lyee
_to the lockers.	_alla custodia automatica.	_AHL-lah koo-STOH dyah ow-toh-MAH-tee-kah
Please be careful!	**Faccia attenzione, per favore!**	**FAH-chah aht-tehn-TSYOH-neh, pehr fah-VOH-reh**
How much is it?	Quant'è?	kwahn-TEH?

AIRPORT TRANSPORTATION AND SERVICES

Do you know where . . . is?	Sa dov'è . . .	sah doh-VEH . . .
_Alitalia	_l'Alitalia?	_lah-lee-TAH-lyah?
_the information booth	_l'ufficio informazioni?	_luhf-FEE-choh een-fohr-mah-TSYOH-nee?
_the ticket counter	_la biglietteria?	_lah bee-lyeht-teh-REE-ah?
_the luggage check-in	_l'accettazione bagagli?	_lah-cheht-tah-TSY-OH-neh bah-GAH-lyee?
_the duty-free shop	_il negozio duty-free?	_eel neh-GOH-tsyoh duty-free?
_the currency exchange	_l'ufficio cambio?	_loof-FEE-choh KAHM-byoh?
_the lost baggage office	_l'ufficio oggetti smarriti?	_loof-FEE-choh ohd-JEHT-tee smahr-REE-tee?
_the car rental	_l'autonoleggio?	_low-toh-noh-LEHD-joh?
_the taxi stand	_la fermata dei taxi?	_lah fehr-MAH-tah day TAHK-see?

31

_the phone	_il telefono?	_eel teh-LEH-foh-noh?
_the travel agency	_l'agenzia viaggi?	_lah-jehn-TSEE-ah VYAHD-jee?
_the booking agency	_l'ufficio prenotazioni?	_luhf-FEE-choh preh-noh-tah-TSYOH-nee?

FLIGHT ARRANGEMENTS

Is there a direct flight to Rome?	C'è un volo diretto per Roma? (or) . . . senza scalo . . . ?	cheh oon VOH-loh dee-REHT-toh pehr ROH-mah? . . . SEHN-tsah SKAH-loh . . . ?
What time does it leave?	A che ora parte?	ah keh OH-rah PAHR-teh?
What time does the plane take off?	A che ora decolla l'aereo?	ah keh OH-rah deh-KOHL-lah lah-EH-reh-oh?
What's the flight number?	Qual è il numero del volo?	kwah-LEH eel NOO-meh-roh dehl VOH-loh?
What's the seat number?	Qual è il numero del posto?	kwah-LEH eel NOO-meh-roh dehl POH-stoh?
I would like . . . _a one-way ticket.	Vorrei . . . _un biglietto di sola andata.	vohr-RAY . . . _oon bee-LYEHT-toh dee SOH-lah ahn-DAH-tah
_a round-trip ticket.	_un biglietto di andata e ritorno.	_oon bee-LYEHT-toh dee ahn-DAH-tah eh ree-TOHR-noh
_a first-class ticket.	_di prima classe.	_dee PREE-mah KLAHS-seh
_a seat in tourist class.	_un posto in classe turistica.	_oon POH-stoh een KLAHS-seh too-REE-stee-kah
_a no-smoking section seat.	_un posto nella sezione non fumatori.	_oon POH-stoh NEHL-lah seh-TSYOH-neh nohn foo-mah-TOH-ree

_a window seat.	_un posto vicino al finestrino.	_oon POH-stoh vee-CHEE-noh ahl fee-neh-STREE-noh
_an aisle seat.	_un posto vicino al corridoio.	_oon POH-stoh vee-CHEE-noh ahl kohr-ree-DOH-yoh
_luggage tags.	_dei cartellini.	_day kahr-tehl-LEE-nee
This is my carry-on luggage.	**Questo è il mio bagaglio a mano.**	**KWEH-stoh eh eel MEE-oh bah-GAH-lyoh ah MAH-noh**
May I have my boarding pass?	Posso avere la carta d'imbarco?	POHS-soh ah-VEH-reh lah KAHR-tah deem-BAHR-koh?
What is the arrival time?	**A che ora si arriva?**	**ah keh OH-rah see ahr-REE-vah?**
What time will we land?	Quando atterriamo?	KWAHN-doh aht-tehr-RYAH-moh?
Do I need to change planes?	Devo cambiare aereo?	DEH-voh kahm-BYAH-reh ah-EH-reh-oh?
Can I make a connection in . . . for . . . ?	Posso prendere una coincidenza a . . . per . . . ?	POHS-soh PREHN-deh-reh OO-nah ko-een-chee-DEHN-tsah ah . . . pehr . . . ?
From what gate does the flight leave?	**Da che uscita parte il volo?**	**dah keh oo-SHEE-tah PAHR-teh eel VOH-loh?**
I would like to . . . my reservation.	Vorrei . . . la mia prenotazione.	vohr-RAY . . . lah MEE-ah preh-noh-tah-TSYOH-neh
_confirm	_confermare	_kohn-fehr-MAH-reh
_cancel	_annullare (or) cancellare	_ahn-nuhl-LAH-reh kahn-chehl-LAH-reh
_change	_cambiare	_kahm-BYAH-reh
I missed the plane.	Ho perso l'aereo.	oh PEHR-soh lah-EH-reh-oh
Will my ticket be good for the next flight?	Il biglietto è valido per il prossimo volo?	eel bee-LYEHT-toh eh VAH-lee-doh pehr eel PROHS-see-moh VOH-loh?

33

COMMON AIRPORT TERMS AND SIGNS

LINEE NAZIONALI	LEE-neh-eh nah-tsyoh-NAH-lee	National Airlines
LINEE INTERNAZIONALI	LEE-neh-eh een-tehr-nah-tsyoh-NAH-lee	International Airlines
VOLI NAZIONALI	VOH-lee nah-tsyoh-NAH-lee	Domestic Flights
VOLI INTERNAZIONALI	VOH-lee een-tehr-nah-tsyoh-NAH-lee	International Flights
PARTENZE	pahr-TEHN-tseh	Departures
ARRIVI	ahr-REE-vee	Arrivals
USCITA	oo-SHEE-tah	Departure Gate
TOELETTE	toh-eh-LEHT	Restroom(s)
UOMINI/SIGNORI	WOH-mee-nee/see-NYOH-ree	Men's Restroom
DONNE/SIGNORE	DOHN-neh/see-NYOH-reh	Women's Restroom

Aboard the Aircraft

VIETATO FUMARE	vyeh-TAH-toh foo-MAH-reh	No Smoking
ALLACCIARE LE CINTURE DI SICUREZZA	ahl-laht-CHAH-reh leh cheen-TOO-reh dee see-koo-REHTS-sah	Fasten Your Seat Belts

ABOUT THE CURRENCY

In Italy, the monetary unit is the *euro* (EH-oo-roh), which replaced the *lira* in January 2002. The euro is divided into 100 cents and is symbolized as €.

Coins: 1, 2, 5, 10, 20, and 50 *centesimi*; 1 and 2 euros.

Banknotes: 5, 10, 20, 50, 100, 200, and 500 euros.

You will find the best exchange rates at ATMs in the Cirrus and Plus networks and at banks, which are open weekdays between 8:30 AM and 1:30 PM and between 2:30 or 2:45 PM and 3:30 or 3:45 PM, with slight regional variations. You can also exchange money at some hotels and at exchange offices. Remember that you usually need your passport to change money at banks. At ATMs in Italy, you can use only four-digit PIN numbers; note that transaction fees may be higher than at home. Major credit cards are widely accepted. Make sure they have been programmed for use at ATMs if you want to use them to get cash advances.

CHANGING MONEY

Where is . . .	Dov'è . . .	doh-VEH . . .
_the nearest bank?	_la banca più vicina?	_lah BAHN-kah pyoo vee-CEE-nah?
_automatic cash machine?	_un bancomat?	_oon BAHN-koh-maht?
Where can I change . . .	Dove posso cambiare . . .	DOH-veh POHS-soh kam-BYAH-reh . . .
_some dollars?	_dei dollari?	_day DOHL-lah-ree?
_some money?	_dei soldi?	_day SOHL-dee?
_this check?	_questo assegno?	_KWEH-stoh ahs-SEH-nyoh?
Is the bank open?	È aperta la banca?	eh ah-PEHR-tah lah BAHN-kah?
No, it's closed.	No, è chiusa.	noh, eh KYOO-zah
Is there a currency exchange nearby?	C'è un ufficio di cambio qui vicino?	cheh oon oof-FEE-choh dee KAHM-byoh kwee vee-CHEE-noh?

I wish to cash a traveler's check.	Desidero cambiare un travellers cheque.	deh-ZEE-deh-roh kahm-BYAH-reh oon TREH-vehl-lehr check
Do you accept . . .	Accettate . . .	ah-cheht-TAH-teh . . .
_personal checks?	_assegni personali?	_ahs-SEH-nyee pehr-soh-NAH-lee?
_a money order?	_un vaglia?	_oon VAH-lyah?
What's the exchange rate?	Qual è il cambio?	kwah-LEH eel KAHM-byoh?
How much is the dollar worth today?	**Quanto vale il dollaro oggi?**	**KWAHN-toh VAH-leh eel DOHL-lah-roh OHD-jee?**
Do you need . . .	**Ha bisogno . . .**	**ah bee-ZOH-nyoh . . .**
_my identification card?	_della carta d'identità?	_DEHL-lah KAHR-tah dee-dehn-tee-TAH?
_my passport?	**_del passaporto?**	**_dehl pahs-sah-POHR-toh?**
_another document?	_di un altro documento?	_dee oon AHL-troh doh-koo-MEHN-toh?
Where do I sign?	**Dove firmo?**	**DOH-veh FEER-moh?**
Can you give me . . .	Può darmi . . .	pwoh DAHR-mee . . .
_large bills?	_banconote di grosso taglio?	_bahn-koh-NOH-teh dee GROHS-soh TAH-lyoh?
_small bills?	_banconote di piccolo taglio?	_bahn-koh-NOH-teh dee PEEK-koh-loh TAH-lyoh?
_some change?	_moneta spicciola? (or) spiccioli?	_moh-NEH-tah SPEET-choh-lah? SPEET-choh-lee?
_five ten-euro bills?	_cinque banconote da dieci euro.	_CEEN-kweh bahn-koh-NOH-teh dah DYEH-chee eh-OO-roh?
I want to send a telex to my bank.	Vorrei mandare un telex alla mia banca.	vohr-RAY mahn-DAH-reh oon TEH-lehks AHL-lah MEE-ah BAHN-kah

| Has my money arrived? | È arrivato il mio denaro? | eh ahr-ree-VAH-toh eel MEE-oh deh-NAH-roh? |

DIALOGUE   At the Bank (In Banca)

Cliente:	Vorrei cambiare mille dollari.	vohr-RAY kahm-BYAH-reh MEEL-leh DOHL-lah-ree
Cassiere:	Certamente. Il cambio oggi è a un euro. Sono mille euro.	cher-tah-MEHN-teh. eel KAHM-byoh OHD-jee eh ah oon eh-OO-roh. SOH-noh mee-leh EH-oo-roh.
Cliente:	Va bene. Ecco i travellers cheques.	vah BEH-neh. EHK-koh ee TREH-vehl-lehr checks
Cassiere:	Li firmi, per favore.	lee FEER-mee pehr fah-VOH-reh
Cliente:	D'accordo. Eccoli, e questo è il mio passaporto.	dahk-KOHR-doh. EHK-koh-lee, eh KWEH-stoh eh eel MEE-oh pahs-sah-POHR-toh
Cassiere:	Grazie. Ecco i Suoi soldi.	GRAH-tsyeh. EHK-koh ee soo-OY SOHL-dee

Customer:	I would like to change 1,000 dollars.
Teller:	Certainly, sir. The rate is one euro to the dollar today. That would be one thousand euros.
Customer:	Fine. Here are my traveler's checks.
Teller:	Would you please sign them?
Customer:	Of course. Here they are, and this is my passport.
Teller:	Thank you. Here's your money.

PAYING THE BILL

How much does it cost?	Quanto costa?	KWAHN-toh KOH-stah?
The bill, please.	Il conto, per favore.	eel KOHN-toh pehr fah-VOH-reh
How much do I owe you?	Quanto Le devo?	KWAHN-toh leh DEH-voh?
Is service included?	Il servizio è incluso?	eel sehr-VEE-tsyoh eh een-KLOO-soh?
This is for you.	Questo è per Lei.	KWEH-stoh eh pehr lay

TIPPING

Most restaurants include a service charge of about 15% on the bill, but you may tip your waiter with small change as well. If the menu reads *servizio e coperte a parte,* or "service not included," you should leave a 5%–10% tip.

At a hotel bar, tip about €.50 for each round or two of drinks, €.10 for drinks standing up in a bar or café and €.25 for table service. Tip restroom attendants €.20 and tip checkroom attendants €.30.

Railway and airport porters charge a fixed rate per suitcase that is usually posted. Tip an additional €.50 per person if the porter is very helpful. Tip taxi drivers 5%–10% (remember that cab drivers sometimes add extra charges for luggage and always add a surcharge at night and for pickups).

Give the *portiere* (concierge) about 15% of the bill, or €2.50–€5. Leave room-cleaning staff €.50 per day, or up to €5 per week; bellboys €1–€2 for carrying luggage; doormen €.50–€1 for calling a cab; and €.30–€.50 for valet or room service.

Barbers and hairdressers should be tipped €1–€4, depending on the services rendered.

EXPLORING ON FOOT

It is hard to dispute the old saying that the best way to see a city is to explore it on foot. Many guidebooks provide self-guided walking tours of the most interesting landmarks and areas in major cities such as Milan, Venice, Florence, Rome, and Naples. Handy little map guides to the smaller cities can be found at bookstores, newsstands, tobacco stores, train and bus stations, and all tourist offices. And of course most Italians are happy to give you directions. They are more likely to refer to distances in meters, *metri* (MEH-tree), than in blocks, or streets, *vie* (VEE-eh), since street patterns in Italian cities are usually twisty and irregular.

Excuse me, . . .	Scusi, . . .	SKOO-zee . . .
_sir	_signore	_see-NYOH-reh
_madam	_signora	_see-NYOH-rah
_miss	_signorina	_see-nyoh-REE-nah
Where is . . .	**Dov'è . . .**	**doh-VEH**
St. Peter's Square?	**Piazza San Pietro?**	**PYAH-tzah sahn PYEH-troh**
_the train station?	_la stazione?	_lah stah-TSYOH-neh?
_the bus stop?	_la fermata dell'autobus?	_lah fehr-MAH-tah dehl-OW-toh-boos?
_the subway?	_la metropolitana?	_lah meh-troh-poh-lee-TAH-nah?
_the ticket office?	_la biglietteria?	_lah bee-lyeht-teh-REE-ah?
Is it far?	**È lontano?**	**eh lohn-TAH-noh?**
How can I get there?	**Come ci si arriva?**	**KOH-meh chee see ahr-REE-vah?**
Where can I get a map of the city?	Dove posso trovare una pianta della città?	DOH-veh POHS-soh troh-VAH-reh OO-nah PYAHN-tah DEHL-lah cheet-TAH?
Where can I find this address?	**Dov'è questo indirizzo?**	**doh-VEH KWEH-stoh een-dee-REET-tsoh?**

I think I am lost.	Penso di essermi perso(-a).	PEHN-soh dee EHS-sehr-mee PEHR-zoh(ah)
Can you show me on my map?	Può mostrarmelo sulla pianta?	pwoh moh-STRAHR-meh-loh SUHL-lah PYAHN-tah?

Here are a few possible answers to your questions:

Sempre diritto.	SEHM-preh dee-REET-toh	It's straight ahead.
Giri a destra/a sinistra.	JEE-ree ah DEH-strah/ah see-NEE-strah.	Turn right/left.
È . . .	eh . . .	It's . . .
_laggiù.	_lahd-JOOH	_down there.
_dietro . . .	_DYEH-troh . . .	_behind . . .
_davanti a . . .	_dah-VAHN-tee ah . . .	_in front of . . .
_accanto a . . .	_ah-KAHN-toh ah . . .	_next to . . .
_al di là di . . .	_ahl dee lah dee . . .	_across . . .
_dopo . . .	_DOH-poh . . .	_after . . .
_vicino a . . .	_vee-CHEE-noh ah . . .	_near . . .
_lontano.	_lohn-TAH-noh	_far.
_oltre . . .	_OHL-treh . . .	_beyond . . .
_all'incrocio.	_ah-leen-KROH-choh	_at the intersection.
_all'angolo.	_ahl-LAHN-goh-loh	_at the corner.
_dopo il semaforo.	_DOH-poh eel seh-MAH-foh-roh	_beyond the traffic light.
Ha sbagliato strada.	ah sbah-LYAH-toh STRAH-dah	You're on the wrong road.
Non ci si può andare a piedi.	nohn chee see pwoh ahn-DAH-reh ah PYEH-dee	You can't get there on foot.

DIALOGUE On the Street (Per la Strada)

Turista:	Scusi, dov'è il museo?	SKOO-see, doh-VEH eel moo-ZEH-oh
Passante:	Non è lontano da qui. Prosegua per questa strada per altri cento metri e giri al primo semaforo a sinistra.	nohn eh lohn-TAH-noh dah kwee. proh-SEH-gwah pehr KWEH-stah STRAH-dah pehr AHL-tree chehn-toh MEH-tree eh JEE-ree ahl PREE-moh sel-MAH-foh-roh ah see-NEE-strah.
Turista:	Grazie. Allora posso andarci a piedi. Quanto tempo ci vuole?	GRAH-tsyeh. ahl-LOH-rah POHS-soh ahn-DAHR-chee ah PYEH-dee. KWAHN-toh TEHM-poh chee VOO-oh-leh?
Passante:	Ci vorranno cinque, dieci minuti. Però oggi è lunedì e il museo è chiuso.	chee vohr-RAHN-noh CHEEN-kweh, DYEH-chee mee-NUH-tee. Peh-ROH OHD-jee EH loo-neh-DEE eh eel moo-ZEH-oh EH KYOO-zoh
Turista:	Peccato. Allora andrò domani. Grazie ancora.	pehk-KAH-toh. ahl-LOH-rah ahn-DROH doh-MAH-nee. GRAH-tsyeh ahn-KOH-rah

....

Tourist:	Excuse me. Where is the museum?
Passerby:	It's not far from here. Continue straight ahead for about a hundred meters, then make a left at the first traffic light.
Tourist:	Thank you. Then, I can walk there. How long will it take?
Passerby:	It will take you five or ten minutes. Anyhow, it's Monday and the museum is closed today.
Tourist:	Too bad. I'll go tomorrow, then. Thanks again.

TAKING A TAXI

Most taxis in Italy are white (though some of the older ones are yellow) with a lighted sign on the roof. You cannot hail a taxi from the street. Go to a taxi stand—located in strategic spots throughout the historic center, *centro storico* (CHEN-troh STOH-ree-koh), of most major towns—or phone a local taxi company. Visitor information centers and your hotel concierge can provide you with a list of reliable taxi companies, and they will even make the call for you. At airports and railway stations, taxis are quite easy to find at taxi stands just outside.

Where is the nearest taxi stand?	Dov'è la fermata dei taxi più vicino?	doh-VEH lah fehr-MAH-tah day TAHK-see pyoo vee-CHEE-noh?
Are there any taxis around here?	Ci sono dei taxi in questa zona?	chee SOH-noh day TAHK-see een KWEH-stah DZOH-nah?
Taxi!	**Taxi!**	**TAHK-see!**
Are you free?	**È libero?**	**eh LEE-beh-roh?**
Are you taken?	È occupato?	eh ohk-koo-PAH-toh?
Please take me . . .	**Per favore, mi porti . . .**	**pehr fah-VOH-reh mee POHR-tee . . .**
_to the airport.	_all'aeroporto.	_ahl-lah-eh-roh-POHR-toh
_to the train station.	_alla stazione.	_AHL-lah stah-TSYOH-neh
_to the bus station.	_alla stazione autolinee.	_AHL-lah stah-TSYOH-neh ow-toh-LEE-neh-eh
_to the center.	_in centro.	_een CHEHN-troh
_to the main square.	_alla piazza principale.	_AHL-lah PYAHT-tsah preen-chee-PAH-leh
_to the hotel.	_all'hotel.	_ahl-loh-TEHL
_to this address.	_a questo indirizzo.	_ah KWEH-stoh een-dee-REET-tsoh
_to this restaurant.	_a questo ristorante.	_ah KWEH-stoh ree-stoh-RAHN-teh

_to this store.	_a questo negozio.	_ah KWEH-stoh neh-GOH-tsyoh
How much is it to . . . ?	Quant'è per . . . ?	kwahn-TEH pehr . . . ?
I'm in a hurry!	**Debbo andare in fretta!/Ho fretta!**	**DEH-boh an-DAH reh een FREHT-tah!/oh FREHT-tah**
Stop here, please!	**Si fermi qui, per favore!**	**see FEHR-mee kwee pehr fah-VOH-reh**
Wait here for me. I'll be right back.	Mi aspetti qui. Torno subito.	mee ah-SPEHT-tee kwee. TOHR-noh SOO-bee-toh
Please drive more slowly.	Per favore, guidi più adagio.	pehr fah-VOH-reh GWEE-dee pyoo ah-DAH-joh
How much do I owe you?	**Quanto le devo?**	**KWAHN-toh leh DEH-voh?**
Keep the change.	**Tenga il resto.**	**TEHN-gah eel REH-stoh**
taxi stand	fermata dei taxi	fehr-MAH-tah day TAHK-see
taxi meter	tassametro	tahs-SAH-meh-troh
taxi fare	tariffa	tah-REEF-fah

ON THE BUS

In Italy, buses are a less expensive way to get around town and to sightsee at the same time. Bus stops are located throughout all Italian cities, according to the urban district lines, and complete itineraries are posted at all bus stops. Tickets must be bought in advance and can be purchased at tobacco stores, newsstands, from automatic ticket machines near main stops, and at bus station booths. You must stamp your ticket in the small validation machine immediately upon boarding. Two types of tickets are available, both valid for one or more rides on all lines. One costs about €.77 and is valid for 60 minutes from the time it is first stamped; the other costs about €1.30 and is valid for three hours. A multiple ticket—valid for four 60-minute periods—costs about €3. A 24-hour tourist ticket costs about €3.10. Bus entrances are in the rear and in the front, while the exit is in the middle. Ticket-stamping (validation) machines are near the two entrances inside the bus. You have to put your ticket into the slot: the date and time will be printed on it, letting you know that your hour-long ride has begun. You may notice that some passengers do not use the machine. This may mean that they have a monthly card, *tesserino* (tehs-seh-REE-noh), which does not need to be inserted in the slot. It can also mean that they are riding without a ticket; every so often, inspectors step in and those found without tickets must pay a substantial fine.

I'm looking for the bus stop.	Cerco la fermata dell'autobus.	CHEHR-koh lah fehr-MAH-tah dehl-LOW-toh-boos
Where is the nearest bus stop?	**Dovè la fermata dell'autobus più vicina?**	**doh-VEH lah fehr-MAH-tah dehl-OW-toh-boos pyoo vee-CHEE-nah?**
What bus do I take to go to . . . ?	Che autobus devo prendere per andare a . . . ?	keh OW-toh-boos DEH-voh PREHN-deh-reh pehr ahn-DAH-reh ah . . . ?
Does this bus go to . . . ?	Quest'autobus va a . . . ?	kweh-STOW-toh-boos vah ah . . . ?
How many stops until . . . ?	Quante fermate ci sono prima di . . . ?	KWAHN-teh fehr-MAH-teh chee SOH-noh PREE-mah dee . . . ?
Which is the closest stop to . . . ?	Qual è la fermata più vicina a . . . ?	kwah-LEH lah fehr-MAH-tah pyoo vee-CHEE-nah ah . . . ?
How long does it take to get to . . . ?	Quanto ci vuole per arrivare a . . . ?	KWAHN-toh chee voo-OH-leh pehr ahr-ree-VAH-reh ah . . . ?
I want to get off at Siena.	**Voglio scendere a Siena.**	**VOH-lyoh SHEHN-deh-reh ah SYEH-nah**
Do I need to change buses?	**Devo cambiare autobus?**	**DEH-voh kahm-BYAH-reh OW-toh-boos?**
Where do I take the bus to return?	Dove prendo l'autobus per ritornare?	Doh-VEH PREHN-doh LOW-toh-boos pehr ree-tohr-NAH-reh?

When is the next bus?	Quando c'è il prossimo autobus?	KWAHN-doh cheh eel PROHS-see-moh OW-toh-boos?
How often does the bus run?	Ogni quanto passa l'autobus?	OH-nyee KWAHN-toh PAHS-sah LOW-toh-boos?
Where is the bus station?	Dov'è la stazione autolinee?	doh-VEH lah stah-TSYOH-neh ow-toh-LEE-nee-eh?
When does the bus for . . . leave?	Quando parte la corriera per . . . ?	KWAHN-doh PAHR-teh lah kohr-RYEH-rah pehr . . . ?
What is the fare to Pisa?	**Quanto costa il biglietto per Pisa?**	**KWAHN-toh KOH-stah eel bee-LYEHT-toh pehr PEE-zah?**
Should I pay when I get on?	Devo pagare quando salgo?	DEH-voh pah-GAH-reh KWAHN-doh SAHL-goh
I would like . . .	Vorrei . . .	vohr-RAY . . .
_a ticket.	_un biglietto.	_oon bee-LYEHT-toh
_a receipt.	_una ricevuta.	_OO-nah ree-cheh-VOO-tah
_a reserved seat.	_un posto prenotato	_oon POH-stoh preh-noh-TAH-toh

USING THE METRO

Only Milan has an efficient, and quite extensive, metro system. In Rome, because the substratum is so rich in archaeological remains, only a few lines could be built, but they connect most of the major tourist attractions.

Where is the nearest subway station?	Dov'è la stazione della metropolitana più vicina?	do-VEH lah stah-TSYOH-neh DEHL-lah meh-troh-poh-lee-TAH-nah pyoo vee-CHEE-nah?
Where can I buy a ticket?	Dove posso comprare un biglietto?	DOH-veh POHS-soh kohm-PRAH-reh oon bee-LYEHT-toh?
How much does it cost?	Quanto costa?	KWAHN-toh KOH-stah?

Is there a map for the metro?	C'è una pianta della metropolitana?	cheh OO-na PYAHN-tah DEHL-lah meh-troh-poh-lee-TAH-nah?
What line goes to . . . ?	Quale linea va a . . . ?	KWAH-leh LEE-neh-ah vah ah . . . ?
Can you tell me when we arrive at . . . ?	Mi può dire quando arriviamo a . . . ?	mee pwoh DEE-reh KWAHN-doh ahr-ree-VYAH-moh ah . . . ?

GOING BY TRAIN

As is the case in most European countries, there is a single state-run system in Italy, which is known as F.S. (*Ferrovie dello Stato*). Traveling by train in Italy is a relaxing way to see the countryside if you travel by day, and can be comfortable overnight on a long stretch, provided that you travel first class and make reservations in advance either at the railway station or at a travel agency. There are two principal types of sleeping cars. The *vagone letto* (vah-GOH-neh LEHT-toh) is a first-class sleeping car with private accommodations. The *carrozza cuccette* (kahr-ROHT-tsah koo-CHEHT-teh) is a second-class couchette car with six bunks per compartment. There are pillows and blankets in each. Always reserve in advance.

Types of Trains

The **Eurostar** is a high-speed train operating on a few main lines, including Naples-to-Rome-to-Florence-to-Milan. Reservations are mandatory on Fridays and Sundays, and they're a good idea the rest of the week, too. A bar car provides light snacks, soft drinks, coffee, beer, and wine.

The **I.C.**, or Intercity train, runs express between all major, large, and medium-sized Italian cities. There's a bar car, and a fare supplement is charged depending on how far you travel. The **Espresso** (eh-SPREHS-soh) is a long-distance train making few stops, while the **Diretto** (dee-REHT-toh) is a shorter distance train that stops at all stations. In the wagon restaurant of dining car, a waiter walks down the aisle just before lunch and dinner taking reservations for a full-course, set-price meal.

Where is . . .	Dov'è . . .	doh-VEH . . .
_the train station?	_la stazione?	_lah stah-TSYOH-neh?
_the ticket window?	_la biglietteria?	_lah bee-lyeht-teh-REE-ah?
_the information office?	_l'ufficio informazioni?	_loof-FEE-choh een-fohr-mah-TSYOH-nee?
_the reservation office?	_l'ufficio prenotazioni?	_loof-FEE-choh preh-noh-tah-TSYOH-nee?
_the waiting room?	_la sala d'aspetto? (or) la sala d'attesa?	_lah SAH-lah dah-SPEHT-toh? . . . lah SAH-lah daht-TEH-zah?
_the first-class compartment?	_lo scompartimento di prima classe?	_loh skohm-pahr-tee-MEHN-toh dee PREE-mah KLAHS-seh?
_the first-class sleeping car?	_il vagone letto?	_eel vah-GOH-neh LEHT-toh?
_the second-class sleeping car?	_le cuccette?	_leh koot-CHEHT-teh?
_the smoking section?	_lo scompartimento fumatori?	_loh skohm-pahr-tee-MEHN-toh foo-mah-TOH-ree?
_the no-smoking section?	_lo scompartimento non fumatori?	_loh skohm-pahr-tee-MEHN-toh nohn foo-mah-TOH-ree?
_the baggage check?	_il deposito bagagli?	_eel deh-POH-zee-toh bah-GAH-lyee?
_the lost and found?	_l'ufficio oggetti smarriti?	_loof-FEE-choh ohd-JEHT-tee smahr-REE-tee?
What train do I take to get to . . . ?	Che treno devo prendere per andare a . . . ?	keh TREH-noh DEH-voh PREHN-deh-reh pehr ahn-DAH-reh ah . . . ?
When does the train leave for . . . ?	Quando parte il treno per . . . ?	KWAHN-doh PAHR-teh eel TREH-noh pehr . . . ?

When does it arrive at . . . ?	Quando arriva a . . . ?	KWAHN-doh ahr-REE-vah ah . . . ?
What kind of train is it?	Che tipo di treno è?	keh TEE-poh dee TREH-noh eh?
Is it an express train?	È un espresso?	eh oon eh-SPREHS-soh?
Is the train . . .	Il treno è . . .	eel TREH-noh eh . . .
_on time?	_in orario?	_een oh-RAH-ryoh?
_late?	_in ritardo?	_een ree-TAHR-doh?
From what platform does the train leave?	**Da che binario parte il treno?**	**dah keh bee-NAH-ryoh PAHR-teh eel TREH-noh?**
Is there a change of trains in . . . ?	Devo cambiare treno a . . . ?	DEH-voh kahm-BYAH-reh TREH-noh ah . . . ?
Does the train stop at . . . ?	Questo treno si ferma a . . . ?	KWEH-stoh TREH-noh see FEHR-mah ah . . . ?
I'd like to reserve a bunk . . .	Vorrei prenotare una cuccetta . . .	vohr-RAY preh-noh-TAH-reh OO-nah koot-CHEHT-tah . . .
_on the top.	_in alto.	_een AHL-toh
_in the middle.	_in mezzo.	_een MEHD-zoh
_on the bottom.	_in basso.	_een BAHS-soh
I'd like a bed in the sleeping car.	Vorrei un posto nel vagone letto.	vohr-RAY oon POH-stoh nehl vah-GOH-neh LEHT-toh
I'd like a . . . ticket.	**Vorrei un biglietto di . . .**	**vohr-RAY oon bee-LYEHT-toh dee . . .**
_round-trip	_andata e ritorno.	_ahn-DAH-tah eh ree-TOHR-noh
_one-way	_sola andata.	_SOH-lah ahn-DAH-tah
_first-class	_prima classe.	_PREE-mah KLAHS-seh
_second-class	**_seconda classe.**	**_seh-KOHN-dah KLAHS-seh**
I'd like to check my bags.	Vorrei depositare i miei bagagli.	vohr-RAY deh-poh-zee-TAH-reh ee mee-AY bah-GAH-lyee

Is this seat taken?	È occupato questo posto?	eh ohk-KOO-pah-toh KWEH-stoh POH-stah?
Sorry, this seat is taken.	Mi dispiace, è occupato.	mee dee-SPYAH-cheh, eh ohk-KOO-pah-toh
No, it's free.	No, è libero.	noh, eh LEE-beh-roh
Please make yourself comfortable.	S'accomodi.	sahk-KOH-moh-dee
Excuse me, may I get by?	Scusi, mi fa passare?	SKOO-zee, mee fah pahs-SAH-reh?
Excuse me, this is my seat.	Scusi, questo è il mio posto.	SKOO-zee, KWEH-stoh eh eel MEE-oh POH-stoh

TRAVELING BY BOAT

When is the next boat to Elba?	A che ora parte il prossimo battello per l'Elba?	ah keh OH-rah PAHR-teh eel PROHS-see-moh baht-TEHL-loh pehr LEHL-bah?
Where does one embark?	Dove ci si imbarca?	DOH-veh chee see eem-BAHR-kah?
Where is the port?	Dov'è il porto?	doh-VEH eel POHR-toh?
How long is the trip?	Quanto tempo dura la traversata?	KWAHN-toh TEHM-poh DOO-rah lah trah-vehr-SAH-tah?
I'd like to take a cruise.	Vorrei fare una crociera.	voh-RAY FAH-reh OO-nah kroh-CHE-rah
Where does the boat stop?	Dove si fa scalo?	DOH-veh see fah SKAH-loh?
How much is a ticket in a single cabin?	Quanto costa un biglietto in cabina singola?	KWAHN-toh KOH-stah oon bee-LYEHT-toh een kah-BEE-nah SEEN-goh-lah?
ship	la nave	lah NAH-veh
boat	il battello	eel baht-TEHL-loh
ferry	il traghetto	eel trah-GET-toh
hydrofoil	l'aliscafo.	lah-lee-SKAH-foh

49

COMMON PUBLIC SIGNS

ENTRATA	ehn-TRAH-tah	Entrance
USCITA	oo-SHEE-tah	Exit
APERTO	ah-PEHR-toh	Open
CHIUSO	KYOO-zoh	Closed
SPINGERE	SPEEN-jeh-reh	Push
TIRARE	tee-RAH-reh	Pull
ALT	ahlt	Stop
PERICOLO	peh-REE-koh-loh	Danger
VIETATO ENTRARE	vyeh-TAH-toh ehn-TRAH-reh	Do Not Enter
GABINETTI	gah-bee-NEHT-tee	Toilets
UOMINI	WOH-mee-nee	Men
DONNE	DOHN-neh	Women
LAVANDINO	lah-vahn-DEE-noh	Sink
ACQUA NON POTABILE	AH-kwah nohn poh-TAH-bee-leh	Not Drinkable Water
RITIRATA	ree-tee-RAH-tah	W.C. (trains)
VIETATO FUMARE	vyeh-TAH-toh foo-MAH-reh	No Smoking
USCITA DI EMERGENZA	oo-SHEE-tah dee eh-mehr-JEHN-tsah	Emergency Exit

n most cases, it's best to make hotel reservations and confirm
n advance, especially during the high season (April through
August). From the very posh to the unpretentious, you can
choose from a variety of accommodations.

hotel	oh-TEHL	hotel, one to five stars
albergo	ahl-BEHR-goh	small hotel, one to five stars
pensione	pehn-SYOH-neh	boardinghouse offering full board, *pensione completa* (pehn-SYOH-neh kohm-PLEH-tah), or half board, *mezza pensione* (MEHD-zah pehn-SYOH-neh)
appartamento ammobiliato	ahp-pahr-tah-MEHN-toh ahm-moh-bee-LYAH-toh	furnished apartment
residence	REH-see-dehns	temporary furnished apartment or studio
ostello	oh-STEHL-loh	youth hostel

DIALOGUE
At the Front Desk (Al Banco Accettazione)

Turista:	Buon giorno. Avete una camera per due persone?	bwohn JOHR-noh. ah-VEH-teh OO-nah KAH-meh-rah pehr DOO-eh pehr-SOH-neh?
Impiegato:	Per quanto tempo?	pehr KWAHN-toh TEHM-poh?
Turista:	Per una settimana.	pehr OO-nah seht-tee-MAH-nah
Impiegato:	Un momento . . . Sì, ho una matrimoniale con bagno al terzo piano.*	oon moh-MEHN-toh . . . see, oh OO-nah mah-tree-moh-NYAH-leh kohn BAH-nyoh ahl TEHR-tsoh PYAH-noh

*Our first floor is the *pianterreno* (pyahn-tehr-REH-noh), ground floor, in Italy. Thus, their *primo piano* (PREE-moh PYAH-noh), first floor, is our second floor, etc.

Turista:	**Quanto viene?**	KWAHN-toh VYEH-neh?
Impiegato:	**Centoeuro per notte.**	CHEHN-toh EH-ooh-roh pehr NOHT-teh
Turista:	**Va bene, la prendo. Posso vederla?**	vah BEH-neh, lah PREHN-doh. POHS-soh veh-DEHR-lah?
Impiegato:	**Certamente. Mi segua per favore.**	chehr-tah-MEHN-teh. mee SEH-gwah pehr fah-VOH-reh

Tourist:	Hello. Do you have a room for two people?
Clerk:	For how long?
Tourist:	For a week.
Clerk:	One moment. Yes, I have a room with a double bed and bath on the third floor.
Tourist:	How much is it?
Clerk:	One hundred euros per night.
Tourist:	Fine, I'll take it. May I see it?
Clerk:	Certainly. Follow me, please.

HOTEL ARRANGEMENTS AND SERVICES

I have a reservation.	Ho fatto la prenotazione.	oh FAHT-toh lah preh-noh-tah-TSYOH-neh
We are going to stay . . .	Resteremo . . .	reh-steh-REH-moh . . .
_tonight.	_stanotte.	_stah-NOHT-teh
_one night.	_una notte.	_OO-nah NOHT-teh
_a few days.	_alcuni giorni.	_ahl-KOO-nee JOHR-nee
_a week.	_una settimana.	_OO-nah seht-tee-MAH-nah
I'd like a room . . .	Vorrei una camera . . .	vohr-RAY OO-nah KAH-meh-rah . . .
_with one bed.	_singola.	_SEEN-goh-lah
_with two beds.	_doppia.	_DOHP-pyah

_with a double bed.	_matrimoniale.	_mah-tree-moh-NYAH-leh
Do you have a room with . . .	**Avete una camera con . . .**	**ah-VEH-teh OO-nah KAH-meh-rah kohn . . .**
_a private bathroom?	_bagno privato?	_BAH-nyoh pree-VAH-toh?
_a bathtub?	_vasca da bagno?	_VAH-skah dah BAH-nyoh?
_a shower?	_doccia?	_DOHT-chah?
_hot water?	_acqua calda?	_AHK-kwah KAHL-dah?
_air-conditioning?	_aria condizionata?	_AH-ryah kohn-dee-tsyoh-NAH-tah?
_heat?	_riscaldamento?	_ree-skahl-dah-MEHN-toh?
_television?	_televisore?	_teh-leh-vee-ZOH-reh?
_radio?	_radio?	_RAH-dyoh?
_a balcony?	_balcone?	_bahl-KOH-neh?
_a view facing the street?	_vista sulla strada?	_VEE-stah SUHL-lah STRAH-dah?
_a view facing the sea?	_vista sul mare?	_VEE-stah suhl MAH-reh?
May I see the room?	**Posso vedere la camera?**	**POHS-soh veh-DEH-reh lah KAH-meh-rah?**
I'll take it.	La prendo.	lah PREHN-doh
Do you have a . . . room?	**Avete una camera . . . ?**	**ah-VEH-teh OO-nah KAH-meh-rah . . . ?**
_quieter	_più silenziosa?	_pyoo see-lehn-TSYOH-zah?
_bigger	_più grande?	_pyoo GRAHN-deh?
_less expensive	_meno cara?	_MEH-noh KAH-rah?
How much is it . . .	**Qual è il prezzo . . .**	**kwah-LEH eel PREHT-soh . . .**
_per night?	_per una notte?	_pehr OO-nah NOHT-teh?
_per week?	_per una settimana?	_pehr OO-nah seht-tee-MAH-nah?

_with all meals?	_pasti inclusi?	_PAH-stee een-KLOO-zee?
_with no meals?	_pasti esclusi?	_PAH-stee eh-SKLOO-zee?
_with breakfast?	**_con la colazione?**	_kohn lah koh-lah-TSYOH-neh?
Does the price include . . .	Il prezzo include . . .	eel PREHT-soh een-KLOO-deh . . .
_service?	_il servizio?	_eel sehr-VEE-tsyoh?
_value-added tax?	_l'I.V.A.?	_LEE-vah?
Does the hotel have . . .	L'hotel ha . . .	loh-TEHL ah . . .
_a restaurant?	_il ristorante?	_eel ree-stoh-RAHN-teh?
_a bar?	_il bar?	_eel bahr?
_a swimming pool?	_la piscina?	_lah pee-SHEE-nah?
_room service?	_il servizio in cámera?	_eel sehr-VEE-tsyoh een KAH-meh-rah?
_a garage?	_il garage?	_eel gah-RAHZH?
_a safe-deposit box?	_la cassaforte?	_lah kahs-sah-FOHR-teh?
_laundry service?	_il servizio di lavanderia?	_eel sehr-VEE-tsyoh dee lah-vahn-deh-REE-ah?
What's my room number?	Qual è il numero della mia cámera?	kwah-LEH eel NOO-meh-roh DEHL-lah MEE-ah KAH-meh-rah?
Please have my bags sent up to my room.	**Può far portare su i bagagli, per favore?**	pwoh fahr pohr-TAH-reh soo ee bah-GAH-lyee, pehr fah-VOH-reh?
This is for your safe.	Questo è da depositare in cassaforte.	KWHEH-stoh eh dah deh-poh-zee-TAH-reh een kahs-sah-FOHR-teh
I'd like to speak with . . .	Vorrei parlare con . . .	vohr-RAY pahr-LAH-reh kohn . . .
_the manager.	_il direttore.	_eel dee-reht-TOH-reh

_the hall porter.	_il portiere.	_eel pohr-TYEH-reh
_the maid.	_la cameriera.	_lah kah-meh-RYEH-rah
_the bellhop.	_il fattorino.	_eel faht-toh-REE-noh
May I have . . .	**Posso avere . . .**	**POHS-soh ah-VEH-reh**
_an extra bed?	_un letto extra?	_oon LEHT-toh EHK-strah?
_a baby crib?	_una culla?	_OO-nah KOOL-lah?
_an ashtray?	_un portacenere?	_oon pohr-tah-CEH-neh-reh?
_another towel?	**_un altro asciugamano?**	**_oo-NAHL-troh ah-shoo-gah-MAH-noh?**
_another pillow?	_un'altro cuscino?	_oo-NAHL-troh koo-SHEE-noh?
_another blanket?	_un'altra coperta?	_oo-NAHL-trah koh-PEHR-tah?
_some hangers?	_degli attaccapanni?	_DEH-lyee ah-tah-kah-PAH-nee
_some soap?	**_del sapone?**	**_dehl sah-POH-neh?**
_some toilet paper?	**_della carta igienica?**	**_DEHL-lah KAHR-tah ee-JEH-nee-kah?**
_some stationery?	_della carta da lettere?	_DEHL-lah KAHR-tah dah LEHT-teh-reh?
_some water?	_dell'acqua?	_dehl-LAHK-kwah?
This room is very . . .	**Questa camera è molto . . .**	**KWEH-stah KAH-meh-rah eh MOHL-toh . . .**
_small.	_piccola.	_PEEK-koh-lah
_cold.	_fredda.	_FREHD-dah
_hot.	_calda.	_KAHL-dah
_dark.	_buia.	_BOO-yah
_noisy.	_rumorosa.	_roo-moh-ROH-zah
The . . . does not work.	**. . . non funziona.**	**nohn foon-TSYOH-nah . . .**
_light	_la luce.	_lah LOO-cheh
_lamp	_la lampadina.	_lah lahm-pah-DEE-nah

_heat	_il riscaldamento.	_eel ree-skahl-dah-MEHN-toh
_air-conditioning	_l'aria condizionata.	_LAH-ryah kohn-dee-tsyoh-NAH-tah
_toilet	_il gabinetto.	_eel gah-bee-NEHT-toh
_hot water	_l'acqua calda.	_LAHK-kwah KAHL-dah
_key	**_la chiave.**	**_lah KYAH-veh**
_lock	_la serratura.	_lah sehr-rah-TOO-rah
May I change to another room?	E'possibile cambiare camera?	eh pohs-SEE-bee-leh KAHM-byah-reh KAH-meh-rah?
Could you make up the room now?	Può fare la camera adesso?	pwoh FAH-reh lah KAH-meh-rah ah-DEHS-soh?
I'm in room 23	**Sono alla ventitrè**	**SOH-noh AHL-lah vehn-tee-TREH**
I'd like to place an order for room number . . .	Vorrei ordinare qualcosa per la cámera numero . . .	vohr-RAY ohr-dee-NAH-reh kwahl-KOH-zah pehr lah KAH-meh-rah NOO-meh-roh . . .
I am leaving tomorrow at 10 A.M.	**Parto domani alle dieci.**	**PAHR-toh doh-MAH-nee AHL-leh DYEH-chee**
Please prepare the bill.	**Per favore, prepari il conto.**	**pehr fah-VOH-reh, preh-PAH-ree eel KOHN-toh**
Could you please call me a cab?	Mi può chiamare un taxi, per cortesia?	mee pwoh kyah-MAH-reh oon TAHK-see, pehr kohr-teh-SEE-ah?
Please have my baggage brought downstairs.	Può far portare giù i bagagli, per favore?	pwoh fahr pohr-TAH-reh joo ee bah-GAH-lyee, pehr fah-VOH-reh?

Even though Italy means pasta to many visitors, you will be amazed at the variety and originality of Italian cooking, which includes rice, meat, fish, poultry, shellfish, cheeses, mouth-watering cakes, and ice creams. Generally, prices vary according to the type of restaurant, however, do check the posted menu to be sure.

autogrill (ow-toh-GREEL)	Restaurant located on an express highway; bar and snack services are also available.
bar/caffè (bahr/kahf-FEH)	The quintessential Italian institution. Life without it would be inconceivable for an Italian. There, the rite of the morning espresso begins, and it is repeated numerous times throughout the day. These establishments serve coffee, tea, soft drinks, beer, liquor, and snacks such as toasts, sandwiches, and pastries. It's the perfect place to hang out, relax, refresh yourself, read, write, talk, watch, and be watched.
enoteca (eh-noh-TEH-kah)	A wine bar selling wines by the glass, salads, mixed cheese and meat plates, and bottles of wine to take away.
gelateria (jeh-lah-teh-REE-ah)	Ice cream parlor that serves gelato (jeh-LAH-toh); rich, tasty ice cream.
locanda (loh-KAHN-dah)	Restaurant usually located outside the city serving simple, local food. Originally an inn providing bed and board.
osteria (oh-steh-REE-ah)	Usually an informal, rustic place, serving simple but very good food at moderate prices.
paninoteca (pah-nee-noh-TEH-kah)	Sandwich bar, where you can sample a great variety of hot and cold sandwiches, *panini* (pah-NEE-nee).
pizzeria (peet-tseh-REE-ah)	Pizza parlor. Pizzas galore. Many different choices for every taste. Other food is often served.

ristorante (ree-stoh-RAHN-teh)	The range of style, ambiance, and price category is impressive. Make sure you check the menu in the window to get an idea of the prices.
rosticceria (roh-steet-cheh-REE-ah)	A place specializing mainly in grilled chicken to take out. Today, thanks to the addition of tables and chairs, you can sometimes eat on the premises.
sala da tè (SAH-lah dah teh)	"Tea room," where pastries and other desserts are served along with tea, coffee, and hot chocolate. Light meals may be offered in some salons.
taverna (tah-VEHR-nah)	Eatery that might lack the refined atmosphere of a restaurant or even a trattoria. However, the food is tasty, well prepared, and inexpensive.
tavola calda/fredda (TAH-voh-lah KAHL-dah/ FREHD-dah)	Hot/cold table. Restaurant resembling a cafeteria. You may buy hot and cold dishes, moderately priced.
trattoria (traht-toh-REE-ah)	Medium-priced restaurant, often family-run, where you can find home cooking, cucina casalinga (koo-CHEE-nah kah-sah-LEEN-gah).

MEALS AND MEALTIMES

Breakfast, *la colazione* or *la prima colazione* (lah koh-lah-TSYOH-neh or lah PREE-mah koh-lah-TSYOH-neh), is a very light meal and is commonly served between 7 and 10 AM at hotels.* If breakfast is included in the price of your room, it usually consists of coffee, tea, or hot chocolate, and fresh bread, butter, and jam. Warm milk is always served on the side so that you can blend equal parts of coffee and milk and make your own *caffè latte* (kahf-feh LAHT-teh), or just add a few drops to your coffee for a *caffè macchiato* (kahf-FEH mahk-KYAH-toh). If breakfast is not included with the price of your hotel room, you will probably find that it is less expensive and more fun at the corner bar, mingling with the locals. Italians usually have *espresso* (eh-SPREHS-soh) or *cappuccino* (kahp-poot-

*In some areas, especially in large towns, the name of a meal can be misleading. Sometimes lunch, *il pranzo*, can be referred to as *la colazione*, or breakfast. Make sure you ask in advance so you won't show up for the wrong meal.

CHEE-noh), steamy, frothy milk added to espresso, and a brioche for breakfast.

Lunch, *la colazione* or *il pranzo* (lah koh-lah-TSYOH-neh or eel PRAHN-dzoh) used to be the big meal of the day. In recent years, shorter midday breaks have led to quicker lunches for many working people. In general, lunch is served between 12:30 and 2:30. Many businesses and most public services close at lunchtime: Stores are closed between 12:30 or 1 PM and 3:30 or 4 PM, depending on the city. At this time you may find that eateries fill up quite quickly. Those who have the time prefer to have a quiet, relaxed lunch at home.

Dinner, *la cena* (lah CHEH-nah), begins later in Italy than in the United States. Restaurants begin serving around 7:30 or 8; however, most Italians don't come in before 9. Evening dining is a leisurely affair, with people lingering over their food and drinks. Some restaurants pour *prosecco* (proh-SEH-koh), Italian bubbly, gratis while you peruse the menu, and many are candlelit. Service is customarily slow—unobtrusive rather than inattentive.

DIALOGUE At the Restaurant (Al Ristorante)

Cameriere:	Desidera?	deh-ZEE-deh-rah?
Cliente:	Non so. Qual è la specialità della casa?	nohn soh. kwah-LEH lah speh-chah-lee-TAH DEHL-lah KAH-zah?
Cameriere:	Oggi Le consiglio le tagliatelle alla bolognese.	OHD-jee leh kohn-SEE-lyoh leh tah-lyah-TEHL-leh AHL-lah boh-loh-NYEH-zeh
Cliente:	Bene. Proviamole!	BEH-neh. proh-VYAH-moh-leh!
Cameriere:	Desidera qualcosa da bere?	deh-ZEE-deh-rah kwahl-KOH-zah dah BEH-reh?
Cliente:	Sì. Una mezza bottiglia di vino bianco e una minerale, per favore.	see. OO-nah MEHD-zah boh-TEE-lyah dee VEE-noh BYAHN-koh eh OO-nah mee-neh-RAH-leh, pehr fah-VOH-reh

| Cameriere: | **Naturale o gassata?** | nah-too-RAH-leh oh gahs-SAH-tah? |
| Cliente: | **Naturale, grazie.** | nah-too-RAH-leh, GRAH-tsyeh |

....

Waiter:	What would you like to order?
Customer:	I don't know. What's the specialty of the house?
Waiter:	Today I would recommend noodles with meat sauce.
Customer:	Fine. I'll try it!
Waiter:	Something to drink?
Customer:	Yes. Half a bottle of white wine and a bottle of mineral water, please.
Waiter:	Natural or carbonated?
Customer:	Natural, thank you.

EATING OUT

Can you recommend a good restaurant?	Può consigliarmi un buon ristorante?	pwoh kohn-see-LYAHR-mee oon bwon ree-stoh-RAHN-teh?
Do you know any good restaurants nearby?	**Conosce un buon ristorante nei dintorni?**	**koh-NOH-sheh oon bwon ree-stoh-RAHN-teh nay deen-TOHR-nee?**
There are several.	Ce ne sono parecchi.	cheh neh SOH-noh pah-REHK-kee
I want a . . . restaurant.	Voglio un ristorante . . .	VOH-lyoh oon ree-stoh-RAHN-teh . . .
_typical	_tipico.	_TEE-pee-koh
_very good	_molto buono.	_MOHL-toh BWOH-noh
Is it expensive?	**È caro?**	**eh KAH-roh?**
No, it's inexpensive.	No, è economico.	noh, eh eh-koh-NOH-mee-koh
What's the name of the restaurant?	Come si chiama il ristorante?	KOH-meh see KYAH-mah eel ree-stoh-RAHN-teh?
It's called . . .	Si chiama . . .	see KYAH-mah . . .

60

Where is it located?	Dove si trova?	DOH-veh see TROH-vah?
Do you need to make reservations?	Si deve prenotare?	see DEH-veh preh-noh-TAH-reh?
I'd like to reserve a table . . .	Vorrei prenotare un tavolo . . .	vohr-RAY preh-noh-TAH-reh oon TAH-voh-loh . . .
_for two people.	_per due (persone).	_pehr DOO-eh (pehr-SOH-neh)
_for this evening.	_per questa sera.	_pehr KWEH-stah SEH-rah
_for tomorrow evening.	_per domani sera.	_pehr doh-MAH-nee SEH-rah
_for 9 P.M.	_per le ventuno.	_pehr leh vehn-TOO-noh
_on the terrace.	_sul terrazzo.	_suhl tehr-RAHT-tsoh
_by the window.	_vicino alla finestra.	_vee-CHEE-noh AHL-lah fee-NEH-strah
_outside.	_all'aperto. (or) fuori.	_ahl-lah-PEHR-toh FWOH-ree
_inside.	_dentro.	_DEHN-troh

RESTAURANT ITEMS

Waiter/Waitress!	Cameriere(-a)!	kah-meh-RYEH-reh (-rah)!
The menu, please.	Il menu, per favore.	eel meh-NOO, pehr fah-VOH-reh
The wine list, please.	La lista dei vini, per piacere.	lah LEE-stah day VEE-nee, pehr pyah-CHEH-reh
Do you have any special local dishes?	Avete piatti locali tipici?	ah-VEH-teh PYAHT-tee loh-KAH-lee TEE-pee-chee?
I'd like . . .	Vorrei . . .	vohr-RAY . . .
_something light.	_qualcosa di leggero.	_kwahl-KOH-zah dee lehd-JEH-roh
_a full meal.	_un pasto completo.	_oon PAH-stoh kohm-PLEH-toh

61

_the dish of the day.	_il piatto del giorno.	_eel PYAHT-toh dehl JOHR-noh
Do you have children's portions?	Avete mezze porzioni per bambini?	ah-VEH-teh MEHD-zeh pohr-TSYOH-nee pehr bahm-BEE-nee?
I'm ready to order.	Sono pronto(-a) per ordinare.	SOH-noh PROHN-toh (-tah) pehr ohr-dee-NAH-reh
To begin, I would like . . .	Per cominciare vorrei . . .	pehr koh-meen-CHAH-reh vohr-RAY . . .
Next . . .	Poi . . .	poy . . .
Finally . . .	Per finire . . .	pehr fee-NEE-reh . . .
That's all.	È tutto.	eh TOOT-toh
Have you finished?	Ha finito?	ah fee-NEE-toh?
Could we have . . .	Potremmo avere . . .	poh-TREHM-moh ah-VEH-reh . . .
_tap water?	_dell'acqua?	_dehl-LAHK-wah?
_silverware?	_delle posate?	_DEHL-leh poh-ZAH-teh?
_a napkin?	_un tovagliolo?	_oon toh-vah-LYOH-loh?
_a fork?	_una forchetta?	_OO-nah fohr-KEHT-tah?
_a knife?	_un coltello?	_oon kohl-TEHL-loh?
_a spoon?	_un cucchiaio?	_oon kook-KYAH-yoh?
_a plate?	_un piatto?	_oon PYAHT-toh?
_a bowl?	_una scodella?	_OO-nah skoh-DEHL-lah?
_a glass?	_un bicchiere?	_oon beek-KYEH-reh?
_a cup?	_una tazza?	_OO-nah TAHT-tsah?
_a demitasse?	_una tazzina?	_OO-nah taht-TSEE-nah?
_a saucer?	_un piattino?	_oon pyaht-TEE-noh?
_a teaspoon?	_un cucchiaino?	_oon kook-kyah-EE-noh?
_some bread?	_del pane?	_dehl PAH-neh?

_some butter?	_del burro?	_dehl BOOR-roh?
_some salt?	_del sale?	_dehl SAH-leh?
_some pepper?	_del pepe?	_dehl PEH-peh?
_some mustard?	_della senape?	_DEHL-lah SEH-nah-peh?
_some ketchup?	_del ketchup?	_dehl KEHCH-ahp?
_some mayonnaise?	_della maionese?	_DEHL-lah mah-yoh-NEH-zeh?
_some lemon?	_del limone?	_dehl lee-MOH-neh?
_some sugar?	_dello zucchero?	_DEHL-loh TSOOK-keh-roh?
_some saccharine?	_della saccarina?	_DEHL-lah sahk-kah-REE-nah?
_a toothpick?	_uno stuzzicadente?	_OO-noh stoot-tsee-kah-DEHN-teh?
_an ashtray?	_un portacenere?	_oon pohr-tah-CHEH-neh-reh?
_a little more . . . ?	_ancora un po' di . . . ?	_ahn-KOH-rah oon poh dee . . . ?

APPETIZERS (ANTIPASTI)

Increasingly, many Italian diners opt for an *antipasto*, or appetizer, skip the pasta course, and head directly to the second course. Or they opt for a pasta as the main course. *Antipasti* may be hot or cold. Here is a sampler of some types of the most common *antipasti* (ahn-tee-PAH-stee).

affettato misto (ahf-feht-TAH-toh MEE-stoh)	mixed cured meats: prosciutto crudo (raw ham), salami, mortadella, sometimes garnished with mixed pickled vegetables
antipasto misto (ahn-tee-PAH-stoh MEE-stoh)	mixed antipasto: usually a combination of prosciutto and other cured meats, crostini (slices of toasted bread with various toppings), and assorted vegetables *sott'olio* (in oil), anchovies, artichoke hearts, and olives

bruschetta (broo-SKEH-TAH)	Toasted bread rubbed with garlic topped w/freshly chopped tomatoes and basil
caprese (kah-PREH-zeh)	slices of mozzarella cheese with tomatoes, basil, and olive oil
cocktail di gamberi (KOHK-tehl dee GAHM-beh-ree)	shrimp cocktail
insalata di frutti di mare (een-sah-LAH-tah dee FROOT-tee dee MAH-reh)	seafood salad made with clams, mussels, squid, prawns, and cuttlefish, seasoned with lemon
prosciutto e melone o fichi (proh-SHOOT-toh eh meh-LOH-neh oh FEE-kee)	prosciutto and slices of melon or figs; very delicious and very refreshing—a typical and popular summer antipasto

PIZZA

Pizza is probably the most popular Italian contribution to fast food, and Italians often make a whole meal out of it. The Italian pizza is usually a single, round-shaped serving, as wide as the whole platter on which it's served. Pizza parlors, *pizzerie* (peet-tseh-REE-eh), offer a great variety of *pizze* (PEET-tseh) and topping combinations. Here are the most popular variations:

calzone (kahl-TSOH-neh)	pizza dough, folded in half, stuffed with a variety of savory fillings, baked in a pizza oven
capricciosa (kah-pree-CHOH-zah)	with tomato, mozzarella, ham, mushrooms, and artichoke hearts
margherita (mahr-geh-REE-tah)	with tomato, mozzarella, and basil
marinara (mah-ree-NAH-rah)	with tomato, oregano, and garlic
napoletana (nah-poh-leh-TAH-nah)	with tomato, mozzarella, anchovies, and oregano
quattro stagioni (KWAHT-troh stah-JOH-nee)	with tomato, mozzarella, ham, sausage, mushrooms, and artichoke hearts, divided into four quadrants (the "four seasons")
romana (roh-MAH-nah)	with tomato, mozzarella, anchovies, capers, and oregano

siciliana
(see-chee-LYAH-nah)

with tomato, anchovies, and
pecorino cheese

SOUPS (MINESTRE IN BRODO)

brodo . . .	BROH-doh . . .	. . . broth
_di cappone	_dee kahp-POH-neh	_capon
_di manzo	_dee MAHN-dzoh	_beef
_di pollo	_dee POHL-loh	_chicken
cacciucco	kaht-CHOOK-koh	spicy seafood chowder
crema . . .	KREH-mah . . .	cream . . . soup
_di asparagi	_dee ah-SPAH-rah-jee	_of asparagus
_di funghi	_dee FOON-ghee	_of mushrooms
_di pomodoro	_dee poh-moh-DOH-roh	_of tomato
minestrone	mee-neh-STROH-neh	vegetable soup
passatelli	pahs-sah-TEHL-lee	spatzos (broth with small dumplings)
passato di piselli	pahs-SAH-toh dee pee-ZEHL-lee	cream of pea soup
passato di verdura	pahs-SAH-toh dee vehr-DOO-rah	cream of vegetable soup
pasta e fagioli	PAH-stah eh fah-JOH-lee	pasta and beans
pastina in brodo	pah-STEE-nah een BROH-doh	broth and tiny pasta disks
stracciatella	straht-chah-TEHL-lah	egg-drop soup
zuppa di pesce	TSOOP-pah dee PEH-sheh	seafood stew

PASTA

Pastasciutta (pah-stah-SHOOT-tah) is the traditional Italian first course, a national treasure, a gastronomic religion. In many parts of Italy, no meal would be conceivable without it. It is traditionally eaten as a first or second course before the meat course. Pasta comes in different shapes, sizes and has many names—*spaghetti, maccheroni, bucatini, fettuccine, tagliatelle, vermicelli, ziti, linguine,* among others.

Typical Pasta Dishes (Piatti di pasta tipici)

agnolotti (ah-nyoh-LOHT-tee)	tiny ravioli stuffed with meat and cabbage, spinach, or pumpkin
cannelloni (kahn-nehl-LOH-nee)	rectangular pieces of pasta, rolled and stuffed, usually with a meat sauce or with ricotta and spinach, then topped with bechamel (white sauce) and baked in the oven
cappelletti (kahp-pehl-LEHT-tee)	round-shaped "little hats" filled with minced chicken or veal and seasoned with cheeses and herbs.
fettuccine (feht-toot-CHEE-neh)	noodles in the form of narrow ribbons, served with a variety of sauces
gnocchi (NYOHK-kee)	potato or semolina dumplings sometimes also made with spinach
lasagne verdi (lah-ZAH-nyeh VEHR-dee)	baked layers of thin spinach noodles, bechamel, meat sauce, and parmesan cheese
ravioli (rah-VYOH-lee)	freshly prepared thin pasta squares filled with chopped chicken, spinach, ricotta, or ground meat
rigatoni (ree-gah-TOH-nee)	macaroni made in large, short, furrowed tubes
spaghetti (spah-GEHT-tee)	semolina pasta made in thin, solid strings
tagliatelle (tah-lyah-TEHL-leh)	flat, ribbons of pasta narrower than fettucine usually served with bolognese meat sauce and parmesan cheese
tortellini (tohr-tehl-LEE-nee)	tiny squares of pasta, twisted and shaped into rings, stuffed with ground turkey or chicken, ham, mortadella, parmesan, and nutmeg, served in broth or topped with sauce
tortelloni (tohr-tehl-LOH-nee)	larger versions of tortellini usually stuffed with ricotta and spinach

RICE (RISO)

Rice is more popular in northern Italy than it is in the south, and it often replaces pasta. It may be served with a sauce or with a variety of ingredients such as beans, herbs and spices, mushrooms, and seafood. Here are some of the most popular:

risi e bisi (REE-zee eh BEE-zee)	rice with green peas and bacon
riso in bianco (REE-zoh een BYAHN-koh)	rice with butter and grated cheese
riso al pomodoro (REE-zoh ahl poh-moh-DOH-roh)	rice with tomato sauce and herbs
risotto (ree-ZOHT-toh)	rice cooked slowly in broth and flavored with butter, parmesan, and herbs
_alla marinara (AHL-lah mah-ree-NAH-rah)	_with seafood
_alla milanese (AHL-lah mee-lah-NEH-zeh)	_with saffron and bone marrow

SAUCES (SALSE E SUGHI)

Pasta would not be pasta without a sauce to make it so tasty. Italy has a wide range of sauces:

aglio, olio, e peperoncino (AH-lyoh, OH-lyoh, eh peh-peh-rohn-CHEE-noh)	garlic, olive oil, and dried red pepper
all'amatriciana (ahl-lah-mah-tree-CHAH-nah)	with tomatoes, bacon, garlic, red peppers, and onions
alla bolognese/al ragù (AHL-lah boh-loh-NYEH-zeh/ ahl rah-GOO)	with tomato paste and a small chopped onion, simmered with carrot and celery sticks, and combined with minced meat, some white or red wine, and a dash of milk or cream
alla carbonara (AHL-lah kahr-boh-NAH-rah)	with eggs, ham or bacon, and cheese
alla carrettiera (AHL-lah kahr-reht-TYEH-rah)	with tomato paste, tuna, and mushrooms

alla marinara (AHL-lah mah-ree-NAH-rah)	with tomatoes, onions, garlic, and oregano, with olives, mussels, and clams, if desired
al pesto (ahl PEH-stoh)	with a pestled mixture of cheese, garlic, basil, pine nuts, and olive oil
al pomodoro (ahl poh-moh-DOH-roh)	with crushed tomatoes and tomato puree, basil, garlic, and olive oil
alla pizzaiola (AHL-lah peet-tsah-YOH-lah)	with fresh tomatoes, garlic, olive oil, and herbs
alla puttanesca (AHL-lah poot-tah-NEH-skah)	with olives, garlic, capers, dried red pepper, and olive oil
alle vongole (AHL-leh VOHN-goh-leh)	with clams, tomatoes, parsley, garlic, and olive oil
besciamella (beh-shah-MEHL-lah)	white sauce made with melted butter, flour, cream, and milk

FISH AND SEAFOOD (PESCE E FRUTTI DI MARE)

I'd like some fish.	Vorrei del pesce.	vohr-RAY dehl PEH-sheh
What kind of seafood do you have?	Che tipo di frutti di mare avete?	keh TEE-poh dee FROOT-tee dee MAH-reh ah-VEH-teh?
acciughe	**aht-CHOO-geh**	**anchovies**
anguilla	ahn-GWEEL-lah	eel
aragosta	**ah-rah-GOH-stah**	**lobster**
aringa	ah-REEN-gah	herring
arselle	ahr-SEHL-leh	scallops
baccalà	bahk-kah-LAH	salt-dried cod
branzino	brahn-DZEE-noh	bass
calamari	kah-lah-MAH-ree	squid
carpa	KAHR-pah	carp
cozze	**KOHT-tseh**	**mussels**
dentice	DEHN-tee-cheh	bream
gamberi	GAHM-beh-ree	shrimps

granchi	GRAHN-kee	crabs
luccio	LOO-choh	pike
lumache di mare	loo-MAH-keh dee MAH-reh	sea snails
merluzzo	mehr-LOOT-tsoh	cod
orata	oh-RAH-tah	sea bream
ostriche	OH-stree-keh	oysters
pesce spada	PEH-sheh SPAH-dah	swordfish
polipo	POH-lee-poh	octopus
ricci	REE-chee	sea urchins
rombo	ROHM-boh	turbot
salmone	sahl-MOH-neh	salmon
sardine	sahr-DEE-neh	sardines
scampi	SKAHM-pee	prawns
seppia	SEHP-pyah	cuttlefish
sgombro	SGOHM-broh	mackerel
sogliola	SOH-lyoh-lah	sole
spigola	SPEE-goh-lah	sea bass
storione	stoh-RYOH-neh	sturgeon
tonno	TOHN-noh	tuna
triglia	TREE-lyah	red mullet
trota	TROH-tah	trout
vongole	VOHN-goh-leh	clams

Preparation Methods for Fish

affogato	ahf-foh-GAH-toh	poached
al cartoccio	ahl kahr-TOHT-choh	baked in parchment
al forno	**ahl FOHR-noh**	**baked**
alla graticola	AHL-lah grah-TEE-koh-lah	broiled
alla griglia	**AHL-lah GREE-lyah**	**grilled**
al vapore	ahl vah-POH-reh	steamed
fritto	**FREET-toh**	**fried**

69

in umido	een OO-mee-doh	stewed
lesso	LEHS-soh	boiled
marinato	mah-ree-NAH-toh	marinated

MEAT (CARNE)

A slice of meat, *una fettina* (unah feht-TEE-nah), usually follows pasta, and is ordered with a side dish, *un contorno* (oon kohn-TOHR-noh), usually a cooked vegetable or salad.

I'd like . . .	Vorrei . . .	voh-RAY . . .
_some beef.	_del manzo.	_dehl MAHN-dzoh
_some lamb.	_dell' agnello.	_dehl-lah-NYEHL-loh
_some pork.	_del maiale.	_dehl mah-YAH-leh
_some veal.	_del vitello.	_dehl vee-TEHL-loh
abbacchio	ahb-BAHK-kyoh	baby lamb
animelle	ah-nee-MEHL-leh	sweetbreads
arrosto	ahr-ROH-stoh	roast
bistecca	bee-STEHK-kah	steak
braciola	brah-CHOH-lah	chop
cervello	cher-VEHL-loh	brain
coppa	KOHP-pah	neck
costoletta	koh-stoh-LEHT-tah	rib
cotoletta	koh-toh-LEHT-tah	cutlet
fegato	FEH-gah-toh	liver
fesa	FEH-zah	round cut
filetto	fee-LEHT-toh	fillet
lingua	LEEN-gwah	tongue
lombata	lohm-BAH-tah	loin
medaglioni	meh-dah-LYOH-nee	round tenderloin
midollo	mee-DOHL-loh	marrow
mortadella	mohr-tah-DEHL-lah	bologna
nodini	noh-DEE-nee	veal chops
pancetta affumicata	pahn-CHEHT-tah ahf-foo-mee-KAH-tah	smoked bacon

polpette	pohl-PEHT-teh	meat balls
polpettone	pohl-peht-TOH-neh	meat loaf
porchetta	pohr-KEHT-tah	suckling pig
prosciutto	proh-SHOOT-toh	Parma ham
rognoni	roh-NYOH-nee	kidneys
rosbif	ROHZ-beef	roast beef
salame	sah-LAH-meh	salami
salsiccia	sahl-SEET-chah	sausage
scaloppine	skah-lohp-PEE-neh	escalope, thin slice of meat

Methods of Meat Preparation

ai ferri	**ahy FEHR-ree**	**barbecued**
al forno	ahl FOHR-noh	baked
alla griglia	AHL-lah GREE-lyah	grilled
allo spiedo	AHL-loh SPYEH-doh	broiled on a spit
arrosto	**ahr-ROHS-stoh**	**roasted**
brasato	**brah-ZAH-toh**	**braised**
farcito	fahr-CHEE-toh	stuffed
fritto	FREET-toh	fried
in umido	een OO-mee-doh	stewed
lesso	LEHS-soh	boiled
saltato	sahl-TAH-toh	sauteed
How do you like your meat?	**Come desidera la carne?**	**KOH-meh deh-ZEE-deh-rah lah KAHR-neh?**
I like it . . .	La preferisco . . .	lah preh-feh-REE-skoh . . .
_rare.	_al sangue.	_ahl SAHN-gweh
_medium.	_poco cotta. (or) cottura media.	_POH-koh KOHT-tah koht-TOO-rah MEH-dyah
_well-done.	_ben cotta.	_behn KOHT-tah

71

Typical Meat Dishes (Piatti di carne tipici)

abbacchio alla romana (ahb-BAHK-kyoh AHL-lah roh-MAH-nah)	a typical Easter dish; spring lamb flavored with garlic and rosemary and roasted with thin wedges of potatoes
fiorentina (fyoh-rehn-TEE-nah)	thick, juicy steak broiled under a flame and flavored with olive oil, salt, pepper, and lemon juice
carpaccio (kahr-PAHT-choh)	thinly sliced beef with oil and lemon, covered with flakes of parmesan cheese
cima alla genovese (CHEE-mah AHL-lah jeh-noh-VEH-zeh)	breast of veal stuffed with hard-boiled eggs, minced shoulder of pork, shelled peas, and marjoram
ossobuco alla milanese (ohs-soh-BOO-koh AHL-lah mee-lah-NEH-zeh)	shin of veal braised in broth with chopped onions, carrots, and tomatoes
saltimbocca alla romana (sahl-teem-BOHK-kah AHL-lah roh-MAH-nah)	veal cutlet rolled up with prosciutto and sage, secured with a toothpick, sauteed in butter, and simmered in wine
vitello tonnato (vee-TEHL-lohtohn-NAH-toh)	slices of cold veal covered with a sauce made of tuna, mayonnaise, lemon juice, anchovies, and capers

POULTRY AND GAME (POLLAME E CACCIAGIONE)

I would like some game.	Vorrei della cacciagione.	vohr-RAY DEHL-lah kaht-chah-JOH-neh
What kind of poultry do you have?	Che tipo di pollame avete?	keh TEE-poh dee pohl-LAH-meh ah-VEH-teh?
allodola	ahl-LOH-doh-lah	lark
anatra	**AH-nah-trah**	**duck**
beccaccia	behk-KAHT-chah	woodcock
cappone	kahp-POH-neh	capon
capretto	kah-PREHT-toh	kid goat

capriolo	kah-pree-OH-loh	roebuck
cervo	CHEHR-voh	deer
cinghiale	cheen-GYAH-leh	wild boar
coniglio	**koh-NEE-lyoh**	**rabbit**
fagiana	fah-JAH-noh	pheasant
faraona	fah-rah-OH-nah	guinea fowl
gallina	gahl-LEE-nah	stewing chicken
lepre	LEH-preh	hare
oca	OH-kah	goose
pernice	pehr-NEE-cheh	partridge
piccione	peet-CHOH-neh	pigeon
pollo	**POHL-loh**	**chicken**
pollo novello	POHL-loh noh-VEHL-loh	spring chicken
quaglia	KWAH-lyah	quail
selvaggina	**sehl-vahd-JEE-nah**	**venison**
tacchino	**tahk-KEE-noh**	**turkey**
tordo	TOHR-doh	mockingbird

VEGETABLES (VERDURA)

asparagi	ah-SPAH-rah-jee	asparagus
barbabietola	bahr-bah-BYEH-toh-lah	beet
broccoli	BROHK-koh-lee	broccoli
carciofi	**kahr-CHOH-fee**	**artichokes**
cardo	KAHR-doh	cardoon
carote	kah-ROH-teh	carrots
cavolfiore	**kah-vohl-FYOH-reh**	**cauliflower**
cavolini di Bruxelles	kah-voh-LEE-nee dee Broos-SEHL	brussels sprout
cavolo	KAH-voh-lah	cabbage
ceci	CHEH-chee	chick peas
cetrioli	cheh-tree-OH-lee	cucumbers
cicoria	chee-KOH-ryah	chicory

cipolle	**chee-POHL-leh**	**onions**
fagioli	fah-JOH-lee	beans
fagiolini	**fah-joh-LEE-nee**	**string beans**
fave	FAH-veh	broad beans
finocchio	fee-NOHK-kyoh	fennel
funghi	**FOON-gee**	**mushrooms**
granoturco	grah-noh-TOOR-koh	corn
indivia	een-DEE-vyah	endive
insalata	een-sah-LAH-tah	salad/lettuce
lattuga	**laht-TOO-gah**	**lettuce**
lenticchie	lehn-TEEK-kyeh	lentils
mais	MAH-ees	corn
melanzana	**meh-lahn-TSAH-nah**	**eggplant**
patate	**pah-TAH-teh**	**potatoes**
peperoni	peh-peh-ROH-nee	peppers
piselli	pee-ZEHL-lee	peas
pomodori	**poh-moh-DOH-ree**	**tomatoes**
porcini	pohr-CHEE-nee	*boletus edulis* mushroom
porro	POHR-roh	leek
radicchio	rah-DEEK-kyoh	radicchio
ravanelli	rah-vah-NEHL-lee	radishes
sedano	SEH-dah-nah	celery
spinaci	**spee-NAH-chee**	**spinach**
tartufi	tahr-TOO-fee	truffles
verza	VEHR-dzah	savoy cabbage
zucca	TSOOK-kah	pumpkin
zucchini	tsook-KEE-nee	green summer squash

HERBS AND SPICES (ODORI E SPEZIE)

aglio	**AH-lyoh**	**garlic**
alloro	ahl-LOH-roh	bay leaves

aneto	ah-NEH-toh	dill
basilico	**bah-ZEE-lee-koh**	**basil**
cannella	kahn-NEHL-lah	cinnamon
capperi	KAHP-peh-ree	capers
chiodi di garofano	KYOH-dee dee gah-ROH-fah-noh	cloves
cipollotti	chee-pohl-LOHT-tee	chives
maggiorana	mahd-joh-RAH-nah	marjoram
menta	MEHN-tah	mint
noce moscata	NOH-cheh moh-SKAH-tah	nutmeg
origano	oh-REE-gah-noh	oregano
prezzemolo	**preht-TSEH-moh-loh**	**parsley**
rosmarino	**roh-smah-REE-noh**	**rosemary**
salvia	SAHL-vyah	sage
timo	TEE-moh	thyme
zafferano	dzahf-feh-RAH-noh	saffron
zenzero	DZEHN-dzeh-roh	ginger

POTATOES (PATATE)

I'd like some . . .	Vorrei delle patate . . .	vohr-RAY-DEHL-leh pah-TAH-teh . . .
_potatoes cooked with butter and parsley.	_al burro.	_ahl BOOR-roh
_potatoes baked with oil and rosemary.	_all'arrosto.	_ahl-ahr-ROH-stoh
_fried potatoes.	_fritte.	_FREET-teh
_boiled potatoes.	_lesse.	_LEHS-seh
_mashed potatoes.	_purè di patate	_poo-REH dee pah-TAH-teh

SALADS (INSALATE)

I'd like . . .	Vorrei un'insalata . . .	vohr-RAY oon een-sah-LAH-tah . . .
_a tomato salad.	_di pomodori.	_dee poh-moh-DOH-ree
_a radicchio salad.	_di radicchi.	_dee rah-DEEK-kee
_a mixed salad.	_mista.	_MEE-stah
_diced cooked vegetables with mayonnaise.	_russa.	_ROOS-sah
_a green salad.	_verde.	_VEHR-deh

CHEESE (FORMAGGI)

Cheese is used extensively in Italian cooking. Here's a list of the most renowned Italian cheeses:

asiago (ah-ZYAH-goh)	soft, pale yellow cheese, a little sharp and with little holes; a winter cheese
Bel Paese (behl pah-EH-zeh)	mild, soft, pale yellow cheese, creamy and quite delicate
caciocavallo (kah-choh-kah-VAHL-loh)	pear-shaped, yellow, hard-textured cheese with a tangy flavor; may be consumed fresh or seasoned for grating
carnia (KAHR-nyah)	soft, yellow cheese with sharp taste
fontina (fohn-TEE-nah)	creamy, soft, yellow cheese, with a mild flavor if consumed within eight months; aged for sharper taste
gorgonzola (gohr-gohn-DZOH-lah)	flavored, pungent, creamy, white cheese with green mold; like blue cheese, but creamier and softer
grana padano (GRAH-nah pah-DAH-noh)	also known as parmigiano-reggiano; yellow, hard cheese, dry and grainy; at its best when seasoned between 24 and 36 months, this is Italy's complement to pasta
mascarpone (mah-skahr-POH-neh)	very soft, creamy, sweet white cheese that looks like whipped cream; made with heavy cream; to be eaten within ten days

mozzarella (moht-tsah-REHL-lah)	moist, soft, white, unsalted cheese made with buffalo's milk
pecorino (peh-koh-REE-noh)	sharp, off-white cheese, made with sheep's milk
provolone (proh-voh-LOH-neh)	hard-textured, sharp, light yellow cheese, at times made with the addition of sheep's milk
ricotta (ree-KOHT-tah)	white, creamy cottage cheese, made only with sheep's milk; can be sweet or strong and salty
robbiola (rohb-BYOH-lah)	moist, off-white, soft cheese with a Brie-like crust, made with cow and sheep's milk
stracchino (strahk-KEE-noh)	soft, creamy, off-white cheese, excellent with fried polenta

FRUIT (FRUTTA)

Served after the cheese, fruit may also be a dessert.

I would like . . .	Vorrei . . .	vohr-RAY . . .
_some fresh fruit	_della frutta fresca	_DEHL-lah FROOT-tah FREH-skah
_a fruit cocktail	_una macedonia	_OO-nah mah-cheh-DOH-nyah
_an apricot	_un'albicocca	_oo-nahl-bee-KOHK-kah
_some pineapple	_dell'ananas	_dehl-LAH-nah-nahs
_some watermelon	_dell'anguria	_dehl-lahn-GOO-ryah
_an orange	**_un'arancia**	**_oo-nah-RAHN-chah**
_a banana	**_una banana**	**OO-nah bah-NAH-nah**
_a persimmon	_un caco	_oon KAH-koh
_some lime	_del cedro	_dehl CHEH-droh
_some cherries	_delle ciliegie	_DEHL-leh chee-LYEH-jeh
_some watermelon	_dell'anguria	_dehl-lahn-GOO-ree-ah
_some dates	_dei datteri	_day DAHT-teh-ree
_some figs	_dei fichi	_day FEE-kee
_some strawberries	**_delle fragole**	**_DEHL-leh FRAH-goh-leh**

_some raspberries	_dei lamponi	_day lahm-POH-nee
_some lemon	_del limone	_dehl lee-MOH-neh
_a tangerine	_un mandarino	_oon mahn-dah-REE-noh
_an apple	**_una mela**	**_OO-nah MEH-lah**
_some melon	_del melone	_dehl meh-LOH-neh
_some blueberries	_dei mirtilli	_day meer-TEEL-lee
_some blackberries	_delle more	_DEHL-leh MOH-reh
_a pear	_una pera	_OO-nah PEH-rah
_a peach	_una pesca	_OO-nah PEH-skah
_a grapefruit	_un pompelmo	_oon pohm-PEHL-moh
_a Sicilian orange	_un tarocco	_oon tah-ROHK-koh
_some white grapes	_dell'uva bianca	_dehl-LOO-vah BYAHN-kah
_some gooseberries	_dell'uva spina	_dehl-LOO-vah SPEE-nah

NUTS AND DRIED FRUIT (NOCI E FRUTTA SECCA)

peanuts	noccioline	noht-choh-LEE-neh
chestnuts	castagne	kah-STAH-nyeh
coconut	cocco	KOHK-koh
dried figs	fichi secchi	FEE-kee SEHK-kee
almonds	mandorle	MAHN-dohr-leh
hazelnuts	nocciole	noht-CHOH-leh
walnuts	noci	NOH-chee
pine nuts	pignoli	pee-NYOH-lee
dried plums	prugne secche	PROO-nyeh SEHK-keh
raisins	uva passa/uvetta	OO-vah PAHS-sah/oo-VEHT-tah

DESSERTS (DOLCI)

To finish your meal, choose from a variety of the tasty cakes and luscious ice creams for which Italy is famous. Here's a list of the most tempting desserts.

millefoglie (meel-leh-FOH-lyeh)	"a thousand leaves" or layers of crisp, light, buttery pastry dough	
tiramisù (tee-rah-mee-SOO)	cake made with sweet, creamy mascarpone cheese and sprinkled with cocoa powder	
zabaglione (dzah-bah-LYOH-neh)	egg yolks, sugar, and Marsala; may be served right away or chilled	
zuccotto (tsook-KOHT-toh)	round sponge cake with chocolate, cream, and candied fruit; best if chilled	
I'd like some dessert.	Vorrei del dolce.	vohr-RAY dehl DOHL-cheh.
I'd like a slice of cake with whipped cream.	Vorrei una fetta di torta con panna montata.	vohr-RAY OO-nah FEHT-tah dee TOHR-tah kohn PAHN-nah mohn-TAH-tah
Waiter, bring me . . .	**Cameriere, mi porti . . .**	**kah-meh-RYEH-reh, mee POHR-tee . . .**
_almond macaroons.	_amaretti.	_ah-mah-REHT-tee
_pudding.	_budino.	_boo-DEE-noh
_a cannolo.	_un cannolo.	_oon kahn-NOH-loh
_spumoni.	_cassata.	_kahs-SAH-tah
_pound cake.	_ciambella.	_chahm-BEHL-lah
_custard preserve.	_crostata.	_kroh-STAH-tah
_some ice cream.	**_del gelato . . .**	**_dehl jeh-LAH-toh . . .**
chocolate	al cioccolato.	ahl chohk-koh-LAH-toh
strawberry	alla fragola.	AHL-lah FRAH-goh-lah
lemon	al limone.	ahl lee-MOH-neh
vanilla	**alla vaniglia.**	**AHL-lah vah-NEE-lyah**
mixed	misto.	MEE-stoh
_some shaved ice . . .	_granita . . .	_grah-NEE-tah . . .
with coffee.	al caffè.	ahl kahf-FEH
with mint syrup.	alla menta.	AHL-lah MEHN-tah
with tamarind syrup.	al tamarindo.	ahl tah-mah-REEN-doh

_sponge cake.	_pan di Spagna.	_pahn dee SPAH-nyah
_apple strudel.	_strudel.	_STROO-dehl
_chocolate truffle.	_tartufo.	_tahr-TOO-foh
_some cake.	**_della torta ...**	**_DEH-lah TOHR-tah ...**
chocolate	**al cioccolato.**	**al chohk-koh-LAH-toh**

NONALCOHOLIC BEVERAGES (BEVANDE ANALCOLICHE)

The most popular nonalcoholic drink in Italy is *caffè espresso* (kahf-FEH eh-SPREHS-soh), which comes in different varieties:

caffè con panna (kahf-FEH kohn PAHN-nah)	coffee with whipped cream
caffè corretto (kahf-FEH kohr-REHT-toh)	coffee with a dash of liquor
	such as sambuca or grappa
caffè lungo (kahf-FEH LOON-goh)	larger cup of weaker coffee; synonym for American coffee
caffè ristretto (kahf-FEH ree-STREHT-toh)	the one and only espresso,
	thick and condensed
caffellatte (kahf-fehl-LAHT-teh)	coffee with milk
cappuccino (kahp-poot-CHEE-noh)	coffee with steamed, frothy milk

Waiter, please bring me ...	Cameriere, per favore mi porti ...	kah-meh-RYEH-reh, pehr fah-VOH-reh mee POHR-tee ...
_some ... water.	**_dell'acqua ...**	**_dehl-LAHK-kwah ...**
cold	fresca.	FREH-skah
ice	con ghiaccio.	kohn GYAHT-choh
carbonated mineral	minerale gassata.	mee-neh-RAH-leh gahs-SAH-tah
noncarbonated mineral	minerale naturale.	mee-neh-RAH-leh nah-too-RAH-leh
tonic	tonica.	TOH-nee-kah
_an orange soda	_un'aranciata.	_oo-nah-rahn-CHAH-tah

_a soda	_una bevanda gassata.	_OO-nah beh-VAHN-dah gahs-SAH-tah
_a bitter	_un bitter.	_oon BEET-tehr
_a . . . coffee.	_un caffè . . .	_oon kahf-FEH . . .
decaffeinated	decaffeinato.	deh-kahf-fay-NAH-toh
_a lemonade.	_una limonata.	_OO-nah lee-moh-NAH-tah
_a(n) . . . juice.	_un succo . . .	_oon SOOK-koh . . .
orange	d'arancia.	dah-RAHN-chah
fruit	di frutta.	dee FROOT-tah
_a cup of tea . . .	_un tè . . .	_oon teh . . .
with milk.	con latte.	kohn LAHT-teh
with lemon.	con limone.	kohn lee-MOH-neh
_an iced tea.	_un tè freddo.	_oon teh FREHD-doh

ALCOHOLIC BEVERAGES (BEVANDE ALCOLICHE)

Aperitifs (Aperitivi)

The *aperitivo* (ah-peh-ree-TEE-voh) is taken leisurely before lunch and dinner as an appetite stimulant. Italians do not usually have cocktails before their meals as Americans do. The aperitifs may be either sweet, like vermouth, or bitter, like campari. Most bars have "un aperitivo della casa" usually fruit based, and always a house specialty. Here are the most common:

americano (ah-meh-ree-KAH-noh)	a combination of sweet vermouth, brandy, bitters, and lemon peel
Bellini (behl-LEE-nee)	chilled dry, white wine or champagne, and peach juice
Campari soda (kahm-PAH-ree SOH-dah)	a bittersweet drink that can be taken neat or mixed with seltzer water or orange juice
Prosecco (proh-SEH-koh)	Italy's answer to champagne; a light, effervescent white wine

81

Phrases for Ordering Drinks

straight	liscio	LEE-shoh
on the rocks	con ghiaccio	kohn GYAHT-choh
with seltzer/soda	con seltz/soda	kohn sehltz/SOH-dah
with water	con acqua	kohn AHK-kwah

Beer (Birra)

Beer is becoming more popular among young Italians, especially accompanying a sandwich, a pizza, or a light meal. However, a glass of beer still costs considerably more than a glass of wine.

I'd like a . . . beer.	Vorrei una birra . . .	vohr-RAY OO-nah BEER-rah . . .
_bottled	_in bottiglia.	_een boht-TEE-lyah
_can of	_in lattina.	_een laht-TEE-nah
_dark	_scura.	_SKOO-rah
_draft	**_alla spina.**	**_AHL-lah SPEE-nah**
_foreign	_estera.	_EH-steh-rah
_light	_bionda.	_BYOHN-dah
_local	**_nazionale.**	**_nah-tsyoh-NAH-leh**
Bring me a beer, please.	Mi porti una birra, per favore.	mee POHR-tee OO-nah BEER-rah, pehr fah-VOH-reh

Wine (Vino)

Italy is one of the great wine-producing countries of the world, with vineyards found from north to south as well as on the islands (such as Sardinia, Elba, and Sicily—to name but a few). Every region of the country, due to its favorable climate and soil conditions, produces notable wine. The vineyards of greatest renown are in Piedmont, Veneto, Tuscany, and Sicily. Here's a list of some of the better-known wines and the regions where they are produced:

Dry White Wine	Sweet White Wine	Red Wine
Albana (Emilia-Romagna)	Aleatico (Isle of Elba)	Barbera (Piedmont)
Est Est Est (Latium)	Malvasia (Sicily)	Bardolino (Veneto)
Frascati (Latium)	Marsala (Sicily)	Barolo (Piedmont)
Orvieto (Umbria)	Verduzzo (Trentino)	Brunello di Montalcino (Tuscany)
Pinot (Veneto)	Vin Santo (Tuscany)	
Soave (Veneto)	Lacrima Christi (Campania)	Chianti (Tuscany)
Verdicchio (Marches)		Corvo (Sicily)
Vernaccia (Tuscany)		Lambrusco (Emilia-Romagna) Valpolicella (Veneto)

Sparkling Wines

Asti Spumante Brut	Berlucchi Brut	Ferrari Brut

Ordering Wine

What wine do you recommend?	Che vino consiglia?	keh VEE-noh kohn-SEE-lyah?
Where does this wine come from?	Di dov'è questo vino?	dee doh-VEH KWEH-stoh VEE-noh?
I'd like . . .	Vorrei . . .	vohr-RAY . . .
_a bottle of . . .	_una bottiglia di . . .	_OO-nah boht-TEE-lyah dee . . .
red wine.	vino rosso.	VEE-noh ROHS-soh
rosé.	vino rosé.	VEE-noh roh-ZEH
white wine.	vino bianco.	VEE-noh BYAHN-koh
dry wine.	vino secco.	VEE-noh SEHK-koh
light wine.	vino leggero.	VEE-noh lehd-JEH-roh
sweet wine.	vino dolce.	VEE-noh DOHL-cheh
full-bodied wine.	vino corposo.	VEE-noh kohr-POH-zoh
sparkling wine.	spumante.	spoo-MAHN-teh

champagne.	champagne.	shahm-PAHN
_a carafe.	_una caraffa.	_OO-nah kah-RAHF-fah
_a glass.	_un bicchiere.	_oon beek-KYEH-reh
_a half-bottle.	_una mezza bottiglia.	_OO-nah MEHD-dzah boht-TEE-lyah
_another bottle.	_un'altra bottiglia.	_oo-NAHL-trah boht-TEE-lyah
_a liter.	_un litro.	_oon LEE-troh
_a local wine.	_del vino locale.	_dehl VEE-noh loh-KAH-leh
_to taste some . . .	_assaggiare un po' di . . .	_ahs-sahd-JAH-reh oon poh dee . . .
_to see the wine list.	_vedere la lista dei vini.	_veh-DEH-reh lah LEE-stah day VEE-nee
To your health/Cheers!	Salute! (or) Cin cin!	sah-LOO-teh cheen cheen

After-Dinner Drinks (Liquori e digestivi)

Here is a list of some of the more popular after-dinner drinks.

bitters	un amaro	oo-nah-MAH-roh
brandy	un brandy	oon BREHN-dee
cognac	un cognac	oon KOH-nyahk
grappa	una grappa	OO-nah GRAHP-pah
limoncello		(lee-mohn-CHEH-loh)
sambuca	una sambuca	OO-nah sahm-BOO-kah
vin santo		(VEEN SAHN-toh)

The bitter Fernet Branca, Branca Menta, China Martini, and Amaro Averna are well-known digestive drinks. You may also want to try the strong northern Italian aquavit, grappa, or, on the sweeter side, the anise-flavored *sambuca* or the almond-flavored *amaretto*.

SPECIAL DIETS

| I am on a diet. | Sono a dieta. | SON-noh ah DYEH-tah |
| I am on a special diet. | Seguo una dieta speciale. | SEH-gwoh OO-nah DYEH-tah speh-CHAH-leh |

I am a vegetarian.	Sono vegetariano (-a).	SOH-noh veh-jeh-tah-RYAH-noh (-nah)
Do you have vegetarian dishes?	Servite piatti vegetariani?	sehr-VEE-teh PYAHT-tee veh-jeh-tah-RYAH-nee?
I am allergic to . . .	Sono allergico(-a) a . . .	SOH-noh ahl-LEHR-jee-koh(-kah) ah . . .
I can't eat . . .	Devo evitare . . .	DEH-voh eh-vee-TAH-reh . . .
_salt.	_il sale.	_eel SAH-leh
_fat.	_i grassi.	_ee GRAHS-see
_sugar.	_lo zucchero	_loh TSOOK-keh-roh
_flour.	_la farina.	_lah fah-REE-nah
I am diabetic.	Soffro di diabete.	SOHF-froh dee dyah-BEH-teh
I don't eat pork.	Non mangio carne di maiale.	nohn MAHN-joh KAHR-neh dee mah-YAH-leh
I want to lose/gain weight.	Voglio dimagrire/ ingrassare.	VOH-lyoh dee-mah-GREE-reh/ een-grahs-SAH-reh

COMPLAINTS

I didn't order this.	Non è quello che avevo ordinato.	nohn eh KWEHL-loh keh ah-VEH-voh ohr-dee-NAH-toh
May I change this?	Posso cambiare questo?	POHS-soh kahm-BYAH-reh KWEH-stoh?
This is too . . .	È troppo . . .	eh TROHP-poh . . .
_rare.	_al sangue.	_ahl SAHN-gweh
_well done.	_cotto.	_KOHT-toh
_tough.	_duro.	_DOO-roh
_salty.	_salato.	_sah-LAH-toh
_bitter.	_amaro.	_ah-MAH-roh
_sweet.	_dolce.	_DOHL-cheh
I don't like it.	Non mi piace.	nohn mee PYAH-cheh

85

This is not clean.	Non è pulito.	nohn eh poo-LEE-toh
This is cold.	È freddo.	eh FREHD-doh
It isn't fresh.	Non è fresco.	nohn eh FREH-skoh
This wine tastes of cork.	Il vino sa di tappo.	eel VEE-noh sah dee TAHP-poh
There's a knife missing.	Manca un coltello.	MAHN-kah oon kohl-TEHL-loh

THE BILL (IL CONTO)

Waiter!/Miss! The check, please.	**Cameriere(-a)! Il conto, per favore.**	**kah-meh-RYEH-reh (-rah)! eel KOHN-toh, pehr fah-VOH-reh**
Only one check, please.	Faccia un conto unico, per favore.	FAHT-chah oon KOHN-toh oo-NEE-koh, pehr fah-VOH-reh
Please, give us separate checks.	Conti separati, per cortesia.	KOHN-tee seh-pah-RAH-tee pehr kohr-teh-ZEE-ah
We are going Dutch (literally, Roman).	Facciamo alla romana.	faht-CHAH-moh AHL-lah roh-MAH-nah
Is service included?	**Il servizio è compreso?**	**eel sehr-VEE-tsyoh eh kohm-PREH-zoh?**
What's this amount for?	Per che cos'è quest'importo?	pehr keh koh-ZEH kweh-steem-POHR-toh?
I think there's a mistake.	Penso che ci sia un errore.	PEHN-soh keh chee SEE-ah oon ehr-ROH-reh
The meal was excellent.	È stato un pasto delizioso.	eh STAH-toh oon PAH-stoh deh-lee-TSYOH-soh
The service was very good.	Il servizio è stato ottimo.	eel sehr-VEE-tsyoh eh STAH-toh OHT-tee-moh

SOCIALIZING

Meeting people and making new friends are probably among the most memorable and rewarding aspects of an experience abroad.

DIALOGUE Introductions (Le Presentazioni)

Turista:	**Buon giorno. Mi permetta di presentarmi. Mi chiamo Jim Elliot.**	bwohn JYOHR-noh. mee pehr-MEHT-tah dee preh-zehn-TAHR-mee. mee KYAH-moh Jim Elliot
Sig.ra Rossi:	**Piacere. Io mi chiamo Maria Rossi.**	pyah-CHEH-reh. EE-oh mee KYAH-moh mah-REE-ah ROHS-see
Turista:	**Piacere.**	pyah-CHEH-reh
Sig.ra Rossi:	**È qui in vacanza?**	eh kwee een vah-KAHN-tsah?
Turista:	**Sì, rimarrò due settimane.**	see. ree-mahr-ROH DOO-eh seht-tee-MAH-neh.
Sig.ra Rossi:	**Buona permanenza e si diverta!**	BWOH-nah pehr-mah-NEHN-tsah eh see dee-VEHR-tah!
Turista:	**Grazie. Arrivederci.**	GRAH-tsyeh. ahr-ree-veh-DEHR-chee

....

Tourist:	Hello. Allow me to introduce myself. My name is Jim Elliot.
Mrs. Rossi:	Pleased to meet you. My name is Maria Rossi.
Tourist:	Pleased to meet you.
Mrs. Rossi:	Are you here on vacation?
Tourist:	Yes. I'll be here for two weeks.
Mrs. Rossi:	Have a good stay and enjoy yourself!
Tourist:	Thank you. Good-bye.

FIRST CONVERSATION

I'd like to introduce you to . . .	Vorrei presentarLe . . .	vohr-RAY preh-zehn-TAHR-leh . . .
_Mr. Rossi.	_il signor Rossi.	_eel see-NYOHR ROHS-see
_Mrs. Rossi.	_la signora Rossi.	_lah-see-NYOH-rah ROHS-see
_Miss/Ms. Rossi.	_la signorina Rossi.	_lah see-nyoh-REE-nah ROHS-see
Pleased to meet you.	**Piacere.**	**pyah-CHEH-reh**
A pleasure.	Piacere mio.	pyah-CHEH-reh MEE-oh
Allow me to introduce myself.	Mi permetta di presentarmi.	mee pehr-MEHT-tah dee preh-zehn-TAHR-mee
What's your name?	Come si chiama?	KOH-meh see KYAH-mah?
My name is . . .	**Mi chiamo . . .**	**mee KYAH-moh . . .**
I am . . .	**Sono . . .**	**SOH-noh . . .**
This is . . .	**È . . .**	**eh . . .**
_my husband	_mio marito.	_MEE-oh mah-REE-toh
_my wife.	_mia moglie.	_MEE-ah MOH-lyeh
_my colleague.	_il mio collega (or) la mia collega.	_eel MEE-oh kohl-LEH-gah lah MEE-ah kohl-LEH-gah
_my friend.	_il mio amico (m.).	_eel MEE-ah ah-MEE-koh
	la mia amica (f.).	lah MEE-ah ah-MEE-kah
How are you?	**Come sta?**	**KOH-meh stah?**
Fine, thanks. And you?	**Bene, grazie. E Lei?**	**BEH-neh GRAH-tsyeh. eh LEH-ee?**
How's it going?	Come va?	KOH-meh vah?
It's going well. Thank you.	Bene, grazie.	BEH-neh, GRAH-tsyeh

WHERE ARE YOU FROM?

Where are you from?	Da dove viene? (or) Di dov'è?	dah DOH-veh VYEH-neh? dee doh-VEH?
I come from Italy.	Vengo dall'Italia. (or) Sono italiano (-a).	VEHN-goh dahl-lee-TAH-lyah SOH-noh ee-tah-LYAH-noh(-nah)
I come from . . .	Vengo . . .	VEHN-goh . . .
_Switzerland.	_dalla Svizzera.	_DAHL-lah ZVEET-tseh rah
_Egypt.	_dall'Egitto.	_dahl-leh-JEET-toh
_Austria.	_dall'Austria.	_dahl-LOW-stryah
_Portugal.	_dal Portogallo.	_dahl pohr-toh-GAHL-loh
_the Bahamas.	_dalle Bahamas.	_DAHL-leh bah-HAH-mahz
_the United States.	_dagli Stati Uniti.	_DAH-lyee STAH-tee oo-NEE-tee
I'm going to . . .	Vado . . .	VAH-doh . . .
_Germany.	_in Germania.	_een jehr-MAH-nyah
_Mexico.	_in Messico.	_een MEHS-see-koh
_the Azores.	_alle Azorre.	_AHL-leh ah-DZOHR-reh
_the United States.	_negli Stati Uniti.	_NEH-lyee STAH-tee oo-NEE-tee
Where do you live?	**Dove abita?**	**DOH-veh AH-bee-tah?**

Notes: 1. To express the idea of *from*, use *dal* before a masculine country beginning with a consonant, use *dalla* before a feminine country beginning with a consonant, *dall'* before a masculine or feminine country beginning with a vowel, *dalle* before a feminine country that is plural, and *dagli* before a masculine country that is plural (like the United States).

2. For *in* or *to*, use *in* with both masculine and feminine countries that are singular, no matter how they begin; *alle* with feminine plural countries; *negli* with masculine plural countries.

3. For cities, use *da* alone to express *from*—vengo da Roma (VEHN-goh dah ROH-mah)—and use *a* alone to express *to*—vado a Milano (VAH-doh ah mee-LAH-noh).

I live in . . .	Abito . . .	AH-bee-toh . . .
_the United States.	_negli Stati Uniti.	_NEH-lyee STAH-tee oo-NEE-tee
_New York City.	_a New York.	_ah noo yohrk
That's in the . . .	È a (al). . .	eh ah . . .
_north.	_nord.	_nohrd
_south.	_sud.	_sood
_east.	_est.	_ehst
_west.	_ovest.	_OH-vehst
That's near . . .	È vicino . . .	eh vee-CHEE-noh . . .
_the coast.	_alla costa.	_AHL-lah KOH-stah
_the border.	_al confine.	_ahl kohn-FEE-neh
_the ocean.	_all'oceano.	_ahl-loh-CHEH-ah-noh
_the mountains.	_alle montagne.	_AHL-leh mohn-TAH-nyeh
I am from San Francisco.	Sono di San Francisco.	SOH-noh dee sahn frahn-SEE-skoh
How do you like Italy?	Le piace l'Italia?	leh PYAH-cheh lee-TAH-lyah?
I like it very much.	Mi piace moltissimo.	mee PYAH-cheh mohl-TEES-see-moh
I'm not sure yet.	Non sono ancora sicuro(-a).	nohn SOH-noh ahn-KOH-rah see-KOO-roh(-rah)
I like the people a lot.	Mi piace molto la gente.*	mee PYAH-cheh MOHL-toh lah JEHN-teh
I like the country.	Mi piace il paese.*	mee PYAH-cheh eel pah-EH-zeh
Everything is so . . .	Tutto è così . . .	TUHT-toh eh koh-ZEE . . .
_interesting.	_interessante.	_een-teh-rehs-SAHN-teh

*In Italian, the verb *piacere* agrees with the object. The literal translation of *Mi piace l'Italia* is "Italy is pleasing to me." *Piace* is used when the object is singular, *piacciono* when the object is plural (see also grammar on p. 210).

_different.	_differente.	_deef-feh-REHN-teh
_strange.	_strano.	_STRAH-noh
_wonderful.	_meraviglioso.	_meh-rah-vee-LYOH-zoh
_beautiful.	_bello.	_BEHL-loh
_nice.	_simpatico.	_seem-PAH-tee-koh
_pretty.	_carino.	_kah-REE-noh

CONTINENTS, COUNTRIES, AND NATIONALITIES

Africa	l'Africa	LAH-free-kah
Asia	l'Asia	LAH-zyah
Australia	l'Australia	low-STRAH-lyah
Europe	l'Europa	leh-oo-ROH-pah
North America	l'America del Nord	lah-MEH-ree-kah dehl nohrd
South America	l'America del Sud	lah-MEH-ree-kah dehl sood

Country	Paese (pah-EH-zeh)	Nationality/ Nazionalità (nah-tsyoh-nah-lee-TAH)
Algeria	l'Algeria (lahl-jeh-REE-ah)	algerino(-a) (ahl-jeh-REE-noh[-nah])
Argentina	l'Argentina (lahr-jehn-TEE-nah)	argentino(-a) (ahr-jehn-TEE-noh [-nah])
Australia	l'Australia (low-STRAH-lyah)	australiano(-a) (ow-strah-LYAH-noh [-nah])
Austria	l'Austria (LOW-stryah)	austriaco(-a) (ow-STREE-ah-koh [-kah])
Belgium	il Belgio (eel BEHL-joh)	belga (BEHL-gah)
Bolivia	la Bolivia (lah boh-LEE-vyah)	boliviano(-a) (boh-lee-VYAH-noh [-nah])

91

Brazil	il Brasile (eel brah-ZEE-leh)	brasiliano(-a) (brah-zee-LYAH-noh [-nah])
Canada	il Canada (eel KAH-nah-dah)	canadese (kah-nah-DEH-zeh)
Chile	il Cile (eel CHEE-leh)	cileno(-a) (chee-LEH-noh[-nah])
China	la Cina (lah CHEE-nah)	cinese (chee-NEH-zeh)
Colombia	la Colombia (lah koh-LOHM-byah)	colombiano(-a) (koh-lohm-BYAH-noh [-nah])
Costa Rica	la Costa Rica (lah KOH-stah REE- kah)	costaricano(-a) (koh-stah-ree-KAH- noh[-nah])
Cuba	Cuba (KOO-bah)	cubano(-a) (koo-BAH-noh[-nah])
Denmark	la Danimarca (lah dah-nee-MAHR- kah)	danese (dah-NEH-zeh)
Dominican Republic	la Repubblica Dominicana (lah reh-POOB-blee- kah doh-mee-nee- KAH-nah)	dominicano(-a) (doh-mee-nee-KAH- noh[-nah])
Ecuador	l'Ecuador (leh-kwah-DOHR)	ecuadoriano(-a) (eh-kwah-dohr-YAH- noh[-nah])
Egypt	l'Egitto (leh-JEET-toh)	egiziano(-a) (eh-jee-TSYAH-noh [-nah])
England	l'Inghilterra (leen-geel-TEHR-rah)	inglese (een-GLEH-zeh)
Finland	la Finlandia (lah feen-LAHN-dyah)	finlandese (feen-lahn-DEH-zeh)
France	la Francia (lah FRAHN-chah)	francese (frahn-CHEH-zeh)
Germany	la Germania (lah jehr-MAH-nyah)	tedesco(-a) (teh-DEH-skoh[-skoh])

Greece	la Grecia (lah GREH-chah)	greco(-a) (GREH-koh[-kah])
Holland	l'Olanda (lah-LAHN-dah)	olandese (oh-lahn-DEH-zeh)
Iceland	l'Islanda (lee-SLAHN-dah)	islandese (ee-slahn-DEH-zeh)
India	l'India (LEEN-dyah)	indiano(-a) (een-DYAH-noh[-nah])
Ireland	l'Irlanda (leer-LAHN-dah)	irlandese (eer-lahn-DEH-zeh)
Israel	l'Israele (ee-zrah-EH-leh)	israeliano(-a) (ee-zrah-eh-LYAH-noh [-nah])
Italy	l'Italia (lee-TAH-lyah)	italiano(-a) (ee-tah-LYAH-noh [-nah])
Japan	il Giappone (eel jahp-POH-neh)	giapponese (jahp-poh-NEH-zeh)
Mexico	il Messico (eel MEHS-see-koh)	messicano(-a) (mehs-see-KAH-noh [-nah])
Morocco	il Marocco (eel mah-ROHK-koh)	marocchino(-a) (mah-rohk-KEE-noh [-nah])
New Zealand	la Nuova Zelanda (lah NWOH-vah dzeh-LAHN-dah)	zelandese (dzeh-lahn-DEH-zeh)
Norway	la Norvegia (lah nohr-VEH-jah)	norvegese (nohr-veh-JEH-zeh)
Panama	il Panama (PAH-nah-mah)	panamense (pah-nah-MEHN-zeh)
Paraguay	il Paraguay (eel pah-rah-GWAHY)	paraguaiano(-a) (pah-rah-gwah-YAH-noh[-nah])
Peru	il Perù (eel peh-ROO)	peruviano(-a) (peh-roo-VYAH-noh [-nah])
Poland	la Polonia (lah poh-LOH-nyah)	polacco(-a) (poh-LAHK-koh[-kah])

Portugal	il Portogallo (eel pohr-toh-GAHL-loh)	portoghese (pohr-toh-GEH-zeh)
Puerto Rico	il Porto Rico (eel POHR-toh REE-koh)	portoricano(-a) (pohr-toh-ree-KAH-noh[-nah])
Russia	la Russia (lah ROOS-syah)	russo(-a) (ROOS-soh[-sah])
Spain	la Spagna (lah SPAH-nyah)	spagnolo(-a) (spah-NYOH-loh[-lah])
Sweden	la Svezia (lah ZVEH-tsyah)	svedese (zveh-DEH-zeh)
Switzerland	la Svizzera (lah ZVEET-tseh-rah)	svizzero(-a) (ZVEET-tseh-roh[-rah])
Thailand	la Tailandia (lah tahy-LAHN-dyah)	tailandese (tahy-lahn-DEH-zeh)
Tunisia	la Tunisia (lah too-nee-SEE-ah)	tunisino(-a) (too-nee-SEE-noh [-nah])
Turkey	la Turchia (lah toor-KEE-ah)	turco(-a) (TOOR-koh[-kah])
United States	gli Stati Uniti (lyee STAH-tee oo-NEE-tee)	americano(-a) (ah-meh-ree-KAH-noh [-nah]
Uruguay	l'Uruguai (loo-roo-GWAHY)	uruguaiano(-a) (oo-roo-gwah-YAH-noh-[-nah])
Venezuela	il Venezuela (eel veh-neh-TZWEH-lah)	venezuelano(-a) (veh-neh-tzweh-LAH-noh[-nah])

WHAT DO YOU DO?

Where do you work?	Dove lavora?	DOH-veh lah-VOH-rah?
What do you do?	**Che cosa fa?**	**keh KOH-zah fah?**
What is your profession?*	Che professione esercita?	keh proh-fehs-SYOH-neh eh-SEHR-chee tah?
What's your field?	In quale campo lavora?	een KWAH-leh KAHM-poh lah-VOH-rah?

I am . . .	Sono . . .	SOH-noh . . .
_a businessman.	_un uomo d'affari.	_oon WOH-moh dahf-FAH-ree
_a professor.	_professore (m.). professoressa (f.).	_proh-fehs-SOH-reh proh-fehs-soh-REHS-sah
_a doctor.	_medico (or) dottore (m.). dottoressa (f.).	_MEH-dee-koh doht-TOH-reh doht-toh-REHS-sah
_a lawyer.	_un avvocato.	_oon ahv-voh-KAH-toh
I'm retired.	Sono in pensione (or) pensionato (-a).	SOH-noh een pehn-SYOH-neh pehn-syoh-NAH-toh (-tah)
I am not working anymore.	Non lavoro più.	nohn lah-VOH-roh pyoo

JOBS AND OCCUPATIONS

Professions/ Occupations	Professioni/ Occupazioni	proh-feh-SYOH-nee/ ohk-koo-pah-TSYOH-nee
accountant	ragioniere	rah-joh-NYEH-reh
architect	architetto	ahr-kee-TEHT-toh/tah
artist	artista*	ahr-TEE-stah
baker	fornaio(-a)	fohr-NAH-yoh(-yah)
blacksmith	fabbro	FAHB-broh
butcher	macellaio(-a)	mah-chehl-LAH-yoh (-yah)
cardiologist	cardiologo	kahr-DYOH-loh-goh/gah
carpenter	falegname	fah-leh-NYAH-meh
chef	chef	shehf
clerk	impiegato(-a)	eem-pyeh-GAH-toh (-tah)
cook	cuoco(-a)	KWOH-koh(-kah)

*The masculine form of some professions is used by women as well as men. Masculine forms ending in -a also can be used for both men and women.

95

dentist	dentista	dehn-TEE-stah
doctor	dottore/dottoressa	doh-TOH-reh/doh-toh-REHS-sah
	(or) medico	MEH-dee-koh
electrician	elettricista	eh-leht-tree-CHEE-stah
engineer	ingegnere	een-jeh-NYEH-reh
eye doctor (opthalmologist)	oculista	oh-koo-LEE-stah
lawyer	avvocato	ahv-voh-KAH-toh
locksmith	fabbro ferraio	FAHB-broh fehr-RAH-yoh
maid	cameriera	kah-meh-RYEH-rah
neurologist	neurologo	neh-oo-ROH-loh-goh
nurse	infermiere(-a)	een-fehr-MYEH-reh (-rah)
painter	pittore/pittrice	peet-TOH-reh/peet-TREE-cheh
plumber	idraulico	ee-DROW-lee-koh
salesperson	commesso(-a)	kohm-MEHS-soh(-sah)
sculptor	scultore/scultrice	skool-TOH-reh/skool-TREE-cheh
shoemaker	calzolaio	kahl-tsoh-LAH-yoh
shopkeeper	negoziante	neh-goh-TSYAHN-teh
waiter/waitress	cameriere(-a)	kah-meh-RYEH-reh (-rah)
writer	scrittore/scrittrice	skreet-TOH-reh/skreet-TREE-cheh

MAKING FRIENDS

It's so good to see you.	Che piacere verderLa.	keh pyah-CHEH-reh veh-DEHR-lah
It's nice to be here.	È un piacere essere qui.	eh oon pyah-CHEH-reh ehs-SEH-reh kwee
May I buy you a drink?	Posso offrirLe qualcosa da bere?	POHS-soh ohf-FREER-leh kwahl-KOH-sah dah BEH-reh?

96

Shall we have a drink together?	Beviamo qualcosa insieme?	beh-VYAH-moh kwahl-KOH-zah een-SYEH-meh?
With pleasure.	Con piacere.	kohn pyah-CHEH-reh
Cheers!	Salute!	sah-LOO-teh!
No, thank you.	No, grazie.	noh GRAH-tsyeh
Would you like to go with us to . . .	Vuole venire con noi . . .	voo-OH-leh veh-NEE-reh kohn noy . . .
_a café?	_al bar?	_ahl bahr?
_the theatre?	_a teatro?	_ahl teh-AH-troh?
_to the movies?	_al cinema?	_ahl CHEE-neh-mah?
_to a restaurant?	_al ristorante?	_ahl ree-stoh-RAHN-teh?
Gladly.	Volentieri.	voh-lehn-TYEH-ree
May I bring a friend?	Posso portare un amico(-a)?	POHS-soh pohr-TAH-reh oon-ah-MEE-koh(-kah)?
Do you mind if I smoke?	Le dispiace se fumo?	leh dee-SPYAH-cheh seh FOO-moh?
Not at all.	Per niente. (or) Non affatto.	pehr NYEHN-teh nohn ahf-FAHT-toh
Yes, it bothers me.	Sì, mi dà fastidio.	see, mee dah fah-STEE-dyoh
May I telephone you?	Posso telefonarle?	POHS-soh teh-leh-foh-NAHR-leh?
What's your number?	Qual è il Suo numero di telefono?	kwah-LEH eel SOO-oh NOO-meh-roh dee teh-LEH-foh-noh?
What's your address?	Qual è il Suo indirizzo?	kwah-LEH eel SOO-oh een-dee-REET-soh?
Are you married?	È sposato (-a)?	eh spoh-ZAH-toh (-tah)?
No, I'm . . .	No, sono . . .	noh, SOH-noh . . .
_single (m.).	_celibe (or) scapolo.	_CHEH-lee-beh SKAH-poh-loh
_single (f.).	_nubile.	_NOO-bee-leh
I have . . .	Ho . . .	oh . . .

_a boyfriend.	_il ragazzo.	_eel rah-GAHT-soh
_a girlfriend.	_la ragazza.	_lah rah-GAHT-sah
_a fiancé.	_il fidanzato.	_eel fee-dahn-TSAH-toh
_a fiancée.	_la fidanzata.	_lah fee-dahn-TSAH-tah
I'm divorced.	Sono divorziato (-a).	SOH-noh dee-vohr-TSYAH-toh(-tah)
I'm separated.	Sono separato(-a).	SOH-noh seh-pah-RAH-toh(-tah)
I am a widow(er).	Sono vedova(-o).	SOH-noh VEH-doh-vah(-voh)
I'm alone.	Sono solo(-a).	SOH-noh SOH-loh(-lah)
I'm traveling with a friend.	Viaggio con un amico(-a).	VYAHD-joh kohn oon-ah-MEE-koh(-kah)
You should come visit us (at our house).	Perché non ci viene a trovare?	pehr-KEH nonh cee VYEH-neh ah troh-VAH-reh?
You're so kind!	Molto gentile!	MOHL-toh jehn-TEE-leh!
Are you free . . .	**È libero(-a) . . .**	**eh LEE-beh-roh (-rah) . . .**
_this evening?	_stasera?	_stah-SEH-rah?
_tomorrow?	_domani?	_doh-MAH-nee?
I'll wait for you here.	L'aspetto qui.	lah-SPEHT-toh kwee
I'll pick you up at the hotel.	La vengo a prendere in albergo.	lah VEHN-goh ah PREHN-deh-reh een ahl-BEHR-goh
It's getting late.	**Si sta facendo tardi.**	**see stah fah-CHEHN-doh TAHR-dee**
It's time to go back.	È ora di rientrare.	eh OH-rah dee ryehn-TRAH-reh
We are leaving tomorrow.	Partiamo domani.	pahr-TYAH-moh doh-MAH-nee
Thanks for everything.	Grazie di tutto.	GRAH-tsyeh dee TOOT-toh

had a very good time.	Mi sono divertito (-a) molto.	mee SOH-noh dee-vehr-TEE-toh(-tah) MOHL-toh
We are going to miss you.	Ci mancherà.	chee mahn-keh-RAH
t was nice to have met you.	È stato un piacere aver fatto la Sua conoscenza.	eh STAH-toh oon pyah-CHEH-reh ah-VEHR FAHT-toh lah SOO-ah koh-noh-SHEHN-tsah
Give my best to . . .	Mi saluti . . .	mee sah-LOO-tee . . .
Can I give you a ride?	Posso darLe un passaggio?	POHS-soh DAHR-leh oon pahs-SAHD-joh?
Don't bother, thank you.	Non si disturbi, grazie.	nohn see dee-STOOR-bee, GRAH-tsyeh
can take a taxi.	Posso prendere un taxi.	POHS-soh PREHN-deh-reh oon TAHK-see
Bye.	Arrivederci.	ahr-ree-veh-DEHR-chee

THE FAMILY

have a . . . family.	Ho una famiglia . . .	oh OO-nah fah-MEE-lyah . . .
_big	_numerosa.	_noo-meh-ROH-zah
_small	_piccola.	_PEEK-koh-lah
Here is . . .	Ecco . . .	EHK-koh . . .
_my husband.	_mio marito.	_MEE-oh mah-REE-toh
_my wife.	_mia moglie.	_MEE-ah MOH-lyeh
_my son.	_mio figlio.	_MEE-oh FEE-lyoh
_my daughter.	_mia figlia.	_MEE-ah FEE-lyah
have . . .	Ho . . .	oh . . .
_two sons.	_due maschi.	_DOO-eh MAH-skee
_two daughters.	_due femmine.	_DOO-eh FEHM-mee-neh
_three small children.	_tre bambini.	_treh bahm-BEE-nee

_three children.	_tre figli.	_treh FEE-lyee
Here are my parents!	Ecco i miei genitori!	EHK-koh ee mee-AY jeh-nee-TOH-ree!
Here is . . .	Ecco . . .	EHK-koh . . .
_my father.	_mio padre.	_MEE-oh PAH-dreh
_my mother.	_mia madre.	_MEE-ah MAH-dreh
I have many relatives.	Ho molti parenti.	oh MOHL-tee pah-REHN-tee
I have . . .	Ho . . .	oh . . .
_a brother.	_un fratello.	_oon frah-TEHL-loh
_a sister.	_una sorella.	_OO-nah soh-REHL-lah
_a grandfather.	_un nonno.	_oon NOHN-noh
_a grandmother.	_una nonna.	_OO-nah NOHN-nah
_a grandson/ nephew.	_un nipote.	_oon nee-POH-teh
_a granddaughter/ niece.	_una nipote.	_OO-nah nee-POH-teh
_a cousin (m.).	_un cugino.	_oon koo-JEE-noh
_a cousin (f.).	_una cugina.	_OO-nah koo-JEE-nah
_an aunt.	_una zia.	_OO-nah TSEE-ah
_an uncle.	_uno zio.	_OO-noh TSEE-oh
_in-laws.	_dei suoceri.	_day SWOH-cheh-ree
_a brother-in-law.	_un cognato.	_oon koh-NYAH-toh
_a sister-in-law.	_una cognata.	_OO-nah koh-NYAH-tah
_a father-in-law.	_un suocero.	_oon SWOH-cheh-roh
_a mother-in-law.	_una suocera.	_OO-nah SWOH-cheh-rah
my eldest son	mio figlio maggiore	MEE-oh FEE-lyoh mahd-JOH-reh
my youngest daughter	mia figlia minore	MEE-ah FEE-lyah mee-NOH-reh

IN THE HOME

Make yourself at home.	Faccia come a casa Sua.	FAHT-chah KOH-meh ah KAH-zah SOO-ah
You may sit here.	Prego, s'accomodi qui.	PREH-goh sahk-KOH-moh-dee kwee
What a pretty house!	Che bella casa!	keh BEHL-lah KAH-zah!
I really like this neighborhood.	Mi piace molto questa zona.	mee PYAH-cheh MOHL-toh KWEH-stah ZOH-nah
Here is . . .	Ecco . . .	EHK-koh . . .
_the kitchen.	_la cucina.	_lah koo-CHEE-nah
_the living room.	_il salotto.	_eel sah-LOHT-toh
_the dining room.	_la sala da pranzo.	_lah SAH-lah dah PRAHN-dzoh
_the bedroom.	_la camera da letto.	_lah KAH-meh-rah dah LEHT-toh
_the bathroom.	_il bagno.	_eel BAH-nyoh
_the closets.	_gli armadi.	_lyee ahr-MAH-dee
_the couch.	_il divano.	_eel dee-VAH-noh
_the armchair.	_la poltrona.	_lah pohl-TROH-nah
_the table.	_la tavola.	_lah TAH-voh-lah
_the chairs.	_le sedie.	_leh SEH-dyeh
_the lamp.	_la lampada.	_lah LAHM-pah-dah
_the door.	_la porta.	_lah POHR-tah
_the window.	_la finestra.	_lah fee-NEH-strah
_the ceiling.	_il soffitto.	_eel sohf-FEET-toh
_the floor.	_il pavimento.	_eel pah-vee-MEHN-toh
It's . . .	È . . .	eh . . .
_a house.	_una casa.	_OO-nah KAH-zah
_an apartment.	_un appartamento.	_oon-ahp-pahr-tah-MEHN-toh
_a mansion.	_una casa signorile.	_OO-nah KAH-zah see-nyoh-REE-leh

_a villa.	_una villa.	_OO-nah VEEL-lah
_a condominium.	_un condominio.	_oon kohn-doh-MEE-nyoh
_a country house.	_una casa di campagna.	_OO-nah KAH-zah dee kahm-PAH-nyah
Thanks for the invitation.	Grazie dell'invito.	GRAH-tsyeh dehl-leen-VEE-toh.
You must come and visit us sometime.	Ci venga a trovare qualche volta.	chee VEHN-gah ah troh-VAH-reh KWAHL-keh VOHL-tah

TALKING ABOUT LANGUAGE

Name of languages, *lingue* (LEEN-gweh), or idioms, *idiomi* (ee-DYOH-mee), are usually the same as the masculine form of the nationality. For example, the words for the German and Spanish languages are *tedesco* (teh-DEH-skoh) and *spagnolo* (spah-NYOH-loh). Likewise, to say "I speak Italian" you say *Parlo italiano* (PAHR-loh ee-tah-LYAH-noh), or for "I speak English" you say *Parlo inglese* (PAHR-loh een-GLEH-zeh). Remember that the indefinite article is used with names of languages but commonly omitted after the verb *parlare* (to speak).

I speak Italian.	Parlo italiano.	PAHR-loh ee-tah-LYAH-noh
I like Italian.	Mi piace l'italiano.	mee PYAH-cheh lee-tah-LYAH-noh
Do you speak . . .	**Parla . . .**	**PAHR-lah . . .**
_English?	_inglese?	_een-GLEH-zeh?
_French?	_francese?	_frahn-CHEH-zeh?
_Spanish?	_spagnolo?	_spah-NYOH-loh?
I only speak English.	Parlo solamente inglese.	PAHR-loh soh-lah-MEHN-teh een-GLEH-zeh
I don't speak Italian.	Non parlo italiano.	nohn PAHR-loh ee-tah-LYAH-noh
I speak very little.	Parlo poco.	PAHR-loh POH-koh
I speak a little Italian.	**Parlo un po' d'italiano.**	**PAHR-loh oon poh dee-tah-LYAH-noh**

I want to learn Italian.	Voglio imparare l'italiano.	VOH-lyoh eem-pah-RAH-reh lee-tah-LYAH-noh
I understand.	Capisco.	kah-PEE-skoh
I don't understand.	Non capisco.	nohn kah-PEE-skoh
Can you understand me?	**Mi capisce?**	**mee kah-PEE-sheh?**
Please speak more slowly.	Per favore, parli più adagio.	pehr fah-VOH-reh, PAHR-lee pyoo ah-DAH-joh
Please repeat that.	Può ripetere per favore?	pwoh ree-PEH-teh-reh pehr fah-VOH-reh?
How do you write that?	Come si scrive?	KOH-meh see SCREE-veh?
How do you say "spoon" in Italian?	Come si dice "spoon" in italiano?	KOH-meh see DEE-cheh "spoon" een ee-tah-LYAH-noh?
Is there anyone here who speaks English?	**C'è qualcuno qui che parla inglese?**	**cheh kwahl-KOO-noh kwee keh PAHR-lah een-GLEH-zeh?**
Could you translate this for me?	**Mi può tradurre questo?**	**mee pwoh trah-DOOR-reh KWEH-stoh?**

9   PERSONAL CARE

DIALOGUE
Getting a Haircut (Il Taglio dei Capelli)

Parrucchiere:	A chi tocca?	ah kee TOHK-kah?
Signora:	Tocca a me. Vorrei tagliarmi i capelli.	TOHK-kah ah meh, vohr-RAY tah-LYAHR-mee ee kah-PEHL-lee
Parrucchiere:	Certamente, signora. Come vuole i capelli?	chehr-tah-MEHN-teh, see-NYOH-rah. KOH-meh voo-OH-leh ee kah-PEHL-lee?
Signora:	Li lasci lunghi davanti e ai lati e me li accorci di un paio di centimetri di dietro.	lee LAH-shee LOON-ghee dah-VAHN tee eh ahy LAH-tee eh meh lee ahk-KOHR-chee dee oon PAH-yoh dee chehn-TEE-meh-tree dee DYEH-troh
Parrucchiere:	Bene. Allora prima glieli lavo con un ottimo sciampo alle erbe, e poi, il taglio.	BEH-neh. ahl-LOH-rah PREE-mah LYEH-lee LAH-voh kohn oon OHT-tee-moh SHAHM-poh AHL-leh EHR-beh, eh poy, eel TAH-lyoh
Signora:	D'accordo. Faccia pure.	dahk-KOHR-doh. FAH-chah POO-reh

Hairdresser:	Who's next?
Customer:	I am. I'd like a haircut.
Hairdresser:	Certainly, madam. How would you like it?
Customer:	Long in the front and on the sides, and a couple of centimeters shorter in the back.
Hairdresser:	Well, first I'll wash it with an excellent herbal shampoo, and then, I'll cut it.
Customer:	All right. Go ahead.

AT THE BARBERSHOP

Is there a . . . nearby?	C'è un . . . qui vicino?	cheh oon . . . kwee vee-CHEE-noh?

_barbershop	_barbiere	_bahr-BYEH-reh
_hairdresser	_parrucchiere	_pahr-rook-KYEH-reh
I'd like . . .	**Vorrei . . .**	**vohr-RAY . . .**
_a haircut.	_tagliarmi i capelli.	_tah-LYAHR-mee ee kah-PEHL-lee
_a razor cut.	_un taglio al rasoio.	_oon TAH-lyoh ahl rah-ZOH-yoh
_a shampoo.	_uno sciampo.	_OO-noh SHAHM-poh
_a shave.	**_farmi la barba.**	**_FAHR-mee lah BAHR-bah**
Cut it a bit more . . .	Me li tagli un po' di più . . .	meh lee TAH-lyee oon poh dee pyoo . . .
_right here.	_qui.	_kwee
_in the front.	_davanti.	_dah-VAHN-tee
_on the sides.	_ai lati.	_ahy LAH-tee
_on the neck.	_sul collo.	_suhl KOHL-loh
_in the back.	_dietro.	_DYEH-troh
_on the top.	_in cima.	_een CHEE-mah
Leave it a little longer right here.	Li lasci un po' più lunghi qui.	lee LAH-shee oon poh pyoo LOON-ghee kwee
Cut it short.	Li accorci.	lee ahk-KOHR-chee
Cut it a little shorter.	Un po' più corti.	oon poh pyoo KOHR-tee
Not too short!	Non troppo corti!	nohn TROHP-poh KOHR-tee!
I'd like the part . . .	Vorrei la riga . . .	vohr-RAY lah REE-gah . . .
_on the right.	_a destra.	_ah DEH-strah
_on the left.	_a sinistra.	_ah see-NEE-strah
_down the middle.	_in mezzo.	_een MEHD-dzoh
Also trim my . . .	Può spuntarmi anche . . .	pwoh spoon-TAHR-mee AHN-keh . . .
_beard.	_la barba?	_lah BAHR-bah?

_mustache.	_i baffi?	_ee BAHF-fee?
_sideburns.	_le basette?	_leh bah-ZEHT-teh?
It's fine like that.	**Va bene così.**	**vah BEH-neh koh-ZEE**

AT THE HAIR SALON

I need to go to a hairdresser.	Devo andare dal parrucchiere.	DEH-voh ahn-DAH-reh dahl pahr-rook-KYEH-reh
Is there a beauty parlor in this area?	**C'è un istituto di bellezza in questa zona?**	**cheh oon ee-stee-TOO-toh dee behl-LEHT-tsah een KWEH-stah DZOH-nah?**
Do I need an appointment?	Devo prendere l'appuntamento?	DEH-voh prehn-DEH-reh lahp-poon-tah-MEHN-toh?
Is there a long wait?	C'è molto da aspettare?	cheh MOHL-toh dah ah-speht-TAH-reh?
Can I make an appointment for . . .	**Posso avere l'appuntamento per . . .**	**POHS-soh ah-VEH-reh lahp-poon-tah-MEHN-toh pehr . . .**
_later?	_più tardi?	_pyoo TAHR-dee?
_this afternoon?	**_questo pomeriggio?**	**_KWEH-stoh poh-meh-REED-joh?**
_three o'clock?	_le quindici?	_leh KWEEN-dee-chee?
_tomorrow?	_domani?	_doh-MAH-nee?
I'd like a . . .	**Vorrei fare . . .**	**vohr-RAY FAH-reh . . .**
_shampoo.	_lo sciampo.	_loh SHAHM-poh
_blow-dry.	**_l'asciugatura col phon.**	_lah-shoo-gah-TOO-rah kohl fohn
_set.	_la messinpiega.	_lah mehs-seen-PYEH-gah
_permanent.	_la permanente.	_lah pehr-mah-NEHN-teh
_color rinse.	_un cachet.	_oon kah-SHEH
_dye.	_la tinta.	_lah TEEN-tah
_bleach.	_la decolorazione.	_lah deh-koh-loh-rah-TSYOH-neh

106

_facial.	_una maschera.	_OO-nah MAH-skeh-rah
_manicure.	_il manicure. (or) le mani.	_eel mah-nee-KOOR leh MAH-nee
_pedicure.	_il pedicure. (or) i piedi.	_eel peh-dee-KOOR ee PYEH-dee
_haircut.	_un taglio.	_oon TAH-lyoh
Could I see a color chart?	Mi fa vedere la tabella dei colori?	mee fah veh-DEH-reh lah tah-BEHL-lah day koh-LOH-ree?
I prefer . . .	Preferisco . . .	preh-feh-REE-skoh . . .
_a lighter shade.	_una tinta più chiara.	_OO-nah TEEN-tah pyoo KYAH-rah
_a darker shade.	_una tinta più scura.	_OO-nah TEEN-tah pyoo SKOO-rah
No hairspray, please.	**Niente lacca, per favore.**	**NYEHN-teh LAHK-kah, pehr fah-VOH-reh**
A little gel, please.	Un po' di gel, per piacere.	oon poh dee jehl, pehr pyah-CHEH-reh
That's perfect!	**Perfetto!**	**pehr-FEHT-toh!**

LAUNDRY AND DRY CLEANING

I'm looking for . . .	Cerco . . .	CHEHR-koh . . .
_a laundry.	_una lavanderia.	_OO-nah lah-vahn-deh-REE-ah
_a dry cleaner.	_una tintoria.	OO-nah teen-toh-REE-ah
_a laundromat.	_una lavanderia automatica. (or) a gettone.	_OO-nah lah-vahn-deh-REE-ah ow-toh-MAH-tee-kah ah jeht-TOH-neh
I have some clothes to be . . .	**Ho della roba da far . . .**	**oh DEHL-lah ROH-bah dah fahr . . .**
_washed.	_lavare.	_lah-VAH-reh
_dry-cleaned.	_lavare a secco.	_lah-VAH-reh ah SEHK-koh

107

_ironed.	_stirare.	_stee-RAH-reh
_mended.	_rammendare.	_rahm-mehn-DAH-reh
_stitched.	_cucire.	_koo-CHEE-reh
These clothes are dirty.	Questi vestiti sono sporchi.	KWEH-stee veh-STEE-tee SOH-noh SPOHR-kee
Can they be cleaned today?	Può lavarli oggi?	pwoh lah-VAHR-lee OHD-jee?
When will they be ready?	Quando sono pronti?	KWAHN-doh SOH-noh PROHN-tee?
I need them . . .	Ne ho bisogno . . .	neh oh bee-ZOH-nyoh . . .
_tomorrow.	_domani.	_doh-MAH-nee
_as soon as possible.	_il più presto possibile. (or) al più presto.	_eel pyoo PREH-stoh pohs-SEE-bee-leh ahl pyoo PREH-stoh
I'm leaving tomorrow.	Parto domani.	PAHR-toh doh-MAH-nee
This isn't mine.	Questo non è mio.	KWEH-stoh nohn eh MEE-oh
There's an item missing.	Manca un capo.	MAHN-kah oon KAH-poh
Can you get this stain out?	Può togliere questa macchia?	pwoh TOH-lyeh-reh KWEH-stah MAHK-kyah?
Can you sew on this button?	Può attaccare questo bottone?	pwoh aht-tahk-KAH-reh KWEH-stoh boht-TOH-neh?
Here's my list:	Ecco la lista:	EHK-koh lah LEE-stah
_two shirts	_due camicie	_DOO-eh kah-MEE-cheh
_a suit	_un abito	_oon AH-bee-toh
_eight pairs of socks	_otto paia di calzini	_OHT-toh PAH-yah dee kahl-TSEE-nee

Check with your health insurance company to find out what accident and illness expenses overseas are covered by your policy. Many doctors in Italy speak English, especially in the large cities. The American embassy or consulates are often helpful in locating English-speaking doctors.

You should carry basic medicine such as aspirin and any prescription drugs you are currently using. If you are traveling with prescribed medication be sure to keep the prescription or label handy, so that you can show it to the pharmacist or the customs authorities. Pharmacists are generally helpful and will suggest over-the-counter remedies for minor ailments. They will also take your blood pressure.

DIALOGUE
Finding a Doctor (Alla Ricerca di Un Medico)

Turista:	**Non mi sento bene.**	nohn mee SEHN-toh BEH-neh.
Farmacista:	**Ha bisogno di un medico?**	ah bee-ZOH-nyoh dee oon MEH-dee-koh?
Turista:	**Credo di sì. Me ne può raccomandare uno?**	KREH-doh dee see. meh neh pwoh rahk-koh-mahn-DAH-reh OO-noh?
Farmacista:	**Sì. Ce ne è uno che presta servizio proprio all'ambulatorio qui vicino.**	see. cheh neh eh OO-noh keh PREH-stah sehr-VEE-tsyoh PROH-pryoh ahl-lahm-boo-lah-TOH-ryoh kwee vee-CHEE-noh.
Turista:	**Parla inglese?**	PAHR-lah een-GLEH-zeh?
Farmacista:	**Lui no, ma la sua infermiera sì: è americana.**	LOO-ee noh, mah lah SOO-ah een-fehr-MYEH-rah see: eh ah-meh-ree-KAH-nah.
Tourist:	I don't feel well.	
Pharmacist:	Do you need a doctor?	

Tourist:	I think so. Can you recommend one?	
Pharmacist:	Yes. There is one on duty right at the medical center near here.	
Tourist:	Does he speak English?	
Pharmacist:	No, but his nurse does: she is an American.	

FINDING A DOCTOR

Is there a doctor here?	C'è un dottore qui?	cheh oon doht-TOH-reh kwee?
Could you call me a doctor?	Può chiamarmi un dottore?	pwoh kyah-MAHR-mee oon doht-TOH-reh?
Where is the doctor's office/outpatient clinic?	Dov'è l'ambulatorio?	doh-VEH lahm-boo-lah-TOH-ryoh?
I need a doctor who speaks English.	**Ho bisogno di un dottore che parli inglese.**	**oh bee-ZOH-nyoh dee oon doht-TOH-reh keh PAHR-lee een-GLEH-zeh**
When can I see the doctor?	Quando posso vedere il dottore?	KWAHN-doh POHS-soh veh-DEH-reh eel doht-TOH-reh?
Can the doctor see me now?	Mi può visitare ora?	mee pwoh vee-zee-TAH-reh OH-rah?
It's an emergency.	È un'emergenza.	eh oo-neh-mehr-JEHN-tsah
Do I need an appointment?	Devo prendere l'appuntamento?	DEH-voh PREHN-deh-reh lahp-poon-tah-MEHN-toh?
Can I have an appointment . . .	**Può fissarmi un appuntamento . . .**	**pwoh fees-SAHR-mee oon ahp-poon-tah-MEHN-toh . . .**
_as soon as possible?	_quanto prima?	_QWAHN-toh PREE-mah?
_today?	**_oggi?**	**_OHD-jee?**
_for 2 o'clock?	_per le quattordici?	_pehr leh kwaht-TOHR-dee-chee?

What are the doctor's visiting hours?	A che ora visita il dottore?	ah keh OH-rah vee-ZEE-tah eel doht-TOH-reh?
I need . . .	Ho bisogno di . . .	oh bee-ZOH-nyoh dee . . .
_a general practitioner.	_un medico generico.	_oon MEH-dee-koh jeh-NEH-ree-koh
_a pediatrician.	_un pediatra.	_oon peh-DYAH-trah
_a gynecologist.	_un ginecologo.	_oon jee-neh-KOH-loh-goh
_an eye doctor.	_un oculista.	_oon oh-koo-LEE-stah
_a dentist.	_un dentista.	_oon dehn-TEE-stah

TALKING TO THE DOCTOR

I don't feel well.	Non mi sento bene.	nohn mee SEHN-toh BEH-neh
I'm sick.	Sono ammalato (-a).	SOH-noh ahm-mah-LAH-toh(-tah)
I don't know what I have.	Non so cosa ho.	nohn soh KOH-zah oh
I feel weak.	Mi sento debole.	mee SEHN-toh DEH-boh-leh
I'm feeling dizzy.	Mi gira la testa.	mee JEE-rah lah TEH-stah
I have a fever.	Ho la febbre.	oh lah FEHB-breh
I don't have a temperature.	Non ho la febbre.	nohn oh lah FEHB-breh
I'm nauseated.	Ho la nausea.	oh lah NOW-zeh-ah
I can't sleep.	Non riesco a dormire.	nohn RYEH-skoh ah dohr-MEE-reh
I threw up.	Ho vomitato.	oh voh-mee-TAH-toh
I'm constipated.	Sono costipato(-a).	SOH-noh koh-stee-PAH-toh (-tah)
I have . . .	Ho . . .	oh . . .
_asthma.	_l'asma.	_LAH-smah
_a bite.	_preso un morso.	_PREH-zoh oon MOHR-soh

111

_bruises.	_delle ammaccature	_DEHL-leh ah-mah-kah-TOO-reh
_a bump.	_un bernoccolo.	_oon behr-NOHK-koh-loh
_a burn.	_una bruciatura. (or) una scottatura.	_OO-nah broo-chah-TOO-rah OO-nah skoht-tah-TOO-rah
_something in my eye.	_qualcosa nell' occhio.	_kwahl-KOH-zah nehl OHK-kyoh
_a cold.	_un raffreddore.	_oon rahf-frehd-DOH-reh
_a cough.	_la tosse.	_lah TOHS-seh
_cramps.	_i crampi.	_ee KRAHM-pee
_a cut.	_una ferita.	_OO-nah feh-REE-tah
_the flu.	_l'influenza.	_leen-floo-EHN-tsah
_diarrhea.	_la diarrea.	_lah dyahr-REH-ah
_a headache.	**_mal di testa.**	**_mahl dee TEH-stah**
_a lump.	_un nodulo.	_oon NOH-doo-loh
_a rash.	_un'irritazione.	_oo-neer-ree-tah-TSYOH-neh
_rheumatism.	_i reumatismi.	_ee reh-oo-mah-TEE-zmee
_a sore throat.	**_mal di gola.**	**_mahl dee GOH-lah**
_a sting.	_una puntura d'insetto. (or) sono stato(-a) punto(-a).	_OO-nah poon-TOO-rah deen-SEHT-toh SOH-noh STAH-toh (-tah) POON-toh (-tah)
_a stomach ache.	_mal di stomaco.	_mahl dee STOH-mah-koh
_a sunstroke.	_preso un'insolazione.	_PREH-zoh oo-neen-soh-lah-TSYOH-neh
_a swelling.	_un gonfiore.	_oon gohn-FYOH-reh
My . . . hurt(s).	**Ho male . . .**	**oh MAH-leh . . .**
_stomach	_allo stomaco.	_AHL-loh STOH-mah-koh

112

_neck	_al collo.	_ahl KOHL-loh
_feet	_ai piedi.	_ahy PYEH-dee
I am allergic to . . .	Sono allergico (-a) . . .	SOH-noh ahl-LEHR-jee-koh(-kah) . . .
_penicillin.	_alla penicillina.	_AHL-lah peh-nee-cheel-LEE-nah
_sulfa.	_ai sulfamidici.	_ahy sool-fah-MEE-dee-chee
_certain medicines.	_a certe medicine.	_ah CHER-teh meh-dee-CHEE-neh
Here's the medicine I take.	Questa è la medicina che prendo.	KWEH-stah eh lah meh-dee-CHEE-nah keh PREHN-doh
I've had this pain for two days.	Sono due giorni che avverto questo disturbo.	SOH-noh DOO-eh IOHR-nee keh ahv-VEHR-toh KWEH-stoh dee-STOOR-boh
I had a heart attack four years ago.	Ho avuto un infarto quattro anni fa.	oh ah-VOO-toh oon een-FAHR-toh KWAHT-troh AHN-nee fah
I am three months pregnant.	Sono incinta di tre mesi.	SOH-noh een-CHEEN-tah dee treh MEH-zee
I have menstrual cramps.	Ho dolori mestruali.	oh doh-LOH-ree meh-stroo-AH-lee
What exactly is wrong with me?	**Cosa ho esattamente?**	**KOH-zah OH eh-zah-tah-MEHN-teh?**
Do I need a prescription?	**Ho bisogno di una ricetta?**	**oh bee-ZOH-nyoh dee OO-nah-ree-CHEH-tah?**

Parts of the Body

ankle (left/right)	la caviglia (sinistra/destra)	lah kah-VEE-lyah (see-NEE-strah/ DEH-strah)
appendix	l'appendice	lahp-PEHN-dee-cheh
arm	il braccio	eel BRAHT-choh

113

artery	l'arteria	lahr-TEH-ryah
back	la schiena	lah SKYEH-nah
bladder	la vescica	lah veh-SHEE-kah
bones	le ossa	leh OHS-sah
bowels	l'intestino	leen-teh-STEE-noh
breast	il seno	eel SEH-noh
buttocks	il sedére	eel Seh-DEH-reh
calf	il polpaccio	eel pohl-PAHT-choh
chest	il petto	eel PEHT-toh
	(or) il torace	eel toh-RAH-cheh
ear	l'orecchio	loh-REHK-kyoh
an eye	un occhio	oon OHK-kyoh
eyes	gli occhi	lyee OHK-kee
face	la faccia	lah FAHT-chah
finger	il dito	eel DEE-toh
fingers	le dita	leh DEE-tah
foot	il piede	eel PYEH-deh
forehead	la fronte	lah FROHN-teh
glands	le glandole	leh GLAHN-doh-leh
hair	i capelli	ee kah-PEHL-lee
hair (body)	i peli	ee PEH-lee
hand	la mano	lah MAH-noh
head	la testa	lah TEH-stah
heart	il cuore	eel KWOH-reh
hip	l'anca	LAHN-kah
jaw	la mascella	lah mah-SHEHL-lah
joint	l'articolazione	lahr-tee-koh-lah-TSYOH-neh
kidneys	i reni	ee REH-nee
knee	il ginocchio	eel jee-NOHK-kyoh
leg	la gamba	lah GAHM-bah
lip	il labbro	eel LAHB-broh
liver	il fegato	eel FEH-gah-toh

lungs	i polmoni	ee POHL-moh-nee
mouth	la bocca	lah BOHK-kah
muscle	il muscolo	eel MOO-skoh-loh
nail	l'unghia	LOON-gyah
neck	il collo	eel KOHL-loh
nose	il naso	eel NAH-zoh
penis	il pene	eel PEH-neh
ribs	le costole	leh KOH-stoh-leh
shoulder	la spalla	lah SPAHL-lah
skin	la pelle	lah PEHL-leh
spine	la colonna vertebrale	lah koh-LOHN-nah vehr-teh-BRAH-leh
stomach	lo stomaco	loh STOH-mah-koh
teeth	i denti	ee DEHN-tee
thigh	la coscia	lah KOH-shah
throat	la gola	lah GOH-lah
thumb	il pollice	eel POHL-lee-cheh
toe	il dito del piede	eel DEE-toh dehl PYEH-deh
tongue	la lingua	lah LEEN-gwah
tonsils	le tonsille	leh tohn-SEEL-leh
torso	il torso	eel TOHR-soh
vagina	la vagina	lah vah-GEE-nah
vein	la vena	lah VEH-nah
wrist	il polso	eel POHL-soh

What the Doctor Says

Che sintomi ha?	keh SEEN-toh-mee ah?	What symptoms do you have?
Si spogli.	see SPOH-lyee	Get undressed.
Si spogli fino alla cintola	see SPOH-lyee FEE-noh AHL-lah CHEEN-toh-lah	Undress to the waist.
(or) . . . vita.	. . . VEE-tah.	
Si stenda qui.	see STEHN-dah kwee	Lie down here.

115

Apra la bocca.	AH-prah lah BOHK-kah	Open your mouth.
Tossisca.	tohs-SEE-skah	Cough.
Respiri profondamente.	reh-SPEE-ree proh-fohn-dah-MEHN-teh	Take a deep breath.
Mi dica dove Le fa male.	mee DEE-kah DOH-veh leh fah MAH-leh	Show me where it hurts.
Faccia vedere la lingua.	FAHT-chah veh-DEH-reh lah LEEN-gwah	Stick out your tongue.
Si vesta.	see VEH-stah	Get dressed.
Da quanto tempo soffre di questi disturbi?	dah KWAHN-toh TEHM-poh SOHF-freh dee KWEH-stee dee-STOOR-bee?	How long have you had these pains?
Le misuro . . .	leh mee-ZOO-roh . . .	I'm going to take . . .
_la febbre.	_lah FEHB-breh	_your temperature.
_la pressione.	_lah prehs-SYOH-neh	_your blood pressure.
Ho bisogno di un campione di . . .	oh bee-ZOH-nyoh dee oon kahm-PYOH-neh dee . . .	I need a sample of your . . .
_sangue.	_SAHN-gweh	_blood.
_feci.	_FEH-chee	_stools.
_urina.	_oo-REE-nah	_urine.
Le do un . . .	leh doh oon . . .	I'm going to give you . . .
_analgesico.	_ah-nahl-JEH-zee-koh	_a pain killer.
_un calmante. (or) un sedativo.	_oon kahl-MAHN-teh oon seh-dah-TEE-voh	_a sedative.
Deve . . .	DEH-veh . . .	You need . . .
_fare una radiografia.	_FAH-reh OO-nah rah-dyoh-grah-FEE-ah	_an X ray.
_fare un'iniezione.	_FAH-reh oo-nee-nyeh-TSYOH-neh	_an injection.
_andare all'ospedale.	_ahn-DAH-reh ahl-loh-speh-DAH-leh	_to go to the hospital.

_consultare uno specialista.	_kohn-sool-TAH-reh OO-noh speh-chah-LEE-stah	_to see a specialist.
È grave.	eh GRAH-veh	It's grave.
Non è grave.	nohn eh GRAH-veh	It's not serious.
È . . .	eh . . .	It's . . .
_slogato.	_zloh-GAH-toh	_dislocated.
_rotto.	_ROHT-toh	_broken.
_distorto	_dee-STOHR-toh	_sprained.
_infetto.	_een-FEHT-toh	_infected.
Ha . . .	ah . . .	You have . . .
_l'appendicite.	_lahp-pehn-dee-CHEE-teh	_appendicitis.
_una cistite.	_OO-nah chee-STEE-teh	_cystitis.
_una frattura.	_OO-nah fraht-TOO-rah	_a fracture.
_la gastrite.	_lah gah-STREE-teh	_gastritis.
_l'influenza.	_leen-floo-EHN-tsah	_the flu.
_un' intossicazione da cibo.	_oo-neen-tohs-see-kah-TSYOH-neh dah CHEE-boh	_food poisoning.
_il morbillo.	_eel mohr-BEEL-loh	_measels.
_un osso rotto.	_oon OHS-soh ROHT-toh	_a broken bone.
_la polmonite.	_lah pohl-moh-NEE-teh	_pneumonia.
_la scarlattina.	_lah skahr-laht-TEE-nah	_scarlet fever.
_la dissenteria.	_lah dees-sehn-teh-REE-ah	_dysentery.
_una malattia venerea.	_OO-nah mah-laht-TEE-ah veh-NEH-reh-ah	_a venereal disease.

Patient's Questions

Is it serious?	È grave?	eh GRAH-veh?
Is it contagious?	È contagioso?	eh kohn-tah-JOH-zoh?
How long should I stay in bed?	Quanto tempo devo rimanere a letto?	KWAHN-toh TEHM-poh DEH-voh ree-mah-NEH-reh ah LEHT-toh?
What exactly is wrong with me?	Cosa ho esattamente?	KOH-sah oh eh-zaht-tah-MEHN-teh?
How frequently should I take the medication?	Ogni quante ore devo prendere la medicina?	OH-nyee KWAHN-teh OH-reh DEH-voh PREHN-deh-reh lah meh-dee-CHEE-nah?
How many times a day?	Quante volte al giorno?	KWAHN-teh VOHL-teh ahl JOHR-noh?
Do I need to see you again?	Devo ritornare?	DEH-voh ree-TOHR-nah-reh?
Do I need a prescription?	Ho bisogno di una ricetta?	oh bee-ZOH-nyoh dee OO-nah ree-CHEHT-tah?
When can I start traveling again?	Quando posso riprendere il viaggio?	KWAHN-doh POHS-soh ree-PREHN-deh-reh eel VYAHD-joh?
Can you give me a prescription for . . .	Può farmi una ricetta per . . .	pwoh FAHR-mee OO-nah ree-CHEHT-tah pehr . . .
_a painkiller?	_un analgesico?	_oon ah-nahl-JEH-zee-koh?
_a tranquilizer?	_un tranquillante?	_oon trahn-kweel-LAHN-teh?
Can I have a bill for my insurance?	Mi può fare una ricevuta per la mia assicurazione?	mee pwoh FAH-reh OO-nah ree-cheh-VOO-tah pehr lah MEE-ah ahs-see-koo-rah-TSYOH-neh?
Could you fill out this medical form?	Può compilare questo modulo?	pwoh kohm-pee-LAH-reh KWEH-stoh MOH-doo-loh?

118

AT THE HOSPITAL

Where is the nearest hospital?	Dov'è l'ospedale più vicino?	doh-VEH loh-speh-DAH-leh pyoo vee-CHEE-noh?
Call an ambulance!	Chiami un'ambulanza!	KYAH-mee oo-nahm-boo-LAHN-tsah!
Help me, please.	Mi aiuti, per favore.	mee ah-YOO-tee pehr fah-VOH-reh
Get me to a hospital!	**Mi porti all'ospedale!**	**mee POHR-tee ahl-loh-speh-DAH-leh!**
I need first aid fast!	Ho bisogno del pronto soccorso. È urgente!	oh bee-ZOH-nyoh dehl PROHN-toh sohk-KOHR-sohk eh oor-JEHN-teh!
I was in an accident.	**Ho avuto un incidente.**	**oh ah-VOO-toh oo-neen-chee-DEHN-teh**
I cut . . .	Mi sono tagliato (-a) . . .	mee SOH-noh tah-LYAH-toh(-tah) . . .
_my hand.	_la mano.	_lah MAH-noh
_my leg.	_la gamba.	_lah GAHM-bah
_my face.	_la faccia.	_lah FAHT-chah
_my finger.	_il dito.	_eel DEE-toh
_my neck.	_il collo.	_eel KOHL-loh
I can't move.	Non riesco a muovermi.	nohn RYEH-skoh ah MWOH-vehr-mee
He/she hurt his/her head.	Si è fatto(-a) male alla testa.	see eh FAHT-toh(-tah) MAH-leh AHL-lah TEH-stah
His/her ankle is . . .	Ha la caviglia . . .	ah lah kah-VEE-lyah . . .
_broken.	_rotta.	_ROHT-tah
_swollen.	_gonfia.	_GOHN-fyah
_twisted.	_storta.	_STOHR-tah
_dislocated.	_slogata.	_zloh-GAH-tah
He/she is bleeding heavily.	Perde molto sangue.	PEHR-deh MOHL-toh SAHN-gweh

119

She/he is unconscious.	È priva(-o) di conoscenza.	eh PREE-vah(-voh) dee koh-noh-SHEHN-tsah
He/she has fainted.	È svenuto(-a).	eh zveh-NOO-toh (-tah)
He/she burned himself/herself.	Si è bruciato(-a).	see eh broo-CHAH-toh(-tah)
I got food poisoning.	Ho un'intossicazione da cibo.	oh oo-neen-tohs-see-kah-TSYOH-neh dah CHEE-boh
When can I leave?	Quando sarò dimesso?	KWAHN-doh sah-ROH dee-MEHS-soh?
When will the doctor come?	Quando viene il dottore?	KWAHN-doh VYEH-neh eel doht-TOH-reh?
Where's the nurse?	**Dov'è l'infermiera?**	**doh-VEH leen-fehr-MYEH-rah?**
What are the visiting hours?	Qual'è l'orario di visita?	kwah-LEH loh-RAH-ryoh dee VEE-zee-tah?

THE DENTIST

I need to see a dentist.	Devo andare dal dentista.	DEH-voh ahn-DAH-reh dahl dehn-TEE-stah
I have a toothache.	Ho mal di denti.	oh mahl dee DEHN-tee
It's an emergency.	È un'emergenza.	eh oo-neh-mehr-JEHN-tsah
I'm in a lot of pain.	Mi fa molto male.	mee fah MOHL-toh MAH-leh
My gums are bleeding.	Mi sanguinano le gengive.	mee sahn-GWEE-nah-noh leh jehn-JEE-veh
I've lost a filling.	Mi è venuta via un'otturazione.	mee eh veh-NOO-tah VEE-ah oo-noht-too-rah-TSYOH-neh
I broke a tooth.	Mi si è rotto un dente.	mee see eh ROHT-toh oon DEHN-teh
This tooth hurts.	Mi duole questo dente.	mee DWOH-leh KWEH-stoh DEHN-teh
I don't want to have it extracted.	Non lo voglio togliere.	nohn loh VOH-lyoh TOH-lyeh-reh

Can you fill it . . .	Lo può otturare . . .	loh pwoh oht-too-RAH-reh . . .
_with gold?	_con dell'oro?	_kohn dehl-LOH-roh?
_with silver?	_con dell'argento?	_kohn dehl-lahr-JEHN-toh?
_temporarily?	_provvisoria-mente?	_prohv-vee-zoh-ryah-MEHN-teh?
I want a local anesthetic.	Vorrei l'anestesia locale.	vohr-RAY lah-neh-steh-ZEE-ah loh-KAH-leh
My . . . is broken.	Mi si è rotta . . .	mee see eh ROHT-tah . . .
_denture	_la dentiera.	_lah dehn-TYEH-rah
_crown	_la corona.	_lah koh-ROH-nah
My bridge is broken.	Mi si è rotto il ponte.	mee see eh ROHT-toh eel POHN-teh
Can you fix it?	Lo/la può riparare?	loh/lah pwoh ree-pah-RAH-reh?

What the Dentist Says

Ha . . .	ah . . .	You have . . .
_un'infezione.	_oo-neen-feh-TSYOH-neh	_an infection.
_una carie.	_OO-nah KAH-ryeh	_a cavity.
_un ascesso.	_oo-nah-SHEHS-soh	_an abscess.
Le fa male?	leh fah MAH-leh?	Does it hurt?
Bisogna togliere questo dente.	bee-ZOH-nyah TOH-lyeh-reh KWEH-stoh DEHN-teh	This tooth must come out.
Posso ripararle . . .	POHS-soh ree-pah-RAHR-leh . . .	I can fix . . . for you.
_il ponte.	_eel POHN-teh	_this bridge
_la capsula.	_lah KAHP-soo-lah	_this cap
Ritorni . . .	ree-TOHR-nee . . .	Come back . . .
_domani.	_doh-MAH-nee	_tomorrow.
_fra qualche giorno.	_frah KWAHL-keh JOHR-noh	_in a few days.

121

THE OPTICIAN

If you wear prescription glasses or contact lenses, it's a good idea to take along both an extra pair and a copy of your prescription in case of loss.

I broke . . .	Ho rotto . . .	oh ROHT-toh . . .
_a lens.	_una lente.	_OO-nah LEHN-teh
_the frame.	_la montatura.	_lah mohn-tah-TOO-rah
I have lost my . . .	**Ho perso . . .**	**oh PEHR-soh . . .**
_glasses.	_gli occhiali.	_lyee ohk-KYAH-lee
_a contact lens.	_una lente a contatto.	_OO-nah LEHN-teh ah kohn-TAHT-toh
Can you replace them right away?	**È possibile sostituirli subito?**	**eh pohs-SEE-bee-leh soh-stee-too-EER-lee SOO-bee-toh?**
I'd like soft contact lenses.	Vorrei delle lenti a contatto morbide.	vohr-RAY DEHL-leh LEHN-tee ah kohn-TAHT-toh MOHR-bee-deh
Here's the prescription.	Ecco la ricetta.	EHK-koh lah ree-CHEHT-tah
When can I pick them up?	Quando posso venire a ritirarli?	KWAHN-doh POHS-soh veh-NEE-reh ah ree-tee-RAHR-lee?
Do you have sunglasses?	Avete occhiali da sole?	ah-VEH-teh ohk-KYAH-lee dah SOH-leh?

AT THE PHARMACY

The typical Italian pharmacy is more specialized than its counterpart in the United States. It deals primarily with prescriptions, over-the-counter drugs, and other health products. You'll find household goods and toilet articles at the *drogheria* (droh-geh-REE-ah) or the *supermercato* (soo-perhr-mehr-KAH-toh).

Is there . . . near here?	**C'è . . . qui vicino?**	**cheh . . . kwee vee-CHEE-noh?**
_a pharmacy	_una farmacia	_OO-nah fahr-mah-CHEE-ah

_an all-night pharmacy	_una farmacia di turno	_OO-nah fahr-mah-CHEE-ah dee TOOR-noh
When does the pharmacy open?	Quando apre la farmacia?	KWAHN-doh AH-preh lah fahr-mah-CHEE-ah?
I need something for . . .	**Ho bisogno di qualcosa contro . . .**	**oh bee-ZOH-nyoh dee kwahl-KOH-zah KOHN-troh . . .**
_an allergy.	_l'allergia.	_lahl-lehr-JEE-ah
_a cold.	**_il raffreddore.**	**_eel rahf-frehd-DOH-reh**
_constipation.	_la costapazione	_lah koh-stah-pah-TZYOH-neh
_a cough.	_la tosse.	_lah TOHS-seh
_diarrhea.	_la diarrea.	_lah dyahr-REH-ah
_fever.	_la febbre.	_lah FEHB-breh
_hay fever.	_la febbre da fieno.	_lah FEHB-breh dah FYEH-noh
_a headache.	_l'emicrania.	_leh-mee-KRAH-nyah
_an insect bite.	_una puntura d'insetto.	_OO-nah poon-TOO-rah deen-SEHT-toh
_sunburn.	_una scottatura.	_OO-nah skoht-tah-TOO-rah
_a burn.	_una bruciatura.	_OO-nah broo-chah-TOO-rah
_car sickness.	_il mal d'auto.	_eel mahl DOW-toh
_sea sickness.	_il mal di mare.	_eel mahl dee MAH-reh
_an upset stomach.	**_il mal di stomaco.**	**_eel mahl dee STOH-mah-koh**
_indigestion.	_l'indigestione.	_leen-dee-jeh-STYOH-neh
I'd like . . .	Vorrei . . .	vohr-RAY . . .
_an antiseptic.	_un antisettico.	_oo-nahn-tee-SEHT-tee-koh
_an aspirin.	_un'aspirina	_oo-nah-spee-REE-nah

_some band-aids.	_dei cerotti.	_day cheh-ROHT-tee
_some condoms.	_dei preservativi. (*or*) dei profilattici.	_day preh-zehr-vah-TEE-vee day proh-fee-LAHT-tee-chee
_some contact lens cleaner.	_del detergente per lenti a contatto.	_dehl deh-tehr-JEHN-teh pehr LEHN-tee ah kohn-TAHT-toh
_some solution.	_della soluzione.	_DEHL-la soh-loo-TSYOH-neh
_some contraceptives.	_degli anticoncezionali.	_DEH-lyee ahn-tee-kohn-cheh-tsyoh-NAH-lee
_some cotton.	_del cotone idrofilo.	_dehl koh-TOH-neh ee-DROH-fee-loh
_some cough drops.	_delle pastiglie per la tosse.	_DEHL-leh pah-STEE-lyeh pehr lah TOHS-seh
_a laxative.	_un lassativo.	_oon lahs-sah-TEE-voh
_some mouthwash.	_del collutorio.	_dehl kohl-loo-TOH-ryoh
_some nose drops.	_delle gocce per il naso.	_DEHL-leh GOHT-cheh pehr eel NAH-zoh
_some sanitary napkins.	_degli assorbenti igienici.	_DEH-lyee ahs-sohr-BEHN-tee ee-JEH-nee-chee
_some tampons.	_dei assorbenti interni.	_day ah-sohr-BEHN-tee een-TEHR-nee.
_a thermometer.	_un termometro.	_oon tehr-MOH-meh-troh
_some vitamins.	_delle vitamine.	_DEHL-leh vee-tah-MEE-neh

124

CAR RENTALS

Italy has an excellent, widespread highway system linking all major Italian cities. The most famous is the *Autostrada del Sole* (ow-toh-STRAH-deh dehl SOH-leh), running along the spine of Italy from north to south. Some roadside stops are veritable resort areas, offering restaurants, supermarkets, motels, and cafés.

You may use your valid American driver's license to rent a car in Italy. It's not a bad idea to get an international driver's license, available at a nominal charge from the Canadian and American Automobile Association and in the United Kingdom from the Automobile Association or the Royal Automobile Club. If you wish to have a car upon arrival, it is best to make arrangements with one of the major car-rental agencies before departing, even though many of the major automobile rental companies have branches in Italy.

Always check the advertised daily rate and type of cars offered and also see if taxes and insurance are included. Also, remember that in Europe, manual transmissions are standard and air-conditioning is rare. Your hotel can help you rent a car after your arrival, but keep in mind that making arrangements in advance is usually much cheaper and more convenient.

DIALOGUE
At the Car Rental Agency (All'Autonolleggio)

Turista:	Buon giorno. Vorrei noleggiare una macchina.	bwohn JOHR-noh. vohr-RAY noh-lehd-JAH-reh OO-nah MAHK-kee-nah
Impiegato:	L'ha prenotata?	lah preh-noh-TAH-tah?
Turista:	Purtroppo no. Comunque, non ne ha una disponibile?	poor-TROHP-poh noh. koh-MOON-kweh, nohn neh ah OO-nah dee-spoh-NEE-bee-leh?

Impiegato:	**Sì. Ho una FIAT Uno con cambio automatico. Quanto tempo la vuole tenere?**	see. oh OO-nah FEE-aht OO-noh kohn KAHM-byoh ow-toh-MAH-tee-koh. KWAHN-toh TEHM-poh lah voo-OH-leh teh-NEH-reh?
Turista:	**Una settimana.**	OO-nah seht-tee-MAH-nah
Impiegato:	**Benissimo. E il chilometraggio illimitato è incluso nel prezzo.**	beh-NEES-see-moh, eh eel kee-loh-meh-TRAHD-joh eel-lee-mee-TAH-toh eh een-KLOO-zoh nehl PREHT-tsoh
Turista:	**D'accordo. La prendo.**	dahk-KOHR-doh. lah PREHN-doh
Impiegato:	**Bene. Il passaporto e la patente per favore.**	BEH-neh. eel pahs-sah-POHR-toh eh lah pah-TEHN-teh pehr fah-VOH-reh

---

Tourist:	Hello. I'd like to rent a car.
Clerk:	Do you have a reservation?
Tourist:	Unfortunately I don't. However, do you have one available?
Clerk:	Yes. I have a FIAT Uno with automatic transmission. How long do you want it for?
Tourist:	For a week.
Clerk:	Very well. And unlimited mileage is included in the price.
Tourist:	Perfect. I'll take it.
Clerk:	Very good. Passport and driver's license, please.

Is there a car rental agency nearby?	C'è un autonoleggio qui vicino?	cheh oon ow-toh-noh-LEHD-joh kwee vee-CHEE-noh?
I'd like to rent . . .	**Vorrei noleggiare . . .**	vohr-RAY noh-lehd-JAH-reh . . .
_a car.	_una macchina.	_OO-nah MAHK-kee-nah

_a compact car.	_un'utilitaria.	_oo-noo-tee-lee-TAH-ryah
_a midsize car.	_una vettura di media cilindrata.	_OO-nah veht-TOO-rah dee MEH-dyah chee-leen-DRAH-tah
_a sports car.	_una macchina sportiva.	_OO-nah MAHK-kee-nah spohr-TEE-vah
_a car with automatic transmission.	_una macchina col cambio automatico.	_OO-nah MAHK-kee-nah kohl KAHM-byoh ow-toh-MAH-tee-koh
_a station wagon.	_una familiare.	_OO-nah fah-mee-LYAH-reh
_the least expensive car.	_la meno cara.	_lah MEH-noh KAH-rah
Do you have unlimited mileage?	Il chilometraggio è illimitato?	eel kee-loh-meh-TRAHD-joh eh eel-lee-mee-TAH-toh?
I'd like full insurance coverage.	Vorrei fare l'assicurazione contro ogni rischio.	vohr-RAY FAH-reh lahs-see-koo-rah-TSYOH-neh KOHN-troh OH-nyee REE-skyoh
How much is the rate . . .	Qual è la tariffa . . .	kwah-LEH lah tah-REEF-fah . . .
_per day?	_giornaliera?	_johr-nah-LYEH-rah?
_per week?	_settimanale?	_seht-tee-mah-NAH-leh?
_per month?	_mensile?	_mehn-SEE-leh?
_per kilometer?	_per chilometro?	_pehr kee-LOH-meh-troh?
Do you need a deposit?	Devo lasciare un deposito?	DEH-voh lah-SHAH-reh oon deh-POH-zee-toh?
Do you need my driver's license?	Ha bisogno della patente?	ah bee-ZOH-nyoh DEH-lah pah-TEHN-teh?
Can I leave the car in another city?	Posso lasciare la macchina in un'altra città?	POHS-soh lah-SHAH-reh lah MAHK-kee-nah een oo-NAHL-trah cheet-TAH?

127

THE SERVICE STATION

Where is the nearest service station?	Dov'è il benzinaio più vicino?	doh-VEH eel behn-dzee-NAH-yoh pyoo vee-CHEE-noh?
Fill it, please!	Il pieno, per favore!	eel PYEH-noh, pehr fah-VOH-reh
Give me twenty liters of . . . gasoline.	Mi dia venti litri di benzina . . .	mee DEE-ah VEHN-tee LEE-tree dee behn-DZEE-nah . . .
_regular	_normale.	_nohr-MAH-leh
_super	_super.	_SOO-pehr
_unleaded	_senza piombo.	_SEHN-tsah PYOHM-boh
Fill it with . . .	Metta . . .	MEHT-tah . . .
_diesel.	_del gasolio.	_dehl gah-ZOH-lyoh
_gas/oil mixture. (for mopeds and scooters)	_della miscela.	_DEHL-lah mee-SHEH-lah
Give me 50 Euros of super.	Metta cinquanta di super.	MEHT-tah cheen-kwahn-tah dee SOO-pehr
Please check . . .	Per favore, controlli . . .	pehr fah-VOH-reh, kohn-TROHL-lee . . .
_the battery.	_la batteria.	_lah baht-teh-REE-ah
_the brake fluid.	_l'olio dei freni.	_LOH-lyoh day FREH-nee
_the carburetor.	_il carburatore.	_eel kahr-boo-rah-TOH-reh
_the oil.	_l'olio.	_LOH-lyoh
_the spark plugs.	_le candele.	_leh kahn-DEH-leh
_the spare tire.	_la ruota di scorta.	_lah RWOH-tah dee SKOHR-tah
_the tire pressure.	_le gomme.	_leh GOHM-meh
_the water.	_l'acqua.	_LAHK-kwah
Change the oil.	Cambi l'olio.	KAHM-bee LOH-lyoh

DISTANCES AND LIQUID MEASURES

Distances in Italy, as in most European countries, are expressed in kilometers, *chilometri* (kee-LOH-meh-tree), and liquid measures (for gas and oil) in liters, *litri* (LEE-tree). Unless you are a whiz at mental calculating, converting one system to another can be hard to get used to. The following conversion formulas and charts should help.

DISTANCE CONVERSIONS		LIQUID MEASURE CONVERSIONS	
1 kilometer (km.) =.62 miles		1 liter (l) = .26 gallon	
1 mile = 1.61 km.		1 gallon = 3.78 liters	
Kilometers	**Miles**	**Liters**	**Gallons**
1	0.62	10	2.6
5	3.1	15	4.0
8	5.0	20	5.3
10	6.2	30	7.9
15	9.3	40	10.6
20	12.4	50	13.2
50	31.0	60	15.8
75	46.6	70	18.5
100	62.1		

DRIVING

Get a map before your departure and prepare your itinerary in advance, allowing for plenty of time to sightsee along the way. Any major tourist office in Italy can provide excellent road maps, directions, and advice.

The highways have different names, such as *superstrada* (soo-pehr-STRAH-dah) and *autostrada* (ow-toh-STRAH-dah). Your map will also show the local roads. Highways are subject to a toll based on distance traveled and on the type of vehicle. Toll payment is made upon exit: You must present the ticket you picked up when you first got on the highway. Carry change to save time. On most highways, a special credit card, VIACARD, may be used, and it may be obtained for amounts of €26, €52, or €77 at ACI (*Automobile Club Italiano*) and TCI (*Touring Club Italiano*) offices, at main service areas called *Autogrill*, at the administrative offices of *Autostrade,* and at some tobacconist's shops.

Besides carrying the required driving documents, observe the following traffic regulations: Always carry a triangular reflector, *triangolo* (tree-AHN-goh-loh), to warn others of danger in case you should stop for some reason. No hitchhiking is allowed on highways. The speed limit is 50 kph (31 mph) per hour in town, 110 kph (70 mph) on state and provincial roads, and 130 kph (80 mph) on *autostrade,* unless otherwise indicated.

Remember that Italian traffic sometimes appears to be a chaotic merry-go-round. Not all drivers adhere to speed limits and infractions are quite common. This is not to say that there is no highway enforcement. Speed is monitored and you can get a ticket, *multa* (MOOL-tah), if you exceed the speed limit or run a red light.

Gasoline

Gas stations on the autostrade are open 24 hours and elsewhere Monday through Saturday 7–7. Gas costs about €1.20.

Parking

Especially in its cities, Italy has parking problems, and finding a space is quite difficult during certain hours. All major cities have outdoor parking lots *parcheggi* (pahr-KEHD-jee), watched by attendants. They can be easily identified because they are marked by blue signs that have a *P.* Aside from these parking lots and meters, *parchimetri* (pahr-KEE-meh-tree), you can park anywhere it's allowed, at no expense, by simply posting a parking disk, *disco orario* (DEE-skoh oh-RAH-ryoh), in your windshield, set to show your arrival time. This time cannot exceed 1½ hours. These disks may be obtained at garages, gas stations, tourist offices, etc. If you park in a no-parking zone, your car may be towed away. If you do not find your car where you left it, you should call the city police, *Vigili Urbani* (VEE-jee-lee oor-BAH-nee).

Excuse me, how do I get to . . . ?	Scusi, come si va a . . . ?	SKOO-zee, KOH-meh see vah ah . . . ?
Is this the road to Milan?	**È questa la strada per Milano?**	**eh KWEH-stah lah STRAH-dah pehr Mee-LAH-noh?**
How far is it to . . . from here?	Quanto dista . . . da qui?	KWAHN-toh DEE-stah . . . dah kwee?

Is there a . . . road?	C'è una strada . . .	cheh OO-nah STRAH-dah . . .
_better	_migliore?	_mee-LYOH-reh?
_less congested?	_con meno traffico?	_kohn MEH-noh TRAHF-fee-koh?
Is there a shortcut?	C'è una scorciatoia?	cheh OO-nah skohr-chah-TOH-yah?
Where can I get a road map?	Dove posso avere una carta stradale?	DOH-veh POHS-soh ah-VEH-reh OO-nah KAHR-tah strah-DAH-leh?
I think I'm lost.	Penso di essermi perso.	PEHN-soh dee EHS-sehr-mee PEHR-soh
I think I'm . . .	Credo di aver sbagliato . . .	KREH-doh dee ah-VEHR zbah-LYAH-toh . . .
_on the wrong road.	_strada.	_STRAH-dah
_in the wrong lane.	_corsia.	_kohr-SEE-ah
_at the wrong exit.	_uscita.	_oo-SHEE-tah
We are . . .	Siamo . . .	SYAH-moh . . .
_in the center of town.	_in centro.	_een CHEHN-troh
_in the outskirts.	_in periferia.	_een peh-ree-feh-REE-ah
Are we on the right road?	Siamo sulla strada giusta?	SYAH-moh SOOL-lah STRAH-dah JOO-stah?
How far is . . .	Quanto dista . . .	KWAHN-toh DEE-stah . . .
_the next village?	_il prossimo paese?	_eel PROHS-see-moh pah-EH-zeh?
_the highway?	_l'autostrada?	_low-toh-STRAH-dah?
_the center of town?	_il centro?	_eel CHEHN-troh?
How long does it take by car?	Quanto ci vuole in macchina?	KWAHN-toh chee VOO-oh-leh een MAHK-kee-nah?

131

Do I go . . .	Devo andare . . .	DEH-voh ahn-DAH-reh . . .
_straight ahead?	_diritto?	_dee-REET-toh?
_to the right?	_a destra?	_ah DEH-strah?
_to the left?	_a sinistra?	_ah see-NEE-strah?
_to the traffic light?	_al semaforo?	_ahl seh-MAH-foh-roh?
_to the next corner?	_al prossimo angolo?	_ahl PROHS-see-moh AHN-goh-loh?
Do I make a U-turn here?	Devo fare inversione di marcia qui?	DEH-voh FAH-reh een-vehr-SYOH-neh dee MAHR-chah kwee?
I want to get to . . .	Voglio andare a . . .	VOH-lyoh ahn-DAH-reh ah . . .
What do I do at the next intersection?	Cosa faccio al prossimo incrocio?	KOH-sah FAHT-choh ahl PROHS-see-moh een-KROH-choh?
Where can I park?	Dove posso parcheggiare?	DOH-veh POHS-soh pahr-kehd-JAH-reh?
Can I park here?	Posso parcheggiare qui?	POHS-soh pahr-kehd-JAH-reh kwee?
Is there a parking lot nearby?	**C'è un parcheggio in zona?**	**cheh oon pahr-KEHD-joh een DZOH-nah?**

EMERGENCIES AND CAR PROBLEMS

In case of emergency, the *ACI* (Italian Automobile Club) provides assistance throughout Italy both on highways and roads. If you have car problems while driving on the highway, you can dial 116 on the SOS telephones on yellow poles set at a distance of 2 km apart. If you are not close to one of these phones, wait for the road police.

My car won't start.	La macchina non si mette in moto. (*or*) . . . non parte.	lah MAHK-kee-nah nohn see MEHT-teh een MOH-toh . . . nohn PAHR-teh
Something must be wrong.	C'è qualcosa che non funziona/va.	cheh kwahl-KOH-zah keh nohn foon-TSYOH-nah/vah.

132

I have a flat tire.	Ho una gomma a terra.	oh OO-nah GOHM-mah ah TEHR-rah
I'm out of gas.	Sono senza benzina.	SOH-noh SEHN-tsah behn-DZEE-nah
The battery is dead.	La batteria è scarica.	lah baht-teh-REE-ah eh SKAH-ree-kah
It's overheating.	È surriscaldata.	eh soor-ree-skahl-DAH-tah
I left the keys inside the car.	Ho lasciato le chiavi in macchina.	oh lah-SHAH-toh leh KYAH-vee een MAHK-kee-nah
Can you open the . . .	Può aprire . . .	pwoh ah-PREE-reh . . .
_hood?	_il cofano?	_eel KOH-fah-noh?
_trunk?	_il portabagagli?	_eel pohr-tah-bah-GAH-lyee?
_gas tank?	_il serbatoio?	_eel sehr-bah-TOH-yoh?
Can you change . . .	Può cambiare . . .	pwoh kahm-BYAH-reh . . .
_my battery?	_la batteria?	_lah baht-teh-REE-ah?
_the tire?	_la gomma?	_lah GOHM-mah?
Can you tow the car to a nearby garage?	Può rimorchiare la macchina al garage più vicino?	_pwoh ree-mohr-KYAH-reh lah MAHK-kee-nah ahl gah-RAHZH pyoo vee-CHEE-noh?

Car Repairs

My car has broken down.	Ho la macchina in panne.	oh lah MAHK-kee-nah een PAHN-neh
Can you repair it?	La può riparare?	lah pwoh ree-pah-RAH-reh?
Do you have the part?	Ha il pezzo di ricambio?	ah eel PEHT-tsoh dee ree-KAHM-byoh?
There is something wrong with the . . .	C'è qualcosa che non funziona/va . . .	cheh kwahl-KOH-zah keh nohn foon-TSYOH-nah/vah . . .
_brakes.	_nei freni.	_nay FREH-nee

133

_clutch.	_nella frizione.	_NEHL-lah free-TSYOH-neh
_motor.	_nel motore.	_nehl moh-TOH-reh
_fuel pump.	_nella pompa di alimentazione.	_NEHL-lah POHM-pah dee ah-lee-mehn-tah-TSYOH-neh
_water pump.	_nella pompa dell'acqua.	_NEHL-lah POHM-pah dehl-LAHK-kwah
I have a problem with the . . .	Ho problemi con . . .	oh proh-BLEH-mee kohn . . .
_directional lights.	_le frecce.	_leh FREHT-cheh
_fan belt.	_la cinghia del ventilatore.	_lah CHEEN-gyah dehl vehn-tee-lah-TOH-reh
_gearshift.	_il cambio.	_eel KAHM-byoh
_headlights/ taillights.	_i fari anteriori/ posteriori.	_ee FAH-ree ahn-teh-RYOH-ree/poh-steh-RYOH-ree
_high beams.	_gli abbaglianti.	_lyee ahb-bah-LYAHN-tee
_side lights.	_le luci di posizione.	_leh LOO-chee dee poh-zee-TSYOH-neh
_ignition.	_l'accensione.	_laht-chehn-SYOH-neh
_radiator.	_il radiatore.	_eel rah-dyah-TOH-reh
_spark plugs.	_le candele.	_leh kahn-DEH-leh
_starter.	_lo starter.	_loh STAHR-ter
_stop lights.	_le luci di arresto.	_leh LOO-chee dee ahr-REH-stoh
_transmission.	_l'albero di trasmissione.	_LAHL-beh-roh dee trah-smees-SYOH-neh
_windshield wipers.	_il tergicristallo.	_eel tehr-jee-kree-STAHL-loh
Can you repair . . .	Può riparare . . .	pwah ree-pah-RAH-reh . . .
_the horn?	_il clacson?	_eel KLAHK-sohn?
_the radio?	_la radio?	_lah RAH-dyoh?
_the steering wheel?	_il volante?	_eel voh-LAHN-teh?

134

_the door handle?	_la maniglia?	_lah mah-NEE-lyah?
_the speedometer?	_il tachimetro?	_eel tah-KEE-meh-troh?
How long will it take?	Quanto ci vorrà?	KWAHN-toh chee vohr-RAH?
How much will it cost?	Quanto verrà a costare?	KWAHN-toh vehr-RAH ah koh-STAH-reh?
I need it today.	Ne ho bisogno oggi.	neh oh bee-ZOH-nyoh OHD-jee

ROAD SIGNS

SENSO UNICO	SEHN-soh OO-nee-koh	One Way
STRADA PRINCIPALE	STRAH-dah preen-chee-PAH-leh	Main Raad
PARCHEGGIO	pahr-KEHD-joh	Parking
SUPERSTRADA	soo-pehr-STRAH-dah	Superhighway
AUTOSTRADA	ow-toh-STRAH-dah	highway
DARE LA PRECEDENZA	DAH-reh lah preh-cheh-DEHN-tsah	Yield
RIFORNIMENTO	ree-fohr-nee-MEHN-toh	Gas Station
PERICOLO	peh-REE-koh-loh	Danger Ahead
DISCESA PERICOLOSA	dee-SHEH-zah peh-ree-koh-LOH-zah	Dangerous Descent
CUNETTA (OR) DOSSO	koo-NEHT-tah DOHS-soh	Bumps
STRETTOIA	streht-TOH-yah	Road Narrows
PASSAGGIO A LIVELLO	pahs-SAHD-joh ah lee-VEHL-loh	Railroad Crossing
ZONA DI CIRCOLAZIONE A DOPPIO SENSO SU UNA CARREGGIATA A SENSO UNICO	DZOH-nah dee cheer-coh-lah-TSYOH-neh ah DOHP-pyoh SEHN-soh soo OO-nah kahr-rehd-JAH-tah ah SEHN-soh OO-nee-koh	Two-Way Traffic
STRADA SDRUCCIOLEVOLE	STRAH-dah zdroot-choh-LEH-voh-leh	Slippery Road

135

CURVE PERICOLOSE	KOOR-veh peh-ree-koh-LOH-zeh	Sharp Curves
PASSAGGIO PEDONALE	pahs-SAHD-joh peh-doh-NAH-leh	Pedestrian Crossing
TRANSITO VIETATO AGLI AUTOVEICOLI	TRAHN-zee-toh vieh-TAH-toh AH-lyee ow-toh-veh-EE-koh-lee	No Entry For Motor Vehicles
INCROCIO	een-KROH-choh	Dangerous Intersection
STOP (OR) ALT	stohp ahlt	Stop
DIVIETO DI ACCESSO	dee-VYEH-toh dee aht-CHEHS-soh	No Entry
LIMITE MINIMO DI VELOCITÀ	LEE-mee-teh MEE-nee-moh dee veh-loh-chee-TAH	Minimum Speed
LIMITE DI VELOCITÀ	LEE-mee-teh dee veh-loh-chee-TAH	Speed Limit
DIREZIONE OBBLIGATORIA	dee-reh-TSYOH-neh ohb-blee-gah-TOH-ryah	Direction To Be Followed
TRAFFICO VIETATO AI VEICOLI DI ALTEZZA SUPERIORE AI M. 3.50	TRAHF-fee-koh vyeh-TAH-toh ahy veh-EE-koh-lee dee ahl-TEHT-tsah soo-peh-RYOH-reh ah MEH-tree treh eh cheen-KWAHN-tah	Overhead Clearance 3.50 M.
ROTATORIA	roh-tah-TOH-ryah	Rotary
DIVIETO DI SORPASSO	dee-VYEH-toh dee sohr-PAHS-soh	No Passing
FINE DIVIETO DI SORPASSO	FEE-neh dee-VYEH-toh dee sohr-PAHS-soh	End of No Passing Zone
FINE DIVIETO	FEE-neh dee-VYEH-toh	End of Restriction
DIVIETO DI SVOLTA A SINISTRA	dee-VYEH-toh dee ZVOHL-tah ah see-NEE-strah	No Left Turn
DIVIETO DI INVERSIONE AD "U"	dee-VYEH-toh dee een-vehr-ZYOH-neh ahd oo	No U-Turn
SOSTA VIETATA	SOH-stah vyeh-TAH-tah	No Parking

NO ENTRY FOR MOTOR VEHICLES

DANGEROUS INTERSECTION AHEAD

STOP

NO ENTRY

MINIMUM SPEED (km/hr)

SPEED LIMIT (km/hr)

DIRECTION TO BE FOLLOWED (at the next intersection)

OVERHEAD CLEARANCE (meters)

ROTARY

NO PASSING

END OF NO PASSING ZONE

END OF RESTRICTION

NO LEFT TURN

NO U-TURN

NO PARKING

137

ONE WAY

DEAD END

PARKING

SUPERHIGHWAY

YIELD

GAS

DANGER AHEAD

DANGEROUS
DESCENT

BUMPS

ROAD NARROWS

LEVEL (RAILROAD)
CROSSING

TWO-WAY
TRAFFIC

SLIPPERY ROAD

CAUTION—
SHARP CURVE

PEDESTRIAN
CROSSING

138

Other Signs

PEDAGGIO	peh-DAHD-joh	Toll
CASELLO	kah-ZEHL-loh	Toll Booth
CORSIA	kohr-SEE-ah	Lane
CORSIA DESTRA	kohr-SEE-ah DEH-strah	Right Lane
CORSIA SINISTRA	kohr-SEE-ah see-NEE-strah	Left Lane
LIMITARE LA VELOCITÀ	lee-mee-TAH-reh lah veh-loh-chee-TAH	Reduce Speed
USCITA	oo-SHEE-tah	Exit
LAVORI IN CORSO CONSTRUCTION	lah-VOH-ree een KOHR-soh	Road
DIVIETO DI TRANSITO	dee-VYEH-toh dee TRAHN-zee-toh	No Thorough-Fare
SOSTA A GIORNI ALTERNI	SOH-stah ah JOHR-nee ahl-TEHR-nee	Parking Permitted Alternate Days
VICOLO CIECO	VEE-koh-loh CHEH-koh	NO Through Way
DIVIETO DI SEGNALAZIONI ACUSTICHE	dee-VYEH-toh dee seh-nyah-lah-TSYOH-nee ah-KOO-stee-keh	No Honking

12 COMMUNICATIONS

DIALOGUE   On the Telephone (Al Telefono)

Sig.ra Rossi:	Pronto?	PROHN-toh?
Marco:	Pronto. Sono Marco. Vorrei parlare con Angela, per favore.	PROHN-toh. SOH-noh MAHR-koh. vohr-RAY pahr-LAH-reh kohn AHN-jeh-lah, pehr fah-VOH-reh
Sig.ra Rossi:	Rimanga in linea . . . Mi dispiace ma è uscita.	ree-MAHN-gah een LEE-neh-ah . . . mee dee-SPYAH-cheh mah eh oo-SHEE-tah
Marco:	Sa quando rientra?	sah KWAHN-doh ree-EHN-trah?
Sig.ra Rossi:	Questa sera, verso le otto.	KWEH-stah SEH-rah, VEHR-soh leh OHT-tah
Marco:	Posso lasciare un messaggio?	POHS-soh lah-SHAH-reh oon mehs-SAHD-joh?
Sig.ra Rossi:	Certo, mi dica.	CHER-toh, mee DEE-kah
Marco:	Può dirle di richiamarmi appena rientra? È urgente.	pwoh DEER-leh dee ree-kyah-MAHR-mee ahp-PEH-nah ree-EHN-trah. eh oor-JEHN-teh
Sig.ra Rossi.	Sicuramente, riferirò.	see-koo-rah-MEHN-teh, ree-feh-ree-ROH
Marco:	Grazie. Arrivederla.	GRAH-tsyeh. ahr-ree-veh-DEHR-lah

....

Mrs. Rossi:	Hello?
Marco:	Hello. This is Marco. I would like to speak with Angela, please.
Mrs. Rossi:	Hold the line . . . I'm sorry, but she went out.
Marco:	Do you know when she'll be back?
Mrs. Rossi:	This evening around eight o'clock.
Marco:	Can I leave a message?
Mrs. Rossi:	Certainly.

Marco:	Please tell her to call me as soon as she comes back. It's urgent.
Mrs. Rossi:	Very well. I'll give her the message.
Marco:	Thank you. Good-bye.

TELEPHONES

Pay phones are found in public squares and buildings, on streets, and in bars and cafés. Most only accept phone cards, *carte telefoniche* (KAHR-teh teh-leh-FOH-nee-keh), though some only accept coins. You can buy a phone card for about €2.50 or €5 at tobacco stores or news kiosks. Break off the upper left-hand corner then insert the card into the phone. A digital readout tells you how many euros are left on your card and the number when you dial.

To place a direct call to the United States or Canada, dial 001 + area code + number. To make a collect call from any phone, dial 172–1011. For operator assistance dial 170, and for general information in English dial 176. Rates to the United States are lowest all day on Sunday and 10 PM to 8 AM weekdays and Saturday. Remember that hotels usually add a hefty surcharge to international calls.

Where can I make a phone call?	Da dove posso fare una telefonata?	dah DOH-veh POH-soh FAH-reh OO-nah teh-leh-foh-NAH-tah.
Is there a . . .	C'è . . .	cheh . . .
_public telephone?	_un telefono pubblico?	_oon teh-LEH-foh-noh POOB-blee-koh?
_telephone booth?	_una cabina telefonica?	_OO-nah kah-BEE-nah teh-leh-FOH-nee-kah?
Are tokens needed?	C'è bisogno di gettoni?	cheh bee-ZOH-nyoh dee jeht-TOH-nee?
I would like some tokens.	Vorrei dei gettoni.	vohr-RAY day jeht-TOH-nee
Do you have a phone directory?	Ha un elenco telefonico?	ah oo-neh-LEHN-koh teh-leh-FOH-nee-koh?

141

Operator . . .	Centralinista . . .	chen-trah-lee-NEE-stah . . .
I'd like to call . . .	Vorrei chiamare . . .	vohr-RAY kyah-MAH-reh . . .
_this number.	_questo numero.	_KWEH-stoh NOO-meh-roh
_information.	_il servizio informazioni.	_eel sehr-VEE-tsyoh een-fohr-mah-TSYOH-nee
_the international operator.	_l'operatore internazionale.	_loh-peh-rah-TOH-reh een-tehr-nah-tsyoh-NAH-leh
I'd like to use my credit card.	Vorrei usare la mia carta di credito.	vohr-RAY oo-ZAH-reh lah MEE-ah KAHR-tah dee KREH-dee-toh
I'd like to make . . .	Vorrei fare una telefonata . . .	vohr-RAY FAH-reh OO-nah teh-leh-foh-NAH-tah . . .
_a collect call.	_a carico del destinatario.	_ah KAH-ree-koh dehl deh-stee-nah-TAH-ryoh
_a local call.	_urbana.	_oor-BAH-nah
_a long-distance call.	_interurbana.	_een-teh-roor-BAH-nah
_an overseas call.	_internazionale.	_een-tehr-nah-tsyoh-NAH-leh
_a person-to-person call.	_con preavviso.	_kohn preh-ahv-VEE-zoh
What is the area code for . . . ?	Qual è il prefisso per . . . ?	kwah-LEH eel preh-FEES-son pehr . . . ?

What the Caller Says

Hello!	Pronto!	PROHN-toh!
This is . . .	Sono . . .	SOH-noh . . .
_Mr. Rossi.	_il signor Rossi	eel see-NYOHR ROH-see
_Mrs. . . .	_la signora . . .	_lah see-NYOH-rah . . .
_Miss/Ms. . . .	_la signorina . . .	_lah see-nyah-REE-nah . . .

142

To whom am I speaking?	Con chi parlo?	kohn kee PAHR-loh?
May I speak to Marco?	Posso parlare con Marco?	POHS-soh pahr-LAH-reh kohn MAHR-koh
Speak more slowly, please.	Parli più adagio, per favore.	PAHR-lee pyoo ah-DAH-joh, pehr fah-VOH-reh
Can you repeat?	Può ripètere?	pwoh ree-PEH-teh-reh?
I can't hear you very well.	Non la sento bene.	nohn lah SEHN-toh BEH-neh
Speak louder, please.	Parli più forte, per favore.	PAHR-lee pyoo FOHR-teh, pehr fah-VOH-reh
It's a bad connection.	La linea è disturbata.	lah LEE-neh-ah eh dee-stoor-BAH-tah
I was cut off.	È caduta la linea.	eh kah-DOO-tah lah LEE-neh-ah
I'd like to leave a message.	Vorrei lasciare un messaggio.	vohr-RAY lah-SHAH-reh oon mehs-SAHD-joh
Please tell him/her to call me back at this number . . .	Per favore, gli/le dica di richiamarmi a questo numero . . .	pehr fah-VOH-reh, lyee/leh DEE-kah dee ree-kyah-MAHR-mee ah KWEH-stoh NOO-meh-roh . . .

What the Operator Says

Chi parla?	kee PAHR-lah?	Who's calling?
Rimanga in linea.	ree-MAHN-gah een LEE-neh-ah	Hold the line.
Non risponde nessuno.	nohn ree-SPOHN-deh nehs-SOO-noh	They don't answer.
La linea è occupata.	lah LEE-neh-ah eh ohk-koo-PAH-tah	The line is busy.
Ha sbagliato numero.	ah zbah-LYAH-toh NOO-meh-roh	You got a wrong number
Desidera lasciare un messaggio?	deh-ZEE-deh-rah lah-SHAH-reh oon mehs-SAHD joh?	Do you wish to leave a message?
Ripeta, per favore.	ree-PEH-tah, pehr fah-VOH-reh	Please repeat.

Può chiamare più tardi?	pwoh kyah-MAH-reh pyoo TAHR-dee?	Can you call later?
Con chi desidera parlare?	kohn kee deh-ZEE-deh-rah pahr-LAH-reh?	Who do you want to speak with?
Un momento, per favore.	oon moh-MEHN-toh, pehr fah-VOH-reh	One moment, please.
Non riattacchi.	nohn ryaht-TAHK-kee	Don't hang up.
La vogliono al telefono.	lah VOH-lyoh-noh ahl teh-LEH-foh-noh	You have a call.
C'è una chiamata per Lei.	cheh OO-nah kyah-MAH-tah pehr lay	There is a telephone call for you.
Si è interrotta la comunicazione.	see eh een-tehr-ROHT-tah lah koh-moo-nee-kah-TSYOH-neh	Your call was disconnected.
Desidera che continui a provare?	deh-ZEE-deh-rah keh kohn-TEE-nwee ah proh-VAH-reh?	Do you want me to keep trying?
Il telefono non funziona.	eel teh-LEH-foh-noh nohn foon-TSYOH-nah	The telephone is out of order.

THE POST OFFICE

Mail from Italy to the United States may take one to two weeks. You can speed the process along by sending *posta prioritaria* (Priority Mail). It costs a little bit more but gets there a lot faster. Stamps may be purchased at post offices or tobacco stores, *dal tabaccaio* (dahl tah-bahk-KAH-yoh). Post offices bear the *PT* sign and are usually open from 8:30 AM to 1:50 PM Monday through Friday, 8:30 AM until 11:50 AM on Saturday. The main post office operates from 8:30 AM to 6:30 PM. Red-painted mailboxes can also be usually found outside tobacco stores.

I'm looking for the post office.	Cerco un ufficio postale.	CHER-koh oon oof-FEE-choh poh-STAH-leh
I'd like to mail . . .	Vorrei spedire . . .	vohr-RAY speh-DEE-reh . . .
_a letter	_una lettera.	_OO-nah LEHT-teh-rah
_a postcard.	_una cartolina.	_OO-nah kahr-toh-LEE-nah

144

_a registered letter.	_una raccomandata.	_OO-nah rahk-koh-mohn-DAH-tah
_a special delivery letter.	_una lettera espresso.	_OO-nah LEHT-teh-rah eh-SPREHS-soh
_a certified letter.	_una raccomandata A.R. (con avviso di ricevuta).	_OO-nah rahk-koh-mahn-DAH-tah ah EHR-reh (kohn ahv-VEE-zoh dee ree-cheh-VOO-tah)
_a package.	_un pacco.	_oon PAHK-koh
How many stamps do I need for . . .	Quanti francobolli occorrono per . . .	KWAHN-tee frahn-koh-BOHL-lee ohk-KOHR-roh-noh pehr . . .
_surface mail?	_posta normale?	_POH-stah nohr-MAH-leh?
_airmail?	_posta aerea?	_POH-stah ah-EH-reh-ah?
_a letter	_una lettera	_OO-nah LEHT-teh-rah
_a postcard to the United States?	_una cartolina per gli Stati Uniti?	_OO-nah kahr-toh-LEE-nah pehr lyee STAH-tee oo-NEE-tee?
_five postcards?	_cinque cartoline?	_CHEEN-kweh kahr-toh-LEE-neh?
Which window is it for . . .	Dov'è lo sportello . . .	doh-VEH loh spohr-TEHL-loh . . .
_general delivery?	_del fermo posta?	_dehl FEHR-moh POH-stah?
_money orders?	_dei vaglia postali?	_day VAH-lyah poh-STAH-lee?
_stamps?	_dei francobolli?	_day frahn-koh-BOHL-lee?
Is there mail for me?	C'è posta per me?	cheh POH-stah pehr meh?
I'd also like to buy . . .	Vorrei anche comprare . . .	vohr-RAY AHN-keh kohm-PRAH-reh . . .
_airmail paper and envelopes.	_fogli e buste per posta aerea.	_FOH-lyee eh BOO-steh pehr POH-stah ah-EH-reh-ah

145

_aerograms.	_aerogrammi.	_ah-eh-ro-GRAHM-mee
_a collection of stamps.	_una collezione di francobolli.	_OO-nah kohl-leh-TSYOH-neh dee frahn-koh-BOHL-lee
Where is . . .	Dov'è . . .	doh-VEH . . .
_the mailbox?	_la cassetta della posta . . . (or) la buca?	_lah kahs-SEHT-tah DEHL-lah POH-stah . . . lah BOO-kah?
_the stamp machine?	_il distributore di francobolli?	_eel dee-stree-boo-TOH-reh dee frahn-koh-BOHL-lee?

E-MAIL AND THE INTERNET

Internet cafés are easily found in large and medium-sized towns. Check with visitor information in train stations, or ask your hotel concierge, for exact whereabouts. Some good websites on Italy are www.initaly.com, www.wel.it, and www.italiantourism.com. The site for Ferrovie dello Stato, www.fs-on-line.com, is a good source for train information.

Where is the computer?	Dov'è il computer?	doh-VEH eel kohm-PYOO-tehr
I need to send an e-mail.	Devo mandare un messaggio di posta elettronica.	DEH-voh mahn-DAH-reh oon meh-SAH-joh dee POH-stah eh-leh-TROH-nee-kah
Can I get get on the Internet?	Posso collegarmi con internet?	POH-soh koh-leh-GAHR-mee kohn EEN-tehr-neht
Do you have a Web site?	Avete un sito web?	ah-VEH-teh oon SEE-toh wehb?

FAXES AND TELEGRAMS

There is usually a window at the post office for sending faxes and telegrams. Some hotels conveniently provide fax and telegram services. *ITALICABLE* transmits telegrams abroad; both domestic and international telegrams can be dictated over the phone.

Which window is it for telegrams/a fax?	Qual è lo sportello per i telegrammi/il fax?	kwah-LEH loh spohr-TEHL-loh pehr ee teh-leh-GRAHM-mee/eel fahks?
I would like to send a fax/telegram.	Vorrei mandare un fax/telegramma.	vohr-RAY mahn-DAH-reh oon fahks/teh-leh-GRAHM-mah
How much is it per word?	Quanto costa a parola?	KWAHN-toh KOH-stah ah pah-ROH-lah?
Is there a fax for me?	C'e un fax per me?	cheh oon fahks pehr meh?
Could you give me a telegram form?	Mi può dare un modulo?	mee pwoh DAH-reh oon MOH-doo-loh?
I'd like to wire some money.	Vorrei inviare del denaro.	vohr-RAY een-VYAH-reh dehl deh-NAH-roh

THE MEDIA

Books and Newspapers	Libri e Giornali	LEE-bree eh johr-NAH-lee
Do you have . . . in English?	Ha . . . in inglese?	ah . . . een een-GLEH-zeh?
_newspapers	_giornali	_johr-NAH-lee
_magazines	_riviste	_ree-VEE-steh
_books	_libri	_Lee-bree
_any publications	_pubblicazioni	_poob-blee-kah-TSYOH-nee

Radio and Television	Radio e Televisione	RAH-dyoh eh teh-leh-vee-ZYOH-neh
Is there . . . station?	C'è una stazione . . .	_cheh OO-nah stah-TSYOH-neh . . .
_an English-language	_in inglese?	_een een-GLEH-zeh?
_a music	_che trasmette musica?	_keh trah-SMEHT-teh MOO-zee-kah?
_a news	_che trasmette notizie?	_keh trah-SMEHT-teh noh-TEE-tsyeh?

147

_a weather	_che trasmette le previsioni del tempo?	_keh trah-SMEHT-teh leh preh-vee-ZYOH-nee dehl TEHM-poh?
What number is it on the dial?	Su che programma è?	soo keh proh-GRAHM-mah eh?
What TV channel is it on?	Su che canale è?	soo keh kah-NAH-leh eh?
What time is the program?	A che ora comincia la trasmissione?	ah keh OH-rah koh-MEEN-chah lah trah-smees-SYOH-neh?

Before your trip, you should read something about Italy. In addition to guidebooks, your travel agent or national tourist offices can provide information that will help you plan your itinerary. The Internet is also very useful for research. You'll find a plethora of links to the Web sites of local tourist offices, publications, attractions, and booking services on www.fodors.com. Once you reach your destination, ask your hotel concierge for a map and guide to the city.

DIALOGUE Touring the City (In Giro Per La Città)

Turista:	Quali posti mi consiglia di visitare?	KWAH-lee POH-stee mee kohn-SEE-lyah dee vee-zee-TAH-reh?
Impiegato:	Ci sono molte cose interessanti da vedere.	chee SOH-noh MOHL-teh KOH-seh een-teh-rehs-SAHN-tee dah veh-DEH-reh
Turista:	È lontano il centro storico?	eh lohn-TAH-noh eel CHEHN-troh STOH-ree-koh?
Impiegato:	No. Può prendere l'autobus qui all'angolo. Porta direttamente in centro.	noh. pwoh PREHN-deh-reh LOW-toh-boos kwee ahl-LAHN-goh-loh. POHR-tah dee-reht-tah-MEHN-teh een CHEHN-troh
Turista:	Ci sono molti monumenti antichi?	chee SOH-noh MOHL-tee moh-noo-MEHN-tee ahn-TEE-kee?
Impiegato:	Si. Chiese, palazzi, gallerie, e c'è anche il Museo Archeologico.	see. KYEH-zeh, pah-LAHT-tsee, gahl-leh-REE-eh, eh cheh AHN-keh eel moo-ZEH-oh ahr-keh-oh-LOH-jee-coh
Turista:	Grazie delle informazioni.	GRAH-tsyeh DEHL-leh een-fohr-mah-TSYOH-nee
Tourist:	What places do you recommend visiting?	
Hotel clerk:	There are many interesting things to see.	

Tourist:	Is the historic district far from here?
Hotel clerk:	No. You can take a bus just at the corner. It goes right to the historic district.
Tourist:	Are there many ancient monuments?
Hotel clerk:	Yes. Churches, palaces, galleries, and you can also find the Archaeological Museum.
Tourist:	Thanks for the information.

FINDING THE SIGHTS

Where is the tourist office?	Dov'è l'ufficio turistico?	doh-VEH loof-FEE-choh too-REE-stee-koh?
Can you suggest . . .	Può raccomandarmi . . .	pwoh rahk-koh-mahn-DAHR-mee . . .
_a guided tour?	_un giro organizzato?	_oon JEE-roh ohr-gah-need-DZAH-toh
_an excursion?	_una gita?	_OO-nah JEE-tah?
Are there English-speaking guides?	Ci sono guide che parlano inglese?	chee SOH-noh GWEE-deh keh PAHR-lah-noh een-GLEH-zeh?
We would like a tour guide . . .	Vorremmo una guida . . .	vohr-REHM-moh OO-nah GWEE-dah . . .
_for a day.	_per una giornata.	_peh OO-nah johr-NAH-tah
_for an afternoon.	_per un pomeriggio.	_pehr oon poh-meh-REED-joh
When does the tour begin?	Quando comincia il giro?	KWAHN-doh koh-MEEN-chah eel JEE-roh?
How long does the excursion take?	Quanto dura la gita?	KWAHN-toh DOO-rah lah JEE-tah?
Is breakfast/lunch included?	La colazione/il pranzo è compresa(-o)?	lah koh-lah-TSYOH-neh/eel PRAHN-dzoh eh kohm-PREH-zah (-zoh)?
How much is the excursion, everything included?	Quanto costa la gita, tutto compreso?	KWAHN-toh KOH-stah lah JEE-tah, TOOT-tah kohm-PREH-zoh?

Do you tip the guide?	Si lascia la mancia alla guida?	see LAH-shah lah MAHN-chah AHL-lah GWEE-dah?
Where does the tour begin?	Da dove comincia il giro?	dah DOH-veh koh-MEEN-chah eel JEE-roh?
When do we return to the hotel?	A che ora si ritorna in albergo?	ah keh OH-rah see ree-TOHR-nah een ahl-BEHR-goh?
I'd like to see the . . .	**Vorrei vedere . . .**	**vohr-RAY veh-DEH-reh . . .**
_abbey	_l'abbazia.	_lahb-bah-TSEE-ah
_art gallery.	**_la galleria d'arte.**	**_lah gahl-leh-REE-ah DAHR-teh**
_botanical gardens.	_il giardino botanico.	_ee jahr-DEE-noh boh-TAH-nee-koh
_business district.	_il quartiere degli affari.	_eel kwahr-TYEH-reh DEH-lyee ahf-FAH-ree
_castle.	**_il castello.**	**_eel kah-STEHL-loh**
_catacombs.	_le catacombe.	_leh kah-tah-KOHM-beh
_cathedral.	**_la cattedrale.**	**_lah kaht-teh-DRAH-leh**
_caves.	_le grotte.	_leh GROHT-teh
_cemetery.	_il cimitero.	_eel chee-mee-TEH-roh
_central square.	_la piazza principale.	_lah PYAHT-tsah preen-chee-PAH-leh
_chapel.	_la cappella.	_lah kahp-PEHL-lah
_church.	_la chiesa.	_lah KYEH zah
_cloister.	_il chiostro.	_eel KYOH-stroh
_convent.	_il convento.	_eel kohn-VEHN-toh
_downtown.	_il centro città.	_eel CHEHN-troh cheet-TAH
_flea market.	**_il mercato delle pulci.**	**_eel mehr-KAH-toh DEHL-leh POOL-chee**
_fortress.	_la fortezza.	_lah fohr-TEHT-tsah
_fountains.	_le fontane.	_leh fohn-TAH-neh
_government headquarters.	_il palazzo comunale.	_eel pah-LAHT-tsoh koh-moo-NAH-leh

151

_harbor.	_il porto.	_eel POHR-toh
_historic sites.	**_i luoghi storici.**	**_ee LWOH-ghee STOH-ree-chee**
_library.	_la biblioteca.	_lah bee-blyah-TEH-kah
_market.	_il mercato.	_eel mehr-KAH-toh
_monastery.	_il monastero.	_eel moh-nah-STEH-roh
_monuments.	_i monumenti.	_ee moh-noo-MEHN-tee
_museum . . .	_il museo . . .	_eel moo-ZEH-oh . . .
of art.	d'arte.	DAHR-teh
of modern art.	d'arte moderna.	DAHR-teh moh-DEHR-nah
of natural sciences.	di scienze naturali.	dee SHEHN-tseh nah-too-RAH-lee
_old city.	_la città vecchia.	_lah cheet-TAH VEHK-kyah
_opera house.	_il teatro dell'opera.	_eel teh-AH-troh dehl-LOH-peh-rah
_park.	_il parco.	_eel PAHR-koh
_public gardens.	_i giardini pubblici.	_ee jahr-DEE-nee POOB-blee-chee
_royal palace.	**_il palazzo reale.**	**_eel pah-LAHT-tsoh reh-AH-leh**
_ruins	_le rovine.	_leh roh-VEE-neh
_shopping district	_il centro commerciale.	_eel CHEHN-troh kohm-mehr-CHAH-leh
_square.	_la piazza.	_lah PYAHT-tsah
_stadium.	_lo stadio.	_loh STAH-dyoh
_statue of . . .	_la statua di . . .	_lah STAH-twah dee . . .
_synagogue.	_la sinagoga.	_lah see-nah-GOH-gah
_theater.	_il teatro.	_eel teh-AH-troh
_tomb of . . .	_la tomba di . . .	_lah TOHM-bah dee . . .
_tower.	_la torre.	_lah TOHR-reh
_university.	_l'università.	_loo-nee-vehr-see-TAH
_zoo.	**_il giardino zoologico**	**eel jahr-DEE-noh dzoh-oh-LOH-jee-koh**

Would you take our picture?	Ci fa una foto?	chee fah OO-nah FOH-toh?
One more shot!	Ancora una!	ahn-KOH-rah OO-nah!
Smile!	Sorridete!	soh-ree-DEH-teh!

AT THE MUSEUM

Practically every Italian city has museums and art galleries. Opening times may vary from place to place, but generally their hours are from 8:30 to 4 on weekdays, and 9:30 to 2 on Sunday and holidays. They are usually closed on Monday.

When does the museum open/close?	Quando apre/chiude il museo?	KWAHN-doh AH-preh/KYOO-deh eel moo-ZEH-oh?
Is it open on Sundays?	È aperto la domenica?	eh ah-PEHR-toh lah doh-MEH-nee-kah?
How much is the admission?	Quanto costa l'ingresso?	KWAHN-toh KOH-stah leen-GREHS-soh?
Can I take pictures?	Si possono fare fotografie?	see POHS-soh-noh FAH-reh foh-toh-grah-FEE-eh?
I'm interested in . . .	Mi interessa . . .	mee een-teh-REHS-sah
_antiques.	_l'antichità.	_lahn-tee-kee-TAH
_anthropology.	_l'antropologia.	_lahn-troh-poh-loh-JEE-ah
_archaeology.	_l'archeologia.	_lahr-keh-oh-loh-JEE-ah
_. . . art.	_l'arte . . .	_LAHR-teh . . .
classical	classica.	KLAHS-see-kah
medieval	medievale.	meh-dyeh-VAH-leh
modern	moderna.	moh-DEHR-nah
Renaissance	rinascimentale.	ree-nah-shee-mehn-TAH-leh
_natural history.	_la storia naturale.	_lah STOH-ryah nah-too-RAH-leh
_painting.	_la pittura.	_lah peet-TOO-rah
_sculpture.	_la scultura.	_lah skool-TOO-rah

153

IN THE OLD PART OF TOWN

How many churches are there?	Quante chiese ci sono?	KWAHN-teh KYEH-zeh chee SOH-noh?
Is that church old?	È antica quella chiesa?	eh ahn-TEE-kah KWEHL-lah KYEH-zah?
What religion is it?	Di che culto è?	dee keh COOL-toh eh?
Are there many monuments nearby?	Ci sono molti monumenti qui vicino?	chee SOH-noh MOHL-tee moh-noo-MEHN-tee kwee vee-CHEE-noh?
What does that commemorate?	Che cosa commemora?	keh KOH-zah kohm-MEH-moh-rah?
Whose statue is that?	Di chi è quella statua?	dee kee eh KWEHL-lah STAH-twah?
Who was he/she?	Chi è?	kee eh?

IN THE COUNTRY

Where are the most beautiful landscapes?	Dove si ammirano i paesaggi più belli?	DOH-veh see ahm-MEE-rah-noh ee pah-eh-SAHD-jee pyoo BEHL-lee?
Is there a scenic route to . . . ?	C'è una strada panoramica che porta a . . . ?	cheh OO-nah STRAH-dah pah-noh-RAH-mee-kah keh POHR-tah ah . . . ?
How far is it?	Quanto dista?	KWAHN-to DEE-stah?
Is there any place to eat there?	C'è un posto per mangiare?	cheh oon POH-stoh pehr mahn-JAH-reh?
Are there restrooms?	Ci sono le toelette?	chee SOH-noh leh toh-eh-LEHT-teh?
I like . . .	Mi piacciono . . .	mee PYAHT-choh-noh . . .
_birds.	_gli uccelli.	_lyee oot-CHEHL-lee
_cliffs.	_le scogliere.	_leh skoh-LYEH-reh
_fields.	_i campi.	ee KAHM-pee
_flowers.	_i fiori.	_ee FYOH-ree

_forests.	_le foreste.	_leh foh-REH-steh
_heights.	_le cime.	_leh CHEE-meh
_hills.	_le colline.	_leh kohl-LEE-neh
_meadows.	_i prati.	_ee PRAH-tee
_mountains.	_le montagne.	_leh mohn-TAH-nyeh
_peaks.	_i picchi.	_ee PEEK-kee
_plants.	_le piante.	_leh PYAHN-teh
_waterfalls.	_le cascate.	_leh kah-SKAH-teh
_woods.	_i boschi.	_ee BOH-skee
I also like . . .	Mi piacciono anche . . .	mee PYAHT-choh-noh AHN-keh . . .
_cottages.	_le casette	leh kah-ZEH-teh
_farms.	_le fattorie.	_leh faht-toh-REE-eh
_country houses.	_le case di campagna.	_leh KAH-zeh dee kahm-PAH-nyah
_inns.	_le locande.	_leh loh-KAHN-deh
_villages.	_i villaggi.	_ee veel-LAHD-jee
_vineyards.	_le vigne.	_leh VEE-nyeh
Look! There's a . . .	Guarda! C'è . . .	GWAHR-dah! cheh . . .
_beach.	_una spiaggia.	_OO-nah SPYAHD-jah
_bridge.	_un ponte.	_oon POHN-teh
_castle.	_un castello.	_oon kah-STEHL-loh
_farmhouse.	_una casa colonica.	_OO-nah KAH-zah koh-LOH-nee-kah
_lake.	_un lago.	_oon LAH-goh
_pond.	_uno stagno.	_OO-noh STAH-nyoh
_river.	_un fiume.	_oon FYOO-meh
The view is . . .	Il panorama è . . .	eel pah-noh-RAH-mah eh . . .
_breathtaking.	_incantevole.	_een-kahn-TEH-voh-leh
_magnificent.	_magnifico.	_mah-NYEE-fee-koh

155

RELIGIOUS SERVICES

Roman Catholic churches and cathedrals abound in Italy. Most of the great churches on the traveler's circuit are also fully functional and can be thoroughly appreciated by attending one of the regular masses or a religious service. Remember that you have to dress properly or else you will be refused entrance. No shorts, tank tops, or strapless dresses are allowed. To find Protestant churches, synagogues and mosques ask your hotel concierge or look in the yellow pages, *le pagine gialle* (leh PAH-jee-neh JAHL-leh).

I'd like to visit . . .	Vorrei visitare . . .	vohr-RAY vee-zee-TAH-reh . . .
_a Catholic church.	_una chiesa cattolica.	_OO-nah KYEH-zah koht-TOH-lee-kah
_a mosque.	_una moschea.	_OO-nah moh-SKEH-ah
_a Protestant church.	_una chiesa protestante.	_OO-nah KYEH-zah proh-teh-STAHN-teh
_a synagogue.	_una sinagoga.	_OO-nah see-nah-GOH-gah
When does the . . . begin?	Quando cominicia . . .	KWAHN-doh koh-MEEN-chah . . .
_mass	_la messa?	_lah MEHS-sah?
_service	_la funzione?	_lah foon-TSYOH-neh?
I'm looking for an English-speaking . . .	Cerco un . . . che parli inglese.	CHEHR-koh oon . . . keh PAHR-lee een-GLEH-seh
_minister.	_ministro	_mee-NEE-stroh
_priest.	_prete	_PREH-teh
_rabbi.	_rabbino	_rahb-BEE-noh

Italy is a shopper's paradise. The variety and quality of Italian goods are exceptional. Leather and silk are traditional good buys and are somewhat less expensive than the same articles in the United States. Among the better-known designers, try Ferragamo and Gucci for leather goods, shoes, and scarves; Bruno Magli for shoes; Fendi for furs and accessories. For both haute couture collections, *alta moda* (AHL-tah MOH-dah), and ready-to-wear apparel, look for Armani, Versace, Ferrè, Roberto Cavalli, and Valentino, sold in boutiques. More basic apparel and household goods may be found in department stores, *grandi magazzini* (GRAHN-dee mah-gahd-ZEE-nee).

The areas around Milan's Via Montenapoleone, Florence's Via de' Tornabuoni, Rome's Via Condotti, and Venice's Piazza San Marco offer the finest shopping in general, but many other cities have specialties that interest tourists. Each region features fine craft products that can be purchased from the local artisan's shops, *botteghe* (boht-TEH-geh). Venice is renowned for glassware from Murano and fine laces from Burano. Look for gold, leather, and paper products in Florence. Naples is known for handcrafted mother-of-pearl and coral objects. For richly decorated ceramics, majolica, and pottery, Faenza in Emilia Romagna is world famous, but you can also find them in Umbria, the Marches, Liguria, Tuscany, and the Amalfi Coast.

Business hours may vary from one region to another. In general, store hours are 9 or 9:30 to 12:30 or 1 and from 3:30 or 4 to 7:30 or 8, although in tourist areas some stores stay open all day long. Shops are closed on Sunday as well as a half-day during the week, usually Monday morning or Wednesday, Thursday, or Saturday afternoon.

Prices are fixed at all stores, *negozi* (neh-GOH-tsee), although small shops and handicraft establishments may give a discount if you make a sizable purchase. Look for big sales in August and after Christmas, when you'll see signs in the windows proclaiming *saldi* (SAHL-dee), *sconti* (SKOHN-tee), *occasioni* (ohk-kah-SYOH-nee), *liquidazione* (lee-kwee-dah-TSYOH-neh), or *vendita promozionale* (VEHN-dee-tah proh-moh-tsyoh-NAH-leh).

In general, Italian stores do not give refunds and they often cannot exchange goods because of their limited stock, so make sure of the fit and quality before buying anything. Also, ask for a receipt, *ricevuta fiscale* (ree-cheh-VOO-tah fee-SKAH-leh), so you can apply for a rebate on the *I.V.A.* (EE-vah), the value-added tax, although don't be surprised if you don't get it back. It is not recommended to have your purchases shipped home from the shop; what shows up may not be what you ordered, or may be in pieces, and getting your correct goods or refund may take a battle of wills, lots of paperwork, or even a lawyer. It's best to carry everything with you.

DIALOGUE
At the Leather Store (In un Negozio di Articoli di Pelle)

Cliente:	Buon giorno. Vorrei vedere una borsa per mia moglie e un paio di scarpe per me.	bwohn JOHR-noh, vohr-RAY veh-DEH-reh OO-nah BOHR-sah pehr MEE-ah MOH-lyeh eh oon PAH-yoh dee SKAHR-peh pehr meh
Commessa:	Buon giorno signore. Abbiamo diversi tipi di borse e di scarpe. Che modello preferisce?	bwohn JOHR-noh see-NYOH-reh. ahb-BYAH-moh dee-VEHR-see TEE-pee dee BOHR-seh eh dee SKAHR-peh. keh moh-DEHL-loh preh-feh-REE-sheh?
Cliente:	Per me un paio di mocassini neri e per mia moglie una borsetta di coccodrillo verde.	pehr meh oon PAH-yoh dee moh-kahs-SEE-nee NEH-ree eh pehr MEE-ah MOH-lyeh OO-nah bohr-SEHT-tah dee kohk-koh-DREEL-loh VEHR-deh
Commessa:	Che numero porta?	keh NOO-meh-roh POHR-tah?
Cliente:	Quarantatrè.	kwah-rahn-tah-TREH
Commessa:	Un momento. Ecco la borsetta per la sua signora e i mocassini per lei. Vanno bene?	oon moh-MEHN-toh. EHK-koh lah bohr-SEHT-tah pehr lah SOO-ah see-NYOH-rah eh ee mah-kahs-SEE-nee pehr lay. VAHN-noh BEH-neh?

Cliente:	Sì, sono meravigliosi e la borsa è magnifica. Le scarpe le può mettere in un sacchetto. Per la borsetta, può farmi una confezione regalo, per cortesia?	see, SOH-noh meh-rah-vee-LYOH-zee eh lah BOHR-sah eh mah-NYEE-fee-kah. Leh SKAHR-peh leh pwoh MEH teh-reh een oon sahk-KEHT-toh pehr lah bohr-SEHT-tah, pwoh FAHR-mee OO-nah kohn-feh-TSYOH-neh reh-GAH-loh, pehr kohr-teh-ZEE-ah?
Commessa:	Certamente. Grazie e arrivederla.	chehr-tah-MEHN-teh. GRAH-tsyeh eh ahr-ree-veh-DEHR-lah

....

Customer:	Good morning. I'd like to see a handbag for my wife and a pair of shoes for me.
Salesperson:	Good morning sir. We have different types of bags and shoes. What style would you prefer?
Customer:	A pair of black loafers for me and a green alligator handbag for my wife.
Salesperson:	What's your size?
Customer:	Forty-three (nine and a half).
Salesperson:	Just a moment please. Here's the handbag for your wife and here are your loafers. Do they fit?
Customer:	Yes, they are gorgeous, and the handbag is magnificent. You may put my shoes in a bag. Could you gift wrap my wife's handbag please?
Salesperson:	Certainly. Thank you and good-bye.

TYPES OF STORES

I'm looking for a/an . . .	Cerco . . .	CHEHR-koh . . .
_antique shop.	_un antiquario.	_oon ahn-tee-KWAH-ryoh
_art gallery.	_una galleria d'arte.	_OO-nah gahl-leh-REE-ah DAHR-teh

_bakery.	_un panificio.	_oon pah-nee-FEE-choh
_bookstore.	_una libreria.	_OO-nah lee-breh-REE-ah
_camera shop.	_un negozio di articoli fotografici. (or) . . . di foto-ottica.	_oon neh-GOH-tsyoh dee ahrt-TEE-koh-lee foh-toh-GRAH-fee-chee . . . dee FOH-toh OHT-tee-kah
_clothing store.	_un negozio d'abbigliamento	_oon neh-GOH-tsyoh dahb-bee-lyah-MEHN-toh
_delicatessen.	_una salumeria.	_OO-nah sah-loo-meh-REE-ah
_department store.	_un grande magazzino.	_oon GRAHN-deh mah-gahd-DZEE-noh
_drugstore.	_una farmacia.	_OO-nah fahr-mah-CHEE-ah
_gift shop.	_un negozio di articoli da regalo.	_oon neh-GOH-tsyoh dee ahr-TEE-koh-lee dah reh-GAH-loh
_grocery store.	_un negozio di alimentari. (or) una drogheria.	_oon neh-GOH-tsyoh dah-lee-mehn-TAH-ree OO-nah droh-geh-REE-ah
_jeweler.	_una gioielleria.	_OO-nah joh-yehl-leh-REE-ah
_leather goods store.	_una pelletteria.	_OO-nah pehl-leht-teh-REE-ah
_market.	_un mercato.	_oon mehr-KAH-toh
_newsstand.	_un'edicola.	_oo-neh-DEE-koh-lah
_souvenir shop.	_un negozio di souvenir.	_oon neh-GOH-tsyoh dee soo-veh-NEER

GENERAL SHOPPING EXPRESSIONS

Excuse me.	Scusi.	SKOO-zee
Can you help me?	Mi può aiutare?	mee pwah ah-yoo-TAH-reh?
Where can I find . . . ?	Dove si trova . . . ?	DOH-veh see TROH-vah . . . ?

160

I'm just browsing.	Do solo un'occhiata.	doh SOH-loh oo-nohk-KYAH-tah
Can you show me . . .	Può mostrarmi . . .	pwoh moh-STRAHR-mee . . .
_this?	_questo?	_KWEH-stoh?
_that?	_quello?	_KWEHL-loh?
_the one in the window?	_quello in vetrina?	_KWEHL-loh een veh-TREE-nah?
_something better?	_qualcosa di migliore?	_kwahl-KOH-zah dee mee-LYOH-reh?
_a different color?	_un colore diverso?	_oon koh-LOH-reh dee-VEHR-soh?
_a different style?	_un altro modello?	_oon AHL-troh moh-DEHL-loh?
I'd like a gift for . . .	Vorrei un regalo per . . .	vohr-RAY oon reh-GAH-loh pehr . . .
_an adult.	_un adulto.	_oon ah-DOOL-toh
_a child.	_un bambino.	_oon bahm-BEE-noh
_a girl of seventeen.	_una ragazza di diciassette anni.	_OO-nah rah-GAHT-tsah dee dee-chahs-SEHT-teh AHN-nee
How much is it in . . .	Quant'è in . . .	kwahn-TEH een . . .
_dollars?	_dollari?	_DOHL-lah-ree?
_Euros?	_euro?	_EH-oo-roh
Can you write down the price for me?	Mi può scrivere il prezzo?	mee pwoh SCREE-veh-reh eel PREHT-tsoh?
It's very expensive.	È molto caro.	eh MOHL-toh KAH-roh
Do you have something less expensive?	**Ha qualcosa di meno caro?**	ah kwahl-KOH-zah dee MEH-noh KAH-roh?
Can you give me a discount?	Mi può fare lo sconto?	mee pwoh FAH-reh loh SKOHN-toh?
I do not want to pay more than . . .	Non voglio pagare più di . . .	nohn VOH-lyoh pah-GAH-reh pyoo dee . . .
I'll take it.	Lo prendo.	loh PREHN-doh
I'll take two.	Ne prendo due.	neh PREHN-doh DOO-eh

That will be all.	È tutto.	eh TOOT-toh
Can I pay . . .	Posso pagare . . .	POHS-soh pah-GAH-reh . . .
_in dollars?	_in dollari?	_een DOHL-lah-ree?
_with traveler's checks?	_con travellers cheques?	_kohn TRAH-vehl-lehr chehks?
_with a credit card?	_con la carta di credito?	_kohn lah KAHR-tah dee KREH-dee-tah?
Do I have to pay the value-added tax?	Devo pagare l'I.V.A.?	DEH-voh pah-GAH-reh LEE-vah?
May I have a bag?	Mi dà un sacchetto?	mee dah oon sahk-KEHT-toh?
It's a gift. Can you wrap it?	È un regalo. Me lo può incartare?	eh oon reh-GAH-loh. meh loh pwoh een-kahr-TAH-reh?
Can you . . .	Me lo può . . .	meh loh pwah . . .
_order it?	_ordinare?	_ohr-dee-NAH-reh?
_send it?	_spedire?	_speh-DEE-reh?
_deliver to this address?	_far recapitare a questo indirizzo?	_fahr reh-kah-pee-TAH-reh ah KWEH-stoh een-dee-REET-tsoh?
This is damaged. Do you have another one?	È rovinato. Ne ha un altro?	eh roh-vee-NAH-toh. neh ah oon AHL-troh?
Is it out of stock?	Lo avete esaurito?	loh ah-VEH-teh eh-zow-REE-toh?
Can I exchange this?	Lo posso cambiare?	loh POHS-soh kahm-BYAH-reh?
Here's my receipt.	Ecco la ricevuta.	EHK-koh lah ree-cheh-VOO-tah
I'd like my money back.	Vorrei indietro i soldi.	vohr-RAY een-DYEH-troh ee SOHL-dee
Sorry. I'll look somewhere else.	Mi dispiace. Cercherò da un'altra parte.	mee dee-SPYAH-cheh. chehr-keh-ROH dah oo-NAHL-trah PAHR-teh

CLOTHING

I'd like to buy . . .	Vorrei comprare . . .	vohr-RAY kohm-PRAH-reh . . .
_a bathing cap.	_una cuffia da bagno.	_OO-nah KOOF-fyah dah BAH-nyoh
_a bathing suit.	_un costume da bagno.	_oon koh-STOO-meh dah BAH-nyoh
_a bathrobe.	_un accappatoio.	_oon ahk-kahp-pah-TOH-yoh
_a belt.	_una cintura.	_OO-nah cheen-TOO-rah
_a blouse.	_una camicetta.	_OO-nah kah-mee-CHET-tah
_a bomber jacket.	_un giubbotto.	_oon joob-BOHT-toh
_a bra.	_un reggiseno.	_oon rehd-jee-SEH-noh
_some men's underwear	_delle mutande	_deh-leh moo-TAHN-deh
_some women's underwear	_delle mutandine	_de-leh moo-tahn-DEE-neh
_a cap.	_un berretto.	_oon behr-REHT-toh
_a coat.	_un cappotto.	_oon kahp-POHT-toh
_a dress.	_un vestito.	_oon veh-STEE-toh
_an evening dress.	_un ábito da sera.	_oon AH-bee-toh dah SEH-rah
_gloves.	_dei guanti.	_day GWAHN-tee
_a gown.	_una veste.	_OO-nah VEH-steh
_a handbag.	_una vorsetta.	_OO-nah bohr-SEHT-tah
_a handkerchief.	_un fazzoletto.	_oon faht-tsoh-LEHT-toh
_a hat.	_un cappello.	_oon kahp-PEHL-loh
_a jacket.	_una giacca.	_OO-nah JAHK-kah
_jeans.	_dei jeans.	_day jeens
_a nightgown.	_una camicia da notte.	_OO-nah kah-MEE-chah dah NOHT-teh
_overalls.	_una tuta.	_OO-nah TOO-tah
_an overcoat.	_un soprabito.	_oon soh-PRAH-bee-toh
_pajamas.	_un pigiama.	_oon pee-JAH-mah

163

_panties.	_delle mutandine.	_DEHL-leh moo-tahn-DEE-neh
_pants.	_dei pantaloni.	_day pahn-tah-LOH-nee
_pantyhose.	_dei collant.	_day kohl-LAHN
_a petticoat.	_una sottoveste.	_OO-nah soht-toh-VEH-steh
_a raincoat.	_un impermeabile.	_oon eem-pehr-meh-AH-bee-leh
_a (long, woolen) scarf.	_una sciarpa.	_OO-nah SHAR-pah
_a (square, silk) scarf.	_un foulard.	_oon foo-LAHR
_a . . . shirt.	**_una camicia . . .**	**_OO-nah kah-MEE-chah . . .**
long-sleeved	con le maniche lunghe.	kohn leh MAH-nee-keh LOON-gheh
short-sleeved	con le maniche corte.	kohn leh MAH-nee-keh KOHR-teh
sleeveless	senza maniche.	SEHN-tsah MAH-nee-keh
_(a pair of) shoes.	**_un paio di scarpe.**	**_oon PAH-yoh dee SKAHR-peh**
_shorts.	_dei pantaloni corti.	_day pahn-tah-LOH-nee KOHR-tee
_a skirt.	_una gonna. (or) una sottana.	_OO-nah GOHN-nah OO-nah soht-TAH-nah
_a slip.	_una sottoveste.	_OO-nah soht-toh-VEH-steh
_socks.	_dei calzini.	_day kahl-TSEE-nee
_a sports jacket.	_una giacca sportiva.	_OO-nah JAHK-kah spohr-TEE-vah
_stockings.	_delle calze.	_DEHL-leh KAHL-tseh
_a (man's) suit.	**_un abito.**	**_oon AH-bee-toh**
_a (woman's) suit.	_un tailleur.	_oon tah-YUHR
_suspenders.	_delle bretelle.	_DEHL-leh breh-TEHL-leh
_a sweater.	**_un maglione.**	_oon mah-LYOH-neh

164

_a T-shirt.	_una maglietta. (or) una T shirt.	_OO-nah mah-LYET-tah OO-nah tee shehrt
_a tank top.	_una canottiera.	_OO-nah kah-noht-TYEH-rah
_a tie.	**_una cravatta.**	**_OO-nah krah-VAHT-tah**
_a turtleneck sweater.	_un maglione con il collo alto.	_oon mah-LYOH-neh kohn eel KOHL loh AHL-toh
_an umbrella.	_un ombrello.	_oon ohm-BREHL-loh
_underpants.	_delle mutande.	_DEHL-leh moo-TAHN-deh
_an undershirt.	_una canottiera.	_OO-nah kah-noht-TYEH-rah
_underwear.	_della biancheria intima.	_DEHL-lah byahn-keh-REE-ah EEN-tee-mah
_a vest.	_un gilet.	_oon jee-LEH
_a V-neck pullover.	_un pullover con il collo a V.	_oon pool-LOH-vehr cohn eel KOHL-loh ah voo
My size is . . .	**Porto una misura . . .**	**POHR-toh OO-nah mee-ZOO-rah . . .**
_small.	_piccola.	_PEEK-koh-lah
_medium.	_media.	_MEH-dyah
_large.	_grande. (or) large.	_GRAHN-deh lahrj
_extra large.	_extra large.	_EHK-strah lahrj
I wear size 40.	Porto la quaranta.	POHR-toh lah kwah-RAHN-tah
Can I try it on?	**Posso provarlo?**	**POHS-soh proh-VAHR-loh?**
It fits well.	Mi sta bene.	mee stah BEH-neh
It does not fit me.	Non mi sta bene.	nohn mee stah BEH-neh
Can this be altered?	Lo/la può aggiustare?	loh/lah pwoh ahd-joo-STAH-reh?
Do you have a skirt that's . . .	Avete una gonna . . .	ah-VEH-teh OO-nah GOHN-nah . . .
_longer?	_più lunga?	_pyoo LOON-gah?

_shorter?	_più corta?	_pyoo KOHR-tah?
_bigger?	_più grande?	_pyoo GRAHN-deh?
_smaller?	_più piccola?	_pyoo PEEK-koh-lah?
These pants are . . .	Questi pantaloni sono . . .	KWEH-stee pahn-tah-LOH-nee SOH-noh . . .
_too tight.	_troppo stretti.	_TROHP-poh STREHT-tee
_too loose.	_troppo larghi.	_TROHP-poh LAHR-ghee

Colors and Patterns

I think you would look nice in . . .	La vedo bene in . . .	lah VEH-doh BEH-neh een . . .
_beige.	_beige.	_behzh
_black.	**_nero.**	**_NEH-roh**
_blue.	**_blu.**	**_bloo**
_brown.	_marrone.	_mahr-ROH-neh
_gray.	_grigio.	_GREE-joh
_green.	**_verde.**	**_VEHR-deh**
_orange.	_arancione.	_ah-rahn-CHOH-neh
_pink.	_rosa.	_ROH-zah
_purple.	_viola.	_VYOH-lah
_red.	**_rosso.**	**_ROHS-soh**
_white.	**_bianco.**	**_BYAHN-koh**
_yellow.	_giallo.	_JAHL-loh
I would like to see something . . .	Vorrei vedere qualcosa . . .	vohr-RAY veh-DEH-reh kwahl-KOH-sah . . .
_lighter.	_di più chiaro.	_dee pyoo KYAH-roh
_darker.	_di più scuro.	_dee pyoo SKOO-roh
_in a solid color.	_in tinta unita.	_een TEEN-tah oo-NEE-tah
_with stripes.	_a righe.	_ah REE-geh
_with polka dots.	_a pois.	_ah pwah
_in plaid.	_di scozzese.	_dee skoht-TSEH-zeh
_checked.	_a scacchi.	_ah SKAHK-kee

Materials

I don't like this material.	Non mi piace questo tessuto.	nohn mee PYAH-cheh KWEH-stoh tehs-SOO-toh
I prefer something in . . .	**Preferisco qualcosa in . . .**	**preh-feh-REE-skoh kwahl-KOH-zah een . . .**
_corduroy.	_velluto a coste.	_vehl-LOO-toh ah KOH-steh
_cotton.	**_cotone.**	**_koh-TOH-neh**
_denim.	_tela.	_TEH-lah
_gabardine.	_gabardine.	_gah-bohr-DEEN
_lace.	_pizzo.	_PEET-tsoh
_leather.	_pelle.	_PEHL-leh
_linen.	_lino.	_LEE-noh
_nylon.	_nylon.	_NAHY-lohn
_poplin.	_popeline.	_POHP-leen
_satin.	_raso.	_RAH-zoh
_silk.	**_seta.**	**_SEH-tah**
_suede.	_camoscio.	_kah-MOH-shoh
_terrycloth.	_spugna.	_SPOO-nyah
_velvet.	_velluto.	_vehl-LOO-toh
_wool.	**_lana.**	**_LAH-nah**
_worsted.	_lana pettinata.	_LAH-nah peht-tee-NAH-tah

SHOES

I'd like a pair of . . .	Vorrei un paio di . . .	vohr-RAY oon PAH-yoh dee . . .
_boots.	_stivali.	_stee-VAH-lee
_flats.	_scarpe col tacco basso.	_SKAHR-peh kohl TAHK-koh BAHS-soh
_ankle boots.	_stivaletti.	_stee-vah-LEHT-tee
_high heels.	_scarpe col tacco alto.	_SKAHR-peh kohl TAHK-koh AHL-toh

_shoes.	_scarpe.	_SKAHR-peh
_sneakers.	_scarpe da tennis.	_SKAHR-peh dah TEHN-nees
They fit me well.	Mi vanno bene.	mee VAHN-noh BEH-neh
They don't fit.	Non mi vanno bene.	nohn mee VAHN-noh BEH-neh
They're too . . .	Sono troppo . . .	SOH-noh TROHP-poh . . .
_big.	_grandi.	_GRAHN-dee
_large.	_larghe.	_LAHR-geh
_narrow.	_strette.	_STREHT-teh
_small.	_piccole.	_PEEK-koh-leh
Do you have a larger/smaller size?	Ha un numero più grande/piccolo?	ah oon NOO-meh-roh pyoo GRAHN-deh PEEK-koh-loh?
I do not know my size.	Non so il numero.	nohn soh eel NOO-meh-roh
I'd like the same in black.	Vorrei le stesse in nero.	vohr-RAY leh STEHS-seh een NEH-roh

WOMEN'S CLOTHING SIZES*

Coats, Dresses, Suits, Skirts, Slacks							
U.S.	4	6	8	10	12	14	16	18
Italy	36	38	40	42	44	46	48	50

Blouses, Sweaters						
U.S.	30	32	34	36	38	40	42
Italy	38	40	42	44	46	48	50

Shoes							
U.S.	5–5½	6	6½–7	7½	8	8½	9	9½–10
Italy	35	36	37	38	38½	39	40	41

*It's a good idea to try on all clothing before buying because sizes vary and do not always correlate exactly with U.S. sizes. Also, it is less customary in Italy to return clothing purchased, except at large department stores in major cities.

MEN'S CLOTHING SIZES*

Suits, Coats

U.S.	34	36	38	40	42	44	46	48
Italy	44	46	48	50	52	54	56	58

Sweaters

U.S.	XS-36	S/38	M/40	L/42	XL/44
Italy	42/2	44/3	46–48/4	50/5	52–54/6

Shirts

U.S.	14	14½	15	15½	15¾	16	16½	17	17½	18
Italy	36	37	38	39	40	41	42	43	44	45

Socks

U.S.	9½	10	10½	11	11½	12
Italy	36–37	38–39	40–41	42–43	44–45	46

Shoes

U.S.	6½	7	7½	8	8½	9	9½	10	10½	11	11½
Italy	39	39½	40	41	42	42½	43	43½	44	44½	45

*It's a good idea to try on all clothing before buying because sizes vary and do not always correlate exactly with U.S. sizes. Also, it is less customary in Italy to return clothing purchased, except at large department stores in major cities.

THE JEWELRY STORE

I'd like to see . . .	Vorrei vedere . . .	vohr-RAY veh-DEH-reh . . .
_a bracelet.	_un braccialetto.	_oon braht-chah-LEHT-toh
_a brooch.	_una spilla.	_OO-nah SPEEL-lah
_a chain.	_una catenina.	_OO-nah kah-teh-NEE-nah
_a cigarette case.	_un portasigarette.	_oon pohr-tah-see-gah-REHT-teh
_a clock.	_un orologio.	_oon oh-roh-LOH-joh

_some cufflinks.	_dei gemelli.	_day jeh-MEHL-lee
_some earrings.	_degli orecchini.	_DEH-lyee oh-rehk-KEE-nee
_a gem.	_una pietra preziosa.	_OO-nah PYEH-trah preh-TSYOH-zah
_a necklace.	_una collana.	_OO-nah kohl-LAH-nah
_a pin.	_una spilla.	_OO-nah SPEEL-lah
_a ring.	_un anello.	_oon ah-NEHL-loh
_an engagement ring.	_un anello di fidanzamento.	_oon ah-NEHL-loh dee fee-dahn-tsah-MEHN-toh
_a wedding ring.	_una fede	_OO-nah FEH-deh
_a tie clip.	_un fermacravatte.	_oon fehr-mah-krah-VAHT-teh
_a tie pin.	_una spilla da cravatta.	_OO-nah SPEEL-lah dah krah-VAHT-tah
_a watch.	_un orologio da polso.	_oon oh-roh-LOH-joh dah POHL-so
_a watchstrap.	_un cinturino.	_oon cheen-too-REE-noh
Do you have this . . .	L'avete . . .	lah-VEH-teh . . .
_in 18 carat gold?	_in oro a diciotto carati?	_een OH-roh ah dee-CHOHT-toh kah-RAH-tee?
_gold-plated?	_placato in oro?	_plahk-KAH-toh een OH-roh?
_in platinum?	_in platino?	_een PLAH-tee-noh?
_in silver?	_in argento?	_een ahr-JEHN-toh?
_in stainless steel?	_in acciaio inossidabile?	_een aht-CHAH-yoh ee-nohs-see-DAH-bee-leh?
Can you repair this watch?	Può riparare questo orologio?	pwoh ree-pah-RAH-reh KWEH-stoh oh-roh-LOH-joh?

How many carats is this?	Quanti carati è?	KWAHN-tee kah-RAH-tee-eh?
What is this made out of?	Di che cosa è fatto?	dee keh KOH-zah eh FAHT-toh?
It's . . .	È . . .	eh . . .
_an amethyst.	_un'ametista.	_oo-nah-meh-TEE-stah
_copper.	_di rame.	_dee RAH-meh
_coral.	_di corallo.	_dee koh-RAHL-loh
_crystal.	_di cristallo.	_dee kree-STAHL-loh
_a diamond.	_un diamante.	_oon dyah-MAHN-teh
_an emerald.	_uno smeraldo.	_OO-noh zmeh-RAHL-doh
_ivory.	_d'avorio.	_dah-VOH-ryoh
_jade.	_di giada.	_dee JAH-dah
_onyx.	_d'onice.	_DOH-nee-cheh
_a pearl.	_una perla.	_OO-nah PEHR-lah
_a ruby.	_un rubino.	_oon roo-BEE-noh
_a sapphire.	_uno zaffiro.	_OO-noh dzahf-FEE-roh
_a topaz.	_un topazio.	_oon toh-PAH-tsyoh

THE PHOTO SHOP

Do you sell . . .	Vendete . . .	vehn-DEH-teh . . .
_cameras?	_macchine fotografiche?	_MAHK-kee-neh foh-toh-GRAH-fee-keh?
_movie cameras?	_cineprese?	_chee-neh-PREH-zeh?
_filters?	_filtri?	_FEEL-tree?
_batteries?	_pile?	_PEE-leh?
Do you have . . .	Avete . . .	ah-VEH-teh . . .
_a light meter?	_un esposimetro?	_oon eh-spoh-ZEE-meh-troh?
_a lens?	_un obiettivo?	_oon oh-byeht-TEE-voh?

_a lens cap?	_un copriobiettivo?	_oon koh-pree-oh-byeht-TEE-voh?
_a telephoto lens?	_un teleobiettivo?	_oon teh-leh-oh-byeht-TEE-voh?
_a wide-angle lens?	_un grandangolare?	oon grahn-dahn-goh-LAH-reh?
I'd like a roll of . . .	**Vorrei una pellicola . . .**	**vohr-RAY OO-nah pehl-LEE-koh-lah . . .**
_film for prints.	_per stampe.	_pehr STAHM-peh
_film for slides.	_per diapositive.	_pehr dyah-poh-zee-TEE-veh
_color film.	_a colori.	_ah koh-LOH-ree
_black-and-white film.	_in bianco e nero.	_een BYAHN-koh eh NEH-roh
_35 millimeter film.	_trentacinque millimetri.	_trehn-tah-CHEEN-kweh meel-LEE-meh-tree
_36 exposures.	_per trentasei pose.	_pehr trehn-tah-SAY POH-zeh
How long does it take?	Quanto tempo ci vuole?	KWAHN-toh TEHM-poh chee voo-OH-leh?
I'd like . . .	Vorrei . . .	vohr-RAY . . .
_two prints of each negative.	_due stampe di ogni negativa.	_DOO-eh STAHM-peh dee OH-nyee neh-gah-TEE-vah
_an enlargement of this photo.	_un ingrandimento di questa foto.	_oon een-grahn-dee-MEHN-toh dee KWEH-stah FOH-toh
_prints with a . . .	_foto su carta . . .	_FOH-toh soo KAHR-tah . . .
_glossy finish.	_lucida.	_LOO-chee-dah
_matt finish.	_opaca.	_oh-PAH-kah
When will they be ready?	Quando sono pronte?	KWAHN-doh SOH-noh PROHN-teh?
Do you do camera repairs?	Riparate macchine fotografiche?	ree-pah-RAH-teh MAHK-kee-neh foh-toh-GRAH-fee-keh?

BOOKS, MAGAZINES, AND PAPER GOODS

In an Italian bookstore, *libreria* (lee-breh-REE-ah), you can usually find popular and scholarly books, as well as guides, manuals, and art and photography books. Writing supplies are found at the stationery store, *cartoleria* (kahr-toh-leh-REE-ah). Newspapers and magazines can be found at any outdoor newsstand, *edicola* (eh-DEE-koh-lah).

I'm looking for . . .	Cerco . . .	CHEHR-koh . . .
_a bookstore.	_una libreria.	_OO-nah lee-breh-REE-ah
_a newsstand.	_un'edicola.	_oo-neh-DEE-koh-lah
_a stationery store.	_una cartoleria.	_OO-nah kahr-toh-leh-REE-ah
Is there a bookstore that carries . . . in English?	C'e una libreria che vende . . . in inglese?	cheh OO-nah lee-breh-REE-ah keh VEHN-deh . . . een een-GLEH-zeh?
_books	_libri	_LEE-bree
_magazines	_riviste	_ree-VEE-steh
_newspapers	_giornali	_johr-NAH-lee
Do you have the book . . . by . . . ?	Ha il libro . . . di . . . ?	ah eel LEE-broh . . . dee . . . ?
I'd like a book on . . .	Vorrei un libro di . . .	vohr-RAY oon LEE-broh dee . . .
The title is . . .	È intitolato . . .	eh een-tee-toh-LAH-toh . . .
The author is . . .	L'autore è . . .	low-TOH-reh eh . . .
Do you have it in paperback?	L'avete in edizione tascabile?	lah-VEH-teh een eh-dee-TSYOH-neh tah-SKAH-bee-leh?
Do you have this guidebook in English?	Avete questa guida in inglese?	ah-VEH-teh KWEH-stah GWEE-dah een een-GLEH-zeh?
Do you have an Italian-English dictionary?	Avete un dizionario italiano-inglese?	ah-VEH-teh oon dee-tsyoh-NAH-ryoh ee-tah-LYAH-noh/een-GLEH-zeh?

173

Do you have . . .	Avete . . .	ah-VEH-teh . . .
_a pocket dictionary?	_un dizionario tascabile?	_oon dee-tsyoh-NAH-ryoh tah-SKAH-bee-leh?
_a map?	_una mappa?	_OO-nah MAHP-pah?
_a city map?	_una pianta della città?	_OO-nah PYAHN-tah DEHL-lah cheet-TAH
_a road map?	_una carta stradale?	_OO-nah KAHR-tah strah-DAH-leh?
_a travel guide?	_una guida turistica?	_OO-nah GWEE-dah too-REE-stee-kah?
I'd like . . .	Vorrei . . .	vohr-RAY . . .
_a ballpoint pen.	_una biro. (or) una penna a sfera.	_OO-nah BEE-roh _OO-nah PEHN-nah ah-SFEH-rah
_a calendar.	_un calendario.	_oon kah-lehn-DAH-ryoh
_envelopes.	_delle buste.	_DEHL-leh BOO-steh
_an eraser.	_una gomma.	_OO-nah GOHM-mah
_a fountain pen.	_una stilografica.	_OO-nah stee-loh-GRAH-fee-kah
_a marker.	_un pennarello.	_oon pehn-nah-REHL-loh
_a notebook.	_un quaderno.	_oon kwah-DEHR-noh
_paperclips.	_delle graffette.	_DEHL-leh grahf-FEHT-teh
_a pencil.	_una matita.	_OO-nah mah-TEE-tah
_a pencil sharpener.	_un temperino.	_oon tehm-peh-REE-noh
_a pocket calculator.	_una calcolatrice tascabile.	_OO-nah kahl-koh-lah-TREE-cheh tah-SKAH-bee-leh
_a ruler.	_una riga.	_OO-nah REE-gah
_scotch tape.	_dello scotch.	_DEHL-loh skohch
_a stapler.	_una spillatrice.	_OO-nah spil-lah-TREE-cheh

_staples.	_dei punti metallici.	_day POON-tee meh-TAHL-lee-chee
_stationery.	_della carta da lettere.	_DEHL-lah KAHR-tah dah LEHT-teh-reh
_string.	_dello spago.	_DEHL-loh SPAH-goh
_a typewriter.	_una macchina da scrivere.	_OO-nah MAHK-kee-nah dah SCREE-veh-reh
_a typewriter ribbon.	_un nastro.	_oon NAH-stroh
_wrapping paper.	_della carta da pacchi.	_DEHL-lah KAHR-tah dah PAHK-kee
_a writing pad.	_un bloc notes.	_oon blohk NOH-tehs

TOILETRIES

Perfume and cosmetics are available at many major department stores. You can also find them at a *profumeria* (proh-foo-meh-REE-ah). Other toiletries may be found in a *drogheria* (droh-geh-REE-ah) or in a *farmacia* (fahr-mah-CHEE-ah).

Do you have . . .	Avete . . .	ah-VEH-teh . . .
_after-shave lotion?	_una lozione dopobarba?	_OO-nah loh-TSYOH-neh doh-poh-BAHR-bah?
_bobby pins?	_delle mollette?	_DEHL-leh mohl-LEHT-teh?
	(or) delle forcine?	DEHL-leh fohr-CHEE-neh?
_a brush?	_una spazzola?	_OO-nah SPAHT-tsoh-lah?
_bubble bath?	_un bagnoschiuma?	_oon bah-nyoh-SKYOO-mah?
_cleansing cream?	_una crema detergente?	_OO-nah KREH-mah deh-tehr-JEHN-teh?
_cologne?	_dell'acqua di colonia?	_dehl-LAHK-kwah dee koh-LOH-nyah?
_a comb?	_un pettine?	_oon PEHT-tee-neh?
_condoms?	_dei profilattici?	_day proh-fee-LAHT-tee-chee?

_curlers?	_dei bigodini?	_day bee-goh-DEE-nee?
_a deodorant?	_un deodorante?	_oon deh-oh-doh-RAHN-teh?
_diapers?	_dei pannolini?	_day pahn-noh-LEE-nee?
_an emery board?	_una limetta per unghie?	_OO-nah lee-MEHT-tah pehr OON-gyeh?
_an eye liner?	_un eye liner?	_oon ahy LAHY-nehr?
_an eye pencil?	_una matita per occhi?	_OO-nah mah-TEE-tah pehr OHK-kee?
_eye shadow?	_un ombretto?	_oon ohm-BREHT-toh?
_face powder?	_della cipria?	_DEHL-lah CHEE-pryah?
_foundation?	_un fondo tinta?	_oon FOHN-doh TEEN-tah?
_hairspray?	_della lacca?	_DEHL-lah LAHK-kah?
_hand cream?	_una crema per le mani?	_OO-nah KREH-mah pehr leh MAH-nee?
_lipstick?	_un rossetto?	_oon rohs-SEHT-toh?
_makeup?	**_dei cosmetici?**	**_day koh-ZMEH-tee-chee?**
_mascara?	_della mascara?	_DEH-lah mah-SKAH-rah?
_a mirror?	_uno specchio?	_OO-noh SPEHK-kyoh?
_moisturizing cream?	_una crema idratante?	_OO-nah KREH-mah ee-drah-TAHN-teh?
_mouthwash?	_del collutorio?	_dehl kohl-loo-TOH-ryoh?
_a nail clipper?	_un tagliaunghie?	_oon tahl-yah-OON-gyeh?
_nail polish?	_dello smalto?	_DEHL-loh ZMAHL-toh?
_nail polish remover?	_del solvente per unghie? (or) dell'acetone?	_dehl sohl-VEHN-teh pehr OON-gyeh? _dehl-lah-cheh-TOH-neh?
_nail scissors?	_delle forbicine da unghie?	_DEHL-leh fohr-bee-CHEE-neh dah OON-gyeh?

_perfume?	_del profumo?	_dehl proh-FOO-moh?
_a razor?	_un rasoio?	_oon rah-ZOH-yoh?
_razor blades?	**_delle lamette da barba?**	**_DEHL-leh lah-MEHT-teh dah BAHR-bah?**
_rouge?	_del fard?	_dehl fahrd?
_safety pins?	_delle spille da balia?	_DEHL-leh SPEEL-leh dah BAH-lyah?
_sanitary napkins?	_degli assorbenti igienici?	_DEH-lyee ahs-sohr-BEHN-tee ee-JEH-nee-chee?
_scissors?	_delle forbici?	_DEHL-leh FOHR-bee-chee?
_setting lotion?	_un fissatore per capelli?	_oon fees-sah-TOH-reh pehr kah-PEHL-lee?
_shampoo?	_uno sciampo?	_OO-nah SHAHM-poh?
_shaving cream?	_una crema da barba?	_OO-nah KREH-mah dah BAHR-bah?
_soap?	_una saponetta?	_OO-nah sah-poh-NEHT-tah?
_suntan lotion?	_una crema solare?	_OO-nah KREH-mah soh-LAH-reh?
_talcum powder?	_del talco?	_dehl TAHL-koh?
_tampons?	_dei assorbenti interni?	_day ah-sohr-BEHN-tee een-TEHR-nee?
_tissues?	_dei fazzolettini di carta?	_day faht-tsoh-leht-TEE-nee dee KAHR-tah?
_toilet paper?	_della carta igienica?	_DEHL-lah KAHR-tah ee-JEH-nee-kah?
_a toothbrush?	**_uno spazzolino da denti?**	**_OO-nah spaht-tsoh-LEE-noh dah DEHN-tee?**
_toothpaste?	_del dentifricio?	_dehl dehn-tee-FREE-choh?
_tweezers?	_delle pinzette?	_DEHL-leh peen-TSEHT-teh?

FOOD SHOPPING

I'd like . . .	Vorrei . . .	vohr-RAY . . .
_six cans of Coke.	_sei lattine di coca.	_SAY laht-TEE-neh dee KOH-kah
_a box of chocolates.	_una scatola di cioccolatini.	_OO-nah SKAH-toh-lah dee chohk-koh-lah-TEE-nee
_a bottle of mineral water.	_una bottiglia di acqua minerale.	_OO-nah boht-TEE-lyah dee AHK-kwah mee-neh-RAH-leh
_a dozen eggs.	_una dozzina di uova.	_OO-nah dohd-DZEE-nah dee WOH-vah
_a jar of pickles.	_un vasetto di sottaceti.	_oon vah-SEHT-toh dee soht-tah-CHEH-tee
_a kilo of potatoes.	_un chilo di patate.	_oon KEE-loh dee pah-TAH-teh
_a liter of milk.	_un litro di latte.	_oon LEE-troh dee LAHT-teh
_a piece of cheese.	_un pezzo di formaggio.	_oon PEHT-tsoh dee fohr-MAHD-joh
I'd also like some . . .	Vorrei anche . . .	vohr-RAY AHN-keh . . .
_cereal.	_dei cereali.	day-cheh-reh-AH-lee
_coffee.	_del caffè.	_dehl kahf-FEH
_cookies/crackers.	_dei biscotti.	_day bee-SKOHT-tee
_cold cuts.	_dell'affettato.	_dehl-lahf-feht-TAH-toh

WEIGHTS AND MEASURES

METRIC WEIGHT	U.S.
1 gram (g)	0.035 ounce
28.35 grams	1 ounce
100 grams	3.5 ounce
454 grams	1 pound
1 kilogram (kilo)	2.2 pounds

LIQUIDS	U.S.
1 liter (l)	4.226 cups
1 liter	2.113 pints
1 liter	1.056 quarts
3.785 liters	1 gallon

DRY MEASURE	U.S.
1 litre	0.908 quart
1 decalitre	1.135 pecks
1 hectolitre	2.837 bushels

One inch = 2.54 centimeters
One centimeter = .39 inch

inches	feet	yards	
1 mm.	0.039	0.003	0.001
1 cm.	0.39	0.03	0.01
1 dm.	3.94	0.32	0.10
1 m.	39.40	3.28	1.09

.39 (# of centimeters) = (# of inches)
2.54 (# of inches) = (# of centimeters)

inches	feet	yards	
1 mm.	0.039	0.003	0.001
1 cm.	0.39	0.03	0.01
1 dm.	3.94	0.32	0.10
1 m.	39.40	3.28	1.09

ACTIVITIES AND
15 ENTERTAINMENT

In Italy, people spend their free time in a variety of ways. You will see people sitting in parks or cafés, reading a magazine or a newspaper, drinking espresso, chatting, or just watching other people. Italy's rich cultural life includes world-famous Roman, Renaissance, and Baroque art, as well as film, theater, opera, ballet, and concerts.

Italians are avid sports enthusiasts, both as participants and spectators. If you feel like getting some exercise yourself, you can rent a bicycle, or go skiing, hiking, or swimming as the season permits.

DIALOGUE Swimming (A Nuotare)

Marcello:	Che caldo!	keh KAHL-doh!
Sofia:	Sì. Perché non andiamo a nuotare?	see. pehr-KEH nohn ahn-DYAH-moh ah nwoh-TAH-reh?
Marcello:	Buona idea! Andiamo al mare o in piscina?	BWOH-nah ee-DEH-ah! ahn-DYAH-moh ahl MAH-reh oh een pee-SHEE-nah?
Sofia:	A dire il vero io preferisco il mare. Ma non è pericoloso in questa zona?	ah DEE-reh eel VEH-roh EE-oh preh-feh-REE-skoh eel MAH-reh, mah nohn eh peh-ree-koh-LOH-zoh een KWEH-stah DZOH-nah?
Marcello:	No, il mare oggi è piuttosto calmo.	noh, eel MAH-reh OHD-jee eh pyoot-TOH-stoh KAHL-moh
Sofia:	Bene. Allora ci vediamo in spiaggia tra cinque minuti.	BEH-neh. ahl-LOH-rah chee veh-DYAH-moh een SPYAHD-jah trah CHEEN-kweh mee-NOO-tee.
Marcello:	D'accordo. E non dimenticare l'abbronzante. Il sole picchia forte.	dahk-KOHR-doh. eh nohn dee-mehn-tee-KAH-reh lahb-brohn-DZAHN-teh. eel SOH-leh PEEK-kyah FOHR-teh

Marcello:	It's so hot out!
Sofia:	Yes. Why don't we go swimming?
Marcello:	Good idea! Shall we go to the beach or to the pool?
Sofia:	To tell you the truth I love the sea. But isn't it dangerous around here?
Marcello:	No, today the sea is quite calm.
Sofia:	Good. Then I'll see you on the beach in five minutes.
Marcello:	Right. And don't forget the suntan lotion. The sun is very strong.

SPORTS

At the Beach

Let's go swimming!	Andiamo a nuotare!	ahn-DYAH-moh ah nwoh-TAH-reh!
Where are the finest beaches?	**Dove sono le spiagge più belle?**	**DOH-veh SOH-noh leh SPYAHD-jeh pyoo BEHL-leh?**
How do I get there?	Come ci si arriva?	KOH-meh chee see ahr-REE-vah?
Is it a private or public beach?	È una spiaggia pubblica o privata?	eh OO-nah SPYAHD-jah POOB-blee-kah oh pree-VAH-tah?
Where is the lifeguard?	Dov'è il bagnino?	doh-VEH eel bah-NYEE-noh?
Is it dangerous for children?	È pericoloso per i bambini?	eh peh-ree-koh-LOH-zoh pehr ee bahm-BEE-nee?
The sand is hot but the water is cool.	La sabbia scotta ma l'acqua è fresca.	lah SAHB-byah SKOHT-tah mah LAHK-kwah eh FREH-skah
Are there dangerous currents?	Ci sono correnti pericolose?	chee SOH-noh kohr-REHN-tee peh-ree-koh-LOH-zeh?
No, there are only waves.	No, ci sono solo onde.	noh chee SOH-noh SOH-loh OHN-deh

181

Look at the big waves!	Guarda che cavalloni!	GWAHR-dah keh kah-vahl-LOH-nee!
I'd like to rent . . .	Vorrei noleggiare . . .	vohr-RAY noh-lehd-JAH-reh . . .
_a beach chair.	_un lettino. (or) una sedia a sdraio.	_oon leht-TEE-noh OO-nah SEH-dyah ah SDRAH-yoh
_a beach towel.	_un telo da spiaggia.	_oon TEH-loh dah SPYAHD-jah
_a cabana.	_una cabina.	_OO-nah kah-BEE-nah
_a rowboat.	_una barca a remi.	_OO-nah BAHR-kah ah REH-mee
_a rowboat (light double raft).	_un moscone.	_oon moh-SKOH-neh
	(or) un pattino.	_oon paht-TEE-noh
_a sailboard.	_una tavola a vela.	_OO-nah TAH-voh-lah ah VEH-lah
_a sailboat.	_una barca a vela.	_OO-nah BAHR-kah ah VEH-lah
_skin-diving equipment.	_attrezzatura per pesca subacquea.	_aht-treht-tsah-TOO-rah pehr PEH-skah soo-BAHK-kweh-ah
_a surfboard.	_una tavola da surf. (or) un surfboard.	_OO-nah TAH-voh-lah dah sehrf _oon SEHRF-bohrd
_an umbrella.	_un ombrellone.	_oon ohm-brehl-LOH-neh
_waterskis.	_degli sci d'acqua.	_DEH-lyee shee DAHK-kwah

Poolside

Where is the pool?	Dov'è la piscina?	doh-VEH lah pee-SHEE-nah?
Is the pool . . .	La piscina è . . .	lah pee-SHEE-nah eh . . .
_heated?	_riscaldata?	_ree-skahl-DAH-tah?
_indoors?	_coperta?	_koh-PEHR-tah?
_outdoors?	_scoperta?	_skoh-PEHR-tah?

When does the pool open/close?	A che ora apre/chiude la piscina?	ah keh OH-rah AH-preh/KYOO-deh lah pee-SHEE-nah?

Soccer

Soccer, *il calcio* (eel KAHL-choh), is Italy's national sport, and is played both by children and adults. Professional teams are passionately followed Saturdays and Sundays in stadiums all over Italy. The soccer championship season starts in mid-September and continues until the end of May or beginning of June.

Let's go to the stadium!	Andiamo allo stadio!	ahn-DYAH-moh AHL-loh STAH-dyoh!
I'd like to see a soccer match.	**Vorrei vedere una partita di calcio.**	**vohr-RAY veh-DEH-reh OO-nah pahr-TEE-tah dee KAHL-choh**
Who's playing?	Chi gioca?	kee JOH-kah?
Which is the best team?	Qual è la squadra migliore?	kwah-LEH lah SKWAH-drah mee-LYOH-reh?
Is the stadium near here?	È vicino lo stadio?	eh vee-CHEE-noh loh STAH-dyoh?
How much do the tickets cost?	Quanto costano i biglietti?	KWAHN-toh KOH-stah-noh ee bee-LYEHT-tee?
When does the match begin?	Quando comincia la partita?	KWAHN-doh koh-MEEN-chah lah pahr-TEE-tah?
Are there better seats?	Ci sono posti migliori?	chee SOH-noh POH-stee mee-LYOH-ree?
What's the score?	Qual è il risultato?	kwah-LEH eel ree-zool-TAH-toh?
Who won?	Chi ha vinto?	kee ah VEEN-toh?

Skiing

Would you like to go skiing?	Vuole andare a sciare?	voo-OH-leh ahn-DAH-reh ah shee-AH-reh?
What's the best ski area?	Qual è la stazione sciistica migliore?	kwah-LEH lah stah-TSYOH-neh shee-EE-stee-kah mee-LYOH-reh?

I like Cortina.	Mi piace Cortina.	mee PYAH-cheh kohr-TEE-nah
Are there slopes for beginners?	Ci sono piste per principianti?	chee SOH-noh PEE-steh pehr preen-chee-PYAHN-tee?
I'd like to take some lessons.	Vorrei prendere qualche lezione.	vohr-RAY PREHN-deh-reh KWAHL-keh leh-TSYOH-neh
How are the weather conditions?	Come sono le condizioni del tempo?	KOH-meh SOH-noh leh kohn-dee-TSYOH-nee dehl TEHM-poh
There's lots of snow.	C'è molta neve.	cheh MOHL-tah NEH-veh
Where's the ski lift?	Dov'è la sciovia?	doh-VEH lah shee-oh-VEE-ah?
I'd like to rent . . .	Vorrei noleggiare . . .	voh-RAY noh-lehd-JAH-reh . . .
_skis.	_degli sci.	_DEH-lyee shee
_ski boots.	_degli scarponi da sci.	_DEH-lyee skahr-POH-nee dah shee

Other Sports

I like . . .	Mi piace . . .	mee PYAH-cheh . . .
_baseball.	_il baseball.	_eel BAY-sbohl
_cycling.	_il ciclismo.	_eel chee-KLEE-zmoh
_deep-sea diving.	_la pesca subacquea.	_lah PEH-skah soo-BAHK-kweh-ah
_football.	_il football americano.	_eel FOOT-bohl ah-meh-ree-KAH-noh
_rugby.	_il rugby.	_eel RAHG-bee
_swimming.	_il nuoto.	_eel NWOH-toh
_volleyball.	_la pallavolo.	_lah pahl-lah-VOH-loh
Let's go see . . .	Andiamo a vedere . . .	ahn-DYAH-moh ah veh-DEH-reh . . .
_a horse race.	_una corsa di cavalli.	_OO-nah KOHR-sah dee kah-VAHL-lee
_a tennis match.	_una partita di tennis.	_OO-nah pahr-TEE-tah dee TEHN-nees

Would you like to play . . .	Vuole giocare . . .	voo-OH-leh joh-KAH-reh . . .
_golf?	_a golf?	_ah gohlf?
_tennis?	_a tennis?	_ah TEHN-nees?
Where can I find . . .	Dove posso trovare . . .	DOH-veh POHS-soh troh-VAH-reh . . .
_a golf course?	_un campo da golf?	_oon KAHM-poh dah gohlf?
_a tennis court?	_un campo da tennis?	_oon KAHM-poh dah TEHN-nees?
_a skating rink?	_una pista di pattinaggio?	_OO-nah PEE-stah dee paht-tee-NAHD-joh?
How much is it . . .	Quanto costa . . .	KWAHN-toh KOH-stah . . .
_per hour?	_all'ora?	_ahl-LOH-rah?
_per day?	_al giorno?	_ahl JOHR-noh?
We need to buy some balls.	Dobbiamo comprare delle palle.	dohb-BYAH-moh kohm-PRAH-reh DEHL-leh PAHL-leh
I need a racket.	Ho bisogno di una racchetta.	oh bee-ZOH-nyoh dee OO-nah rahk-KEHT-tah
You play very well.	Gioca benissimo.	JOH-kah beh-NEES-see-moh

MOVIES

A leader in cinematic art, Italy hosts several film festivals. Among them, the most famous is the Venice International Film Festival, organized by the *Biennale* and taking place at the end of August and the beginning of September. There you can preview some of the movies of the coming season, both Italian and foreign.

Let's go to the movies!	Andiamo al cinema!	ahn-DYAH-moh ahl CHEE-neh-mah!
What's playing?	Che cosa danno?	keh KOH-zah DAHN-noh?
Is it in Italian or English?	È in italiano o in inglese?	eh een ee-tah-LYAH-noh oh een een-GLEH-zeh?

185

With subtitles?	Con i sottotitoli?	kohn ee soh-toh-TEE-toh-lee?
Is it dubbed?	È doppiato?	eh dohp-PYAH-toh?
I prefer to see the original version.	Preferisco vedere la versione originale.	preh-feh-REE-skoh veh-DEH-reh lah vehr-ZYOH-neh oh-ree-jee-NAH-leh
What kind of film is it?	**Che genere di film è?**	**keh JEH-neh-reh dee feelm eh?**
I'd like to see . . .	Mi piacerebbe vedere . . .	mee pyah-cheh-REHB-beh veh-DEH-reh . . .
_an action movie.	_un film d'azione.	_oon feelm dah-TSYOH-neh
_an adventure movie.	_un film d'avventura.	_oon feelm dahv-vehn-TOO-rah
_a comedy.	**_un film comico.**	**_oon feelm KOH-mee-koh**
_a detective story.	_un film poliziesco.	_oon feelm poh-lee-TSYEH-skoh
_a drama.	**_un film drammatico.**	**_oon feelm drahm-MAH-tee-koh**
_a horror movie.	_un film dell'orrore.	_oon feelm dehl-lohr-ROH-reh
_a love story.	_una storia d'amore.	_OO-nah STOH-ryah dah-MOH-reh
_a musical.	_un musical.	_oon MYOO-zee-kahl
_a political movie.	_un film politico.	_oon feelm poh-LEE-tee-koh
_a science fiction movie.	_un film di fantascienza.	_oon feelm dee fahn-tah-SHEHN-tsah
_a tearjerker.	_un film sentimentale.	_oon feelm sehn-tee-menhn-TAH-leh
_a thriller.	**_un giallo.**	**_oon JAHL-loh**
_a war movie.	_un film di guerra.	_oon feelm dee GWEHR-rah
_a western.	_un western.	_oon WEH-stehrn

THEATER, CONCERTS, OPERA, AND BALLET

The performing arts, particularly opera, are an essential part of Italian culture. The celebrated Teatro alla Scala in Milan is perhaps the most famous opera house in the world. In the summer, spectacular operas are performed outdoors at the Arena Sferisterio in Macerata (July) and at the Terme di Caracalla in Rome (July/August). In the breathtakingly beautiful Arena di Verona, before the performance begins, it is customary for the audience to light up small candles that flicker like stars. Pesaro offers a Rossini Opera Festival beginning in mid-August; Torre del Lago, near Lucca, features Puccini's operas in an open-air theater in July and August, and Ravenna presents both opera and ballet in the majestic Rocca di Brancaleone, an ancient fortress built by the Venetians. Two important festivals of the performing arts are the Maggio Musicale Fiorentino (opera, concerts, ballet, drama), held in Florence in May/June, and the Festival of Two Worlds (art exhibits, ballet, concerts, drama, opera) in Spoleto from late June to mid-July. Also notable are the Music and Drama Festival, a review of films, music, and stage plays held in Taormina's Greek theater in July and August, and the Shakespeare Festival at the Roman theater of Verona. The famous International Ballet Festival is held at Nervi near Genoa in July.

What's playing at the theater?	Che cosa danno al teatro?	keh KOH-zah DAHN-noh ahl teh-AH-troh?
What kind of play is it?	Che tipo di spettacolo è?	keh TEE-poh dee speht-TAH-koh-loh eh?
Who is . . .	Chi è . . .	kee eh . . .
_the author?	_l'autore?	_low-TOH-reh?
_the director?	_il regista?	_eel reh-JEE-stah?
Are there tickets for tonight?	Ci sono biglietti per questa sera?	chee SOH-noh bee-LYEHT-tee pehr KWEH-stah SEH-rah?
How much are they?	Quanto costano?	KWAHN-toh KOH-stah-noh?
I'd like . . .	Vorrei . . .	vohr-RAY . . .
_an orchestra seat.	_un posto in platea.	_oon POH-stoh een plah-TEH-ah

_a mezzanine seat.	_un posto in prima galleria.	_oon POH-stoh een PREE-mah gahl-leh-REE-ah
_a balcony seat.	_un posto in seconda galleria.	_oon POH-stoh een seh-KOHN-dah gahl-leh-REE-ah
_seats up front.	_dei posti davanti.	_day POH-stee dah-VAHN-tee
_seats in back.	_dei posti di dietro.	_day POH-stee dee DYEH-troh
_seats on the side.	_dei posti laterali.	_day POH-stee lah-teh-RAH-lee
_tickets for the matinee.	_dei biglietti per lo spettacolo del pomeriggio.	_day bee-LYEHT-tee pehr loh speht-TAH-koh-loh dehl poh-meh-REED-joh
_tickets for the evening.	_dei biglietti per lo spettacolo serale.	_day bee-LYEHT-tee pehr loh speht-TAH-koh-loh seh-RAH-leh
A program, please.	Un programma, per favore.	oon proh-GRAHM-mah, pehr fah-VOR-reh
I'd like to see . . .	**Vorrei vedere . . .**	**vohr-RAY veh-DEH-reh . . .**
_a ballet.	**_un balletto.**	**_oon bahl-LEHT-toh**
_a comedy.	_una commedia.	_OO-nah kohm-MEH-dyah
_a concert.	_un concerto.	_oon kohn-CHEHR-toh
_an opera.	**_un'opera.**	**_oo-NOH-peh-rah**
_an operetta.	_un'operetta.	_oo-noh-peh-REHT-tah
_a musical.	**_una commedia musicale.**	**_OO-nah kohm-MEH-dyah moo-zee-KAH-leh**
_a variety show.	_uno spettacolo di varietà.	_OO-noh speh-TAH-koh-loh dee vah-ryeh-TAH
Who's playing?	Chi recita?	kee REH-chee-tah?

Who's singing?	Chi canta?	kee KAHN-tah?
Who's dancing?	Chi balla?	kee BAHL-lah?
Who's the conductor?	Chi è il direttore d'orchestra?	kee eh eel dee-reht-TOH-reh dohr-KEH-strah?

CLUBS, DISCOS, AND CABARETS

In Italy, particularly in large cities, some restaurants are also nightclubs or cabarets, where you can have dinner and see a show. On weekends, many nightclubs host live music. Reservations are sometimes required for the better-known clubs, or for featured shows. For the younger crowds there are discos and disco pubs which often play the latest from both sides of the Atlantic.

Why don't we go dancing tonight!	Perché non andiamo a ballare questa sera!	pehr-KEH nohn ahn-DYAH-moh ah bahl-LAH-reh KWEH-stah SEH-rah!
I like dancing a lot.	Mi piace molto ballare.	mee PYAH-cheh MOHL-toh bah-LAH-reh
Can you suggest . . .	Può consigliarmi . . .	pwoh kohn-see-LYAHR-mee . . .
_a good disco?	_una buona discoteca?	_OO-nah BWOH-nah dee-skoh-TEH-kah?
_a good nightclub?	_un buon night-club?	_un bwohn "night club"?
Good evening.	Buona sera.	BWOH-nah SEH-rah
We would like a table . . .	Vorremmo un tavolo . . .	vohr-REHM-moh oon TAH-voh-loh . . .
_near the dance floor.	_vicino alla pista.	_vee-CHEE-noh AHL-lah PEE-stah
_near the stage.	_vicino alla scena.	_vee-CHEE-noh AHL-lah SHEH-nah

189

16 GRAMMAR IN BRIEF

With this book, you can find and use essential phrases without formal study of Italian grammar. However, by learning some of the basic grammatical patterns, you will be able to construct an unlimited number of your own sentences and greatly increase your range of expression.

DEFINITE ARTICLES

Articles have different forms to agree with nouns in gender—masculine or feminine—and in number—singular or plural.

Masculine Singular

il (noun begins with a consonant)

il libro (the book)

l' (noun begins with a vowel)

l'albero (the tree)

lo (noun begins with s + consonant, or z)

lo stadio, lo zingaro (the stadium, the gypsy)

Masculine Plural

il becomes i

i libri (the books)

l' and lo become gli

gli alberi, gli stadi, gli zaffiri (the trees, the stadiums, the saffires)

Feminine Singular

la (noun begins with any consonant)

la casa, la sala, la scuola, la zia (the house, the hall, the school, the aunt)

l' (noun begins with a vowel)

l'agenda (the agenda)

Feminine Plural

le (for all forms)

le case, le sale, le scuole, le zie (the houses, the halls, the schools, the aunts)

INDEFINITE ARTICLES

Masculine Singular

un (before nouns beginning
with vowels and consonants)

un amico, un libro, un sasso
(a friend, a book, a stone)

uno (before nouns beginning
with s + consonant or z)

uno studente, uno zio (a
student, an uncle)

Masculine Plural

dei (before nouns beginning
with a consonant)

dei libri, dei sassi (some
books, some stones)

degli (before nouns beginning
with a vowel, s +
consonant, or z)

degli amici, degli studenti,
degli zii (some friends,
some students, some uncles)

Feminine Singular

un' (before nouns beginning
with a vowel)

un'amica, un'automobile (a
friend, a car)

una (before nouns beginning
with any consonant)

una casa, una sala, una
scuola, una zia (a house, a
hall, a school, an aunt)

Feminine Plural

delle (before vowels and
consonants)

delle amiche, delle case,
delle sale, delle scuole,
delle zie (some friends,
some houses, some halls
some schools, some aunts)

The following chart summarizes the forms of the articles:

Definite—"the"	Singular	Plural
Masculine	il	i
	l', lo	gli
Feminine	l', la	le

Indefinite	Singular—"a, an"	Plural—"some"
Masculine	un, uno	dei/degli
Feminine	un', una	delle

NOUNS

All nouns in Italian are either masculine or feminine (there is no neuter). As a general rule, all masculine nouns end in -o in the singular and -i in the plural. All feminine nouns end in -a in the singular and -e in the plural. However, there are also nouns ending in -e in the singular, which may be either masculine or feminine. Whether masculine or feminine, they both end in -i in the plural. When you come across nouns ending in -e, it's advisable to learn them with the proper definite article so that you will immediately recognize the gender.*

	Singular	Plural
m. (book)	il libro	i libri
f. (house)	la casa	le case
m. (flower)	il fiore	i fiori
f. (car)	l'automobile	le automobili

*m. and f. refer to masculine and feminine.

ADJECTIVES

Descriptive Adjectives

Adjectives agree in gender and number with the noun they modify. They usually follow the noun:

il ragazzo italiano (the Italian boy)

il vino bianco (the white wine)

They *always* follow the noun when modified by the adverb *molto* (very):

una ragazza molto bella (a very beautiful girl)

When the adjective ends in -e it does not change to agree with the noun in gender:

un uomo intelligente (an intelligent man)

una donna intelligente (an intelligent woman)

To make an adjective plural, follow the same rules given for the nouns:

Singular	Plural
ragazzo italiano (Italian boy)	ragazzi italiani (Italian boys)
ragazza spagnola (Spanish girl)	ragazze spagnole (Spanish girls)
bambino francese (French child [m.])	bambini francesi (French children)
bambina inglese (English child [f.])	bambine inglesi (English children)

If an adjective modifies two or more nouns of different gender, the masculine plural form must be used, and the article repeated before each noun:

I giornali e le riviste sono interessanti. (The papers and magazines are interesting.)

Some common adjectives may precede the noun. They are:

bello (beautiful), **brutto** (ugly), **buono** (good), **cattivo** (bad), **grande** (big), **piccolo** (small), **giovane** (young), **vecchio** (old)

Demonstrative Adjectives

Questo (this, these):

questo, questa (this)   **questi, queste** (these)

Quello (that, those) has several different forms that follow the pattern of the definite articles (for reference see the chart on p. 201:

quel, quell', quello, quella (that)	quei, quegli, quelle (those)
quel libro (that book)	quei libri (those books)
quell'amico (that friend) quello studente (that student)	quegli amici/studenti (those friends/students)
quella casa (that house)	quelle case (those houses)

Possessive Adjectives

Possessive adjectives denote ownership. In Italian they agree in gender and number with the thing possessed, not with the possessor as they do in English. They precede the noun.

	Singular		Plural	
	Masculine	**Feminine**	**Masculine**	**Feminine**
my	il mio	la mia	i miei	le mie
your (familiar sing.)	il tuo	la tua	i tuoi	le tue
your (polite sing.)	il Suo	la Sua	i Suoi	le Sue
his/her	il suo	la sua	i suoi	le sue
our	il nostro	la nostra	i nostri	le nostre
your (familiar plural)	il vostro	la vostra	i vostri	le vostre
your (polite plural)	il Loro	la Loro	i Loro	le Loro
their	il loro	la loro	i loro	le loro

Here are some examples:

la mia camera (my room)

la sua casa (his/her house)

il suo appartamento (his/her apartment)

i nostri libri (our books)

le loro valigie (their suitcases)

In some expressions, the possessive adjective is used without the definite article and is placed after the noun:

a casa mia/tua/sua (at my/your/his/her place)

da parte Sua (on your behalf [polite form])

È colpa sua. (It's his/her fault.)

Important: Possessive adjectives are used without the article with a singular, unmodified noun expressing family relationship, except for *their*, which always requires the article:

mio padre (my father), **tua madre** (your mother), **suo fratello** (his/her brother), **nostra sorella** (our sister), **vostra zia** (your aunt), but **il loro cugino** (their cousin)

If the noun denoting family relationship is modified by an adjective or a suffix, then the possessive retains the article.

il mio caro padre (my dear father), **la mia cara madre** (my dear mother), **il mio fratellino** (my little brother)

Possessive adjectives are less-often used in Italian than they are in English, especially when possession is evident and particularly with parts of the body or articles of clothing:

Ho lasciato i guanti a casa. (I left my gloves at home.)

Mi fa male la testa. (My head aches.)*

COMPARATIVES

Italian has three comparatives: equality (*uguaglianza*), majority (*maggioranza*), and minority (*minoranza*).

1. Comparison of Equality (as . . . as) adjective + *come:*

Il mio appartamento è grande come il tuo. (My apartment is as large as yours.)

2. Comparison of Majority (-er . . . than/more . . . than) and Comparison of Minority (less . . . than/fewer . . . than)

(a) *più* (more)/*meno* (less) . . . *di* (by itself or combined with the definite article) when two different persons or items are compared:

Questa ragazza è più alta di Maria. (This girl is taller than Maria.)

Il mio libro è più interessante del tuo. (My book is more interesting than yours.)

(b) *più* (more)/*meno* (less) . . . *che,* when two words are compared and related to the same subject:

Questa ragazza è più elegante che bella. (This girl is more elegant than beautiful.)

(c) *più* (more)/*meno* (less) . . . *di quel/quello che* + verb:

Studia più di quel/quello che tu pensi. (He studies more than you think.)

SUPERLATIVES

Italian has two superlatives:

1. Relative Superlative, *superlativo relativo* **(the most/the least/the . . . -est.)** The relative superlative is formed by placing the appropriate definite article before *più* or *meno*. The second term, of/in, is translated with *di,* either by itself or combined with the definite article:

Quest'uomo è il più ricco del mondo. (This man is the richest in the world.)

Lei è la più/meno famosa delle sorelle. (She is the most/least famous of the sisters.)

2. Absolute Superlative, *superlativo assoluto* **(very + adjective).** Italians are very fond of the *-issimo* form, which agrees in gender and number:

È un quadro bellissimo. (It's a very beautiful painting.)

È una rivista interessantissima. (It's a very interesting magazine.)

Of course, you can also use the invariable adverb *molto* (very) before the adjective:

È un quadro molto bello. (It's a very beautiful painting.)

È una stampa molto vecchia. (It's a very old print.)

Irregular Comparatives and Superlatives

Some adjectives have irregular comparatives and superlatives in addition to the regular forms.

Positive	Comparative	Relative Superlative	Absolute Superlative
good	better	the best	very good
buono (regular)	più buono(-a)	il(la) più buono(-a)	buonissimo
(irregular)	migliore	il/la migliore	ottimo
bad	worse	the worst	very bad
cattivo (regular)	più cattivo(-a)	il(la) più cattivo(-a)	cattivissimo (-a)
(irregular)	peggiore	il/la peggiore	pessimo(-a)

Positive	Comparative	Relative Superlative	Absolute Superlative
big/great	bigger/greater	the biggest/greatest	very big/great
grande (regular)	più grande	il/la più grande	grandissimo (-a)
(irregular)	maggiore	il/la maggiore	massimo(-a)
small/little	smaller	the smallest	very small
piccolo (regular)	più piccolo (-a)	il(la) più piccolo(-a)	piccolissimo (-a)
(irregular)	minore	il/la minore	minimo(-a)

lento	**lenta**	**lentamente**
serio	**seria**	**seriamente**

Remember, *maggiore* and *minore* are also used to express age:

mio fratello maggiore   (my older brother)

mia sorella minore   (my younger sister)

ADVERBS

In English, -*ly* is added to an adjective to form an adverb. Italian forms adverbs by adding -*mente* to the feminine form of the adjective:

If the adjective ends in -*le* or -*re*, the final *e* is dropped before adding -*mente*:

facile	**facilmente**
particolare	**particolarmente**

Note that some common adverbs have their own form, or the same form as the adjectives:

Their Own Form	Adjective Form
allora then	chiaro clearly
ancora yet	forte loud
bene well	giusto right
così so	piano slow
già already	sodo hard (as in lavorare sodo—to work hard)
insieme together	veloce fast
male badly	vicino near
meglio better	
peggio worse	
sempre always	
spesso often	
subito at once	
tardi late	

PRONOUNS

Pronouns stand for or replace nouns. They perform several distinct functions.

Subject Pronouns

These pronouns are the subjects of sentences or clauses, and are usually found at the beginning of the sentence. In Italian, subject pronouns are usually omitted because the verb ending indicates who is performing the action:

Vado al cinema. (I am going to the movies.)

Mangiamo il gelato. (We eat ice cream.)

Direct Object Pronouns

They represent persons or things that receive the action of the verb. They answer the question Whom? or What? They are used with transitive verbs, that is, with those verbs that take an object:

Vedi Maria? Sì _la_ vedo questo pomeriggio. (Do you see Maria? Yes, I'll see her this afternoon.)

Capisci l'italiano? Sì, _lo_ capisco un po'. (Do you understand Italian? Yes, I understand it a little.)

As seen from the above examples, Italian direct object pronouns are usually placed before the conjugated verb. With an infinitive, however, they follow and are attached to the infinitive, which drops the final -e:

Ti piace guardare la televisione? Sì, mi piace guardar_la_. (Do you like to watch television? Yes, I like to watch it.)

Indirect Object Pronouns

They receive the action of the verb indirectly: the action is done to or for the indirect object. They answer the question To whom? or For whom?

Parlo a Mario. _Gli_ parlo. (I speak to him.)

Parlo a Maria. _Le_ parlo. (I speak to her.)

The placement of indirect object pronouns is the same as for direct objects. They usually precede a conjugated verb, the only exception being _loro_ (to them), which always follows:

Parlo agli amici. _Gli_ parlo. (I speak to my friends. I speak to them.)

Again, with an infinitive the indirect object pronoun is attached to the infinitive, which drops the final -e. With *loro,* the infinitive may retain its final -e (optional) and the pronoun is never attached:

Ho bisogno di veder*la*. (I need to see her.)

Preferisco parlar(e) loro. (I prefer to speak to them.)

Pronouns as Objects of Prepositions

They always follow the preposition:

Vado con lei. (I'm going with her.)

Lo faccio per te. (I'm doing this for you.)

The following chart shows the forms of all the pronouns mentioned above.

Subject		Direct Object		Indirect Object		After a Preposition	
I	io	me	mi	to me	mi	me	me
you (familiar)	tu	you	ti	to you	ti	you	te
you (polite)*	Lei	you	La	to you	Le	you	Lei
he	lui	him	lo	to him	gli	him	lui
she	lei	her	la	to her	le	her	lei
we	noi	us	ci	to us	ci	us	noi
you (familiar)	voi	you	vi	to you	vi	you	voi
you (polite)	Loro	you	Li (m.) Le (f.)	to you	. . . Loro	you	Loro
they	loro	them	li (m.) le (f.)	to them	. . . loro	them	loro

*Note that these words are capitalized in written Italian to show a great deal of respect.

Note: Tu, Lei, voi, Loro. Italian has preserved a distinction between familiar and formal "you" both in the singular and in the plural.

Dare del tu, or to use the *tu* form with someone, is reserved for children, close friends, and relatives. *Dare del Lei,* or to use the *Lei* polite form, is reserved for people with whom you are not familiar, people you have just met, people whose name is preceded by a title such as Mr. or Dr., and finally with people you hold in esteem and reverence. Never confuse the *tu* and the *Lei* forms. Therefore, if you are addressing a friend of yours and want to ask "How are you?" you will say, *Come stai (tu)*? If you are addressing a doctor or lawyer, you will say, *Come sta (Lei)*? In the plural the *voi* and *Loro* forms have now become almost interchangeable in favor of *voi: Come state (voi)*?

Relative Pronouns

In English, relative pronouns are often omitted. In Italian they must always be expressed. They are:

che	who, whom, which, that (invariable; refers to persons and things):
	l'uomo che parla (the man who speaks)
	i libri che devo leggere (the books I must read)
cui	whom, that, which (always after a preposition; refers to persons and things and is invariable):
	l'appartamento in cui vivo (the apartment I live in)
	l'uomo a cui parlo (the man I'm talking to)
il/la cui, i/le cui	whose, of which (used to express possession; the article agrees in gender and number with the noun following cui, that is, with the person or thing possessed):
	il signore la cui moglie è italiana (the man whose wife is Italian)
	l'edificio i cui inquilini sono in vacanza (the building whose tenants are on vacation)
il/la quale, i/le quali	(the one) who, whom (used instead of che to avoid ambiguity; the article will express the gender and number of the antecedent, the subject of the sentence):
	L'amico di Maria il quale arriva oggi (Mary's friend who is arriving today).
	La sorella di Paolo la quale è al mare (Paul's sister who is at the seaside).

Interrogative Pronouns

chi	who, whom (invariable)
che, che cosa, cosa	what (invariable and interchangeable)

quale/quali	which (one/ones)
quanto(-a), quanti(-e)	how much, how many
Chi parla italiano?	Who speaks Italian?
Che cosa hai visto?	What did you see?
Quali hai letto?	Which ones did you read?
Quanti hanno parlato?	How many did speak?

Demonstrative Pronouns

They are less complicated than the demonstrative adjectives because *questo* (this) and *quello* (that) as pronouns only have four regular forms, according to gender and number.

Singular		Plural	
questo, questa	this (one)	questi, queste	these (ones)
quello, quella	that (one)	quelli, quelle	those (ones)

Questo è buono e quello è cattivo. (This one is good, and that one is bad.)

Queste sono belle e quelle sono brutte. (These are beautiful, and those are ugly.)

NEGATIVE SENTENCES

To form the negative in Italian place the word *non* in front of the verb. For example:

Parlo Italiano. (I speak Italian.)

Non parlo italiano. (I don't speak Italian.)

Other words that are used with the negative *non* are:

affatto (at all)	Non sono affatto contento. (I am not at all happy.)
ancora (yet)	Non ho ancora mangiato. (I haven't eaten yet.)
mai (never)	Non ha mai soldi. (He never has money.)
nulla/niente (nothing)	Non sanno niente.* (They don't know anything/They know nothing.)
nessuno (no one)	Non conosco nessuno.* (I don't know anyone./I know no one.)

201

| neanche/nemmeno/neppure (not even) | Non vengo neanche se mi preghi. (I won't come, not even if you beg me.) |
| più (more, longer) | Non abita più qui. (He doesn't live here any more.) |

As you may have noticed from the examples, Italian uses double negatives. At times there can be as many as three negatives in a sentence:

Non ha detto niente a nessuno. (He did not say anything to anyone. Literally: He did not say nothing to no one.)

*Notice that both *sapere* and *conoscere* mean to know. *Sapere* is used when referring to facts, *conoscere* when referring to people and places. Also note that the personal pronoun is not used here. The meaning is implied by the particular verb conjugation.

QUESTIONS

Questions are easy to form in Italian. The simplest way is to raise the intonation of your voice at the end of a statement to indicate a question, as you would do in English:

| Statement (flat voice) | Andiamo al ristorante. (We are going to the restaurant.) |
| Question (raising voice) | Andiamo al ristorante? (Shall we go to the restaurant?) |

Wh- questions are another major category. These are the questions that in English begin with *wh-*:

who?	chi?	Chi arriva oggi? (Who is arriving today?)
what?	che cosa?	Che cosa leggi? (What are you reading?)
where?	dove?	Dove vai a quest'ora? (Where are you going at this time?)
when?	quando?	Quando parte il treno? (When does the train leave?)
why?	perché?	Perché mangi adesso? (Why are you eating now?)

These questions are formed as follows:

wh- word + verb + subject

PREPOSITIONS

The most common prepositions in Italian are:

to	a	ah
from	da	dah
of	di	dee
in	in	een
on	su	soo
	(or) sopra	SOH-prah
with	con	kohn
about	circa	CHEER-kah
	(or) di	dee
according to	secondo	seh-KOHN-doh
across	attraverso	aht-trah-VEHR-soh
after	dopo	DOH-poh
against	contro	KOHN-troh
among/between	tra	trah
	(or) fra	frah
at	a	ah
at (plus name of person or profession)*	da	dah
besides	inoltre	ee-NOHL-treh
by/for	per	pehr
during	durante	doo-RAHN-teh
except	eccetto	eht-CHEHT-toh
over	sopra	SOH-prah
through	attraverso	aht-trah-VEHR-soh
	(or) per	pehr
towards	verso	VEHR-soh
under	sotto	SOHT-toh
without	senza	SEHN-tsah

---

*At the doctor's would be translated *dal* (*da + il*) *dottore.* At Marco's (house) is *da Marco.*

CONTRACTIONS

In Italian some prepositions combine with the definite article to make one word. The most common are:

Prepositions	Articles						
	+il	+lo	+l'	+la	+i	+gli	+le
a (to)	al	allo	all'	alla	ai	agli	alle
da (from)	dal	dallo	dall'	dalla	dai	dagli	dalle
di (of)	del	dello	dell'	della	dei	degli	delle
in (in)	nel	nello	nell'	nella	nei	negli	nelle
su (on)	sul	sullo	sull'	sulla	sui	sugli	sulle

Note the following idiomatic forms:

alla radio (on the radio)

alla televisione (on TV)

al telefono (on the phone)

sul giornale (in the newspaper)

VERBS

There are three verb conjugations in Italian. In the infinitive, all verbs end in either -*are*, -*ere*, or -*ire*. Verbs ending in -*ire* fall into two categories: the regular ones (those whose ending -*ire* is usually preceded by two consonants such as *dormire*—*rm* before *ire* (to sleep), and the so-called *isco* verbs, namely those whose ending -*ire* is only preceded by one consonant, such as *capire*—*p* before *ire* (to understand). The *isco* verbs add -*isc*- between the stem of the verb, *cap*- in this case, and the ending for all forms except *noi* (we) and *voi* (you).

	1st Conjugation	2nd Conjugation	3rd Conjugation	
	Parlare (to speak)	**Ripetere** (to repeat)	**Dormire** (to sleep)	**Capire** (-*isc*) (to understand)
(io)	parlo	ripeto	dormo	capisco
(tu)	parli	ripeti	dormi	capisci
(lui/lei/Lei)	parla	ripete	dorme	capisce
(noi)	parliamo	ripetiamo	dormiamo	capiamo
(voi)	parlate	ripetete	dormite	capite
(loro/Loro)	parlano	ripetono	dormono	capiscono

For the third-person plural, *loro*, the stress is on the stem: *parlano* (PAHR-lah-noh), *ripetono* (ree-PEH-toh-noh), *dormono* (DOHR-moh-noh), and *capiscono* (kah-PEE-skoh-noh). All regular verbs follow this pattern.

Irregular Verbs

Some commonly used verbs do not follow the patterns given above and have irregular forms. Here are conjugations of a few of the most common irregular verbs.

	Essere (to be)	Avere (to have)	Andare (to go)	Venire (to come)
(io)	sono	ho	vado	vengo
(tu)	sei	hai	vai	vieni
(lui/lei/Lei)	è	ha	va	viene
(noi)	siamo	abbiamo	andiamo	veniamo
(voi)	siete	avete	andate	venite
(loro/Loro)	sono	hanno	vanno	vengono

	Dare (to give)	Dire (to say/tell)	Fare (to do)	Stare (to be/stay)
(io)	do	dico	faccio	sto
(tu)	dai	dici	fai	stai
(lui/lei/Lei)	dà	dice	fa	sta
(noi)	diamo	diciamo	facciamo	stiamo
(voi)	date	dite	fate	state
(loro/Loro)	danno	dicono	fanno	stanno

	Dovere (must)	Potere (to be able/can)	Volere (want)
(io)	devo (debbo)	posso	voglio
(tu)	devi	puoi	vuoi
(lui/lei/Lei)	deve	può	vuole
(noi)	dobbiamo	possiamo	vogliamo
(voi)	dovete	potete	volete
(loro/Loro)	devono (or) debbono	possono	vogliono

Past Tense

To express an action in the past Italian usually recurs to the structure called *passato prossimo* (present perfect):

subject + present tense of *essere* or *avere* + past participle of main verb

The past participle is formed by adding the appropriate ending to the stem:

Infinitive	Ending	Past Participle
parl-are	-ato	parlato
ripet-ere	-uto	ripetuto
cap-ire	-ito	capito

In this past tense, all verbs are conjugated with either *avere* (to have) or *essere* (to be). All transitive verbs (verbs that take an object) are conjugated with *avere* (whether the object is expressed or not). The past participle is invariable:

We ate (an apple).	Abbiamo mangiato (una mela).
I sang an Italian song.	Ho cantato una canzone italiana.

All intransitive verbs (verbs that do not take an object), such as verbs of motion, are conjugated with the auxiliary *essere*. In this case, the past participle always agrees in gender and number with the subject. Here's a list of the most common verbs conjugated with *essere*:

Verb	Infinitive	Past Participle
to arrive/to leave	arrivare/partire	arrivato(-a)/ partito(-a)
to enter/to leave (go out)	entrare/uscire	entrato(-a)/ uscito(-a)
to go up/to go down	salire/scendere	salito(-a)/ sceso(-a)
to go/to come	andare/venire	andato(-a)/ venuto(-a)
to remain/to return	rimanere/ritornare	rimasto(-a)/ ritornato(-a)
to be born/to die	nascere/morire	nato(-a)/morto(-a)
Mary left for Bologna.	Maria è partita per Bologna.	
The boys have just arrived.	I ragazzi sono appena arrivati.	

Irregular Past Participles

Some of the most commonly used Italian verbs have irregular past participles. A number of these are listed below. They are all conjugated with the auxiliary *avere*,* and the past participle, as mentioned above, is invariable.

Verb	Infinitive	Past Participle
to ask	chiedere	chiesto
to be	essere	stato(-a)
to choose	scegliere	scelto
to do/to make	fare	fatto
to drink	bere	bevuto
to light	accendere	acceso
to offer	offrire	offerto
to open	aprire	aperto
to put	mettere	messo
to read	leggere	letto
to say/to tell	dire	detto
to take	prendere	preso
to turn off	spegnere	spento
to write	scrivere	scritto
We had (took) coffee.	Abbíamo preso il caffè.	
I wrote many cards.	Ho scritto molte cartoline.	

*Note that *essere* is always conjugated with the auxiliary *essere,* and its past participle is *stato(-a)*, just like the past participle of *stare* (to stay):

I have been. **Sono stato(-a).**

Avere has a regular past participle and is conjugated with the auxiliary *avere:*

She has had. **Ha avuto.**

Future Tense

The future tense expresses a future action and is the equivalent of the English "I will" or "I'm going to" + infinitive. The easiest way to form the future in Italian is as follows: drop the final *e* of the infinitive and add the endings *-o, -ai, -a, -emo, -ete, -anno.*

Verbs ending in *-are* change the stem from *-ar* to *-er* and then add the endings.*

Parlare	Ripetere	Dormire	Finire
parlerò	ripeterò	dormirò	finirò
parlerai	ripeterai	dormirai	finirai
parlerà	ripeterà	dormirà	finirà
parleremo	ripeteremo	dormiremo	finiremo
parlerete	ripeterete	dormirete	finirete
parleranno	ripeteranno	dormiranno	finiranno

*The stem for conjugating the future tense of *essere* is *sar-*, and for *avere*, *avr-*.

I'll remember my beautiful holidays in Italy.	Ricorderò le mie belle vacanze in Italia.
We'll buy some shoes in Florence.	Compreremo delle scarpe a Firenze.

Reflexive Verbs

Reflexive verbs are those in which the action of the verb reflects back on the subject. In Italian, reflexive verbs are conjugated with reflexive pronouns, as follows:

subject pronoun (optional) + reflexive pronoun + conjugated verb

Subject	Reflexive Pronoun	Verb (lavarsi, to wash oneself)
io	mi	lavo
tu	ti	lavi
lui/lei/Lei	si	lava
noi	ci	laviamo
voi	vi	lavate
loro/Loro	si	lavano

Mi lavo tutte le mattine. (I wash myself every morning.)

Si rade un giorno sì e un giorno no. (He shaves every other day.)

In compound tenses, reflexive verbs are conjugated with *essere* and the past participle must agree in gender and number:

(Lei) Si è alzata e si è vestita. (She got up and got dressed.)

The reflexive is used in Italian with parts of the body and articles of clothing. The English possessive is replaced by the definite article:

Mi lavo le mani. (I wash my hands.)

Si mette il cappotto. (She puts her coat on.)

With a compound tense and an object in the sentence, the past participle preferably agrees with the subject rather than with the object:

Mario si è lavato la faccia. (Mario washed his face.)

Carla si è messa i guanti. (Carla put her gloves on.)

Here, *lavato* agrees with Mario, not *la faccia,* and *messa* agrees with Carla, not with *i guanti.* Some common verbs can be made reflexive by dropping the final *-e* and by adding *-si* to the infinitive. For example:

alzare	to lift	alzarsi	to get up
chiamare	to call	chiamarsi	to be named
lavare	to wash	lavarsi	to wash oneself
svegliare	to wake (someone) up	svegliarsi	to wake up
vestire	to dress	vestirsi	to get dressed

Verbs *Essere* and *Stare*

The verb "to be" is expressed in Italian by two different verbs: *essere* and *stare* (see irregular verbs section for conjugation). *Essere* is used most of the time. *Stare* is used:

1. In courtesy expressions to express how one feels with an adverb like *bene* or *male,* such as *Come sta?* (How are you?), and their answers *Sto bene/male/così così.* (I'm well/not well/so so.) However, with an adjective, one must use *essere: Sono stanco.* (I am tired.), *Sono contenta.* (I am happy.)

2. To form the progressive tense, to describe an action in progress:

Sto parlando. (I am speaking.)

Stai scrivendo. (You are writing.)

Sta dormendo. (He is sleeping.)

Note: the gerund is formed as follows:

-are verbs drop *-are* from the infinitive and add *-ando* (*parl-are/parl-ando*).

-ere and *-ire* verbs drop *-ere* and *-ire* and add *-endo* (*scriv-ere/scriv-endo; dorm-ire/dorm-endo*).

Special Uses of *Avere* and *Fare*

In Italian, some idiomatic forms are expressed with the verb *avere* (to have) + noun to describe a state of being, whereas in English the same idioms are usually expressed with "to be" + adjective. For example, "I am hungry" is expressed in Italian as "I have hunger," *Ho fame.*

avere . . . anni	to be . . . years old
avere . . .	to be . . .
_bisogno di . . .	_in need of . . .
_caldo	_warm
_fame	_hungry
_freddo	_cold
_fretta	_in a hurry
_paura	_afraid
_sete	_thirsty
_sonno	_sleepy
avere voglia di . . .	to feel like . . .

Fare (to make) is also used to express "to be," but it refers to weather conditions, and it's always used in the third-person singular:

Che tempo fa? (What's the weather like?)

Fa bel tempo. (The weather is nice.)

To Like (*Piacere*)

Piacere is the equivalent of "to like." However, its construction is different from the English "to like" and more similar to the expression "to be pleasing to." To get it right in Italian, you have to change the sentence around, and use **piace** if the object is singular, **piacciono** if the object is plural.

"I like pasta," becomes "Pasta is pleasing to me." **Mi piace la pasta.**

"I like books," becomes "Books are pleasing to me." **Mi piacciono i libri.**

If the subject of the English sentence is a person, his/her name will be introduced in Italian by the preposition *a*:

A Maria piacciono i fiori. (Mary likes flowers.)

A Carlo piace il calcio. (Carlo likes soccer.)

With a noun, the preposition *a* is contracted with the appropriate definite article:

Ai ragazzi piace nuotare.* (The boys like swimming.)

Alle ragazze piace andare a ballare.* (The girls like to go dancing.)

*With infinitives describing an activity such as *nuotare* and *ballare*, one always uses the third-person singular *piace: Mi piace leggere.* (I like to read.)

Here's an easy chart to remember *piacere*:

I like	mi piace/piacciono
you (familiar) like	ti piace/piacciono
you (polite) like	le piace/piacciono
he likes	gli piace/piacciono
she likes	le piace/piacciono
we like	ci piace/piacciono
you like (familiar)	vi piace/piacciono
you like (polite)	piace/piacciono Loro*
they like	piace/piacciono loro*

*Remember that *loro* and *Loro* always follow the verb: *Questo libro piace (a) loro.* (They like this book.)

ENGLISH-ITALIAN DICTIONARY

The gender of nouns is indicated by m. (masculine) or f. (feminine). Nouns commonly used in the plural are shown in the plural form and are followed by the notation pl.

Adjectives appear in their masculine singular forms. Notice that all adjectives ending in -e may be either masculine or feminine.

Verbs ending in -si are reflexive and are followed by the notation (refl.).

A

a; an un, un', uno (m.), un', una (f.) *(oon, OO-noh, OO-nah)*

able, be potere *(poh-TEH-reh)*

about circa *(CHEER-kah)*

above su, sopra *(soo, SOH-prah)*

abroad all'estero *(ahl-LEH-steh-roh)*

accept accettare *(aht-cheht-TAH-reh)*

accident incidente (m.) *(een-chee-DEHN-teh)*

accompany accompagnare *(ahk-kohm-pah-NYAH-reh)*

according to secondo *(seh-KOHN-doh)*

acquaintance conoscenza (f.) *(koh-noh-SHEHN-tsah)*

across attraverso *(aht-trah-VEHR-soh)*

address indirizzo (m.) *(een-dee-REET-tsoh)*

admission, admittance entrata (f.), ingresso (m.) *(ehn-TRAH-tah, een-GREHS-soh)*

afraid, be avere paura di *(ah-VEH-reh pah-OO-rah dee)*

after dopo *(DOH-poh)*

afternoon pomeriggio (m.) *(poh-meh-REED-joh)*

again ancora, di nuovo *(ahn-KOH-rah, dee NWOH-voh)*

against contro *(KOHN-troh)*

age età (f.) *(eh-TAH)*

agency agenzia (f.) *(ah-jehn-TSEE-ah)*

ago fa (with expressions of time) *(fah)*

agree essere d'accordo *(EHS-seh-reh dahk-KOHR-doh)*

aid aiuto (m.) *(ah-YOO-toh)*
 first aid pronto soccorso (m.) *(PROHN-toh sohk-KOHR-soh)*

air aria (f.) *(AH-ryah)*

air-conditioning aria condizionata (f.) *(AH-ryah kohn-dee-tsyoh-NAH-tah)*

airmail posta aerea (f.) *(POH-stah ah-EH-reh-ah)*

airplane aereo (m.) *(ah-EH-reh-oh)*

airport aeroporto (m.) *(ah-eh-roh-POHR-toh)*

alarm clock sveglia (f.) *(ZVEH-lyah)*

all tutto *(TOOT-toh)*

allow permettere *(pehr-MEHT-teh-reh)*

almost quasi *(KWAH-zee)*

alone solo *(SOH-loh)*

already già *(jah)*

also anche *(AHN-keh)*

always sempre *(SEHM-preh)*

A.M. di mattina *(dee maht-TEE-nah)*

am, I sono, sto *(SOH-noh, stoh)*

American americano(-a) *(ah-meh-ree-KAH-noh)(-nah)*

among tra, fra *(trah, frah)*

amuse divertire, divertirsi (refl.) *(dee-vehr-TEE-reh, dee-vehr-TEER-see)*

and e *(eh)*

another un altro *(oon AHL-troh)*

answer risposta (f.) *(ree-SPOH-stah)*

  to answer rispondere *(ree-SPOHN-deh-reh)*

any qualsiasi *(kwahl-SEE-ah-see)*

anybody, anyone qualcuno *(kwahl-KOO-noh)*

anything qualcosa *(kwahl-KOH-sah)*

apartment appartamento (m.) *(ahp-pahr-tah-MEHN-toh)*

apologize scusarsi (refl.) *(skoo-ZAHR-see)*

appetite appetito (m.), fame (f.) *(ahp-peh-TEE-toh, FAH-meh)*

appetizers antipasto (m.) *(ahn-tee-PAH-stoh)*

apple mela (f.) *(MEH-lah)*

appointment appuntamento (m.) *(ahp-poon-tah-MEHN-toh)*

area code prefisso (indicativo) (m.) *(preh-FEES-soh een-dee-kah-TEE-voh)*

arm braccio (m.) *(BRAHT-choh)*

around attorno *(aht-TOHR-noh)*

arrival arrivo (m.) *(ahr-REE-voh)*

arrive arrivare *(ahr-ree-VAH-reh)*

art arte (f.) *(AHR-teh)*

art gallery galleria d'arte (f.) *(gahl-leh-REE-ah DAHR-teh)*

as come *(KOH-meh)*

ashtray portacenere (m.) *(pohr-tah-CHEH-neh-reh)*

ask chiedere *(KYEH-deh-reh)*

aspirin aspirina (f.) *(ah-spee-REE-nah)*

at a *(ah)*

attention attenzione (f.) *(aht-tehn-TSYOH-neh)*

automatic automatico *(ow-toh-MAH-tee-koh)*

automobile automobile (f.), macchina (f.) *(ow-toh-MOH-bee-leh, MAHK-kee-nah)*

autumn autunno (m.) *(ow-TOON-noh)*

avoid evitare *(eh-vee-TAH-reh)*

awful terribile *(tehr-REE-bee-leh)*

B

baby bebè (m./f.) *(beh-BEH)*

  babysitter bambinaia (f.) *(bahm-bee-NAH-yah)*

back (body part) schiena (f.) *(SKYEH-nah)*

  (behind) dietro a *(DYEH-troh ah)*

bacon pancetta affumicata (f.) *(pahn-CHEHT-tah ahf-foo-mee-KAH-tah)*

bad cattivo *(kaht-TEE-voh)*

badly male *(MAH-leh)*

bag borsa (f.) *(BOHR-sah)*

  handbag borsetta (f.) *(bohr-SEHT-tah)*

  (valise) valigia (f.) *(vah-LEE-jah)*

baggage bagaglio (m.) *(bah-GAH-lyoh)*

  baggage locker custodia automatica (f.) *(koo-STOH-dyah ow-toh-MAH-tee-kah)*

baked al forno *(ahl FOHR-noh)*

bakery panificio (m.) *(pah-nee-FEE-choh)*

bandage benda (f.), fascia (f.) *(BEHN-dah, FAH-shah)*

bank banca (f.) *(BAHN-kah)*

bar bar (m.), caffè (m.) *(bahr, kahf-FEH)*

barber barbiere (m.) *(bahr-BYEH-reh)*

bargain affare (m.) *(ahf-FAH-reh)*

bath bagno (m.) *(BAH-nyoh)*

bathe bagnarsi (refl.) *(bah-NYAHR-see)*

bathing suit costume da bagno (m.) *(koh-STOO-meh dah BAH-nyoh)*

bathrobe accappatoio (m.) *(ahk-kahp-pah-TOH-yoh)*

bathroom stanza da bagno (f.), bagno (m.) *(STAHN-tsah dah BAH-nyoh, BAH-nyoh)*

battery pila (f.) *(PEE-lah)*

be essere *(EHS-seh-reh)*

beach spiaggia (f.) *(SPYAHD-jah)*

beans fagioli (m.pl.) *(fah-JOH-lee)*

beard barba (f.) *(BAHR-bah)*

beautiful bello *(BEHL-loh)*

beauty parlor istituto di bellezza (m.) *(ee-stee-TOO-toh dee behl-LEHT-tsah)*

because perché *(pehr-KEH)*

become diventare *(dee-vehn-TAH-reh)*

bed letto (m.) *(LEHT-toh)*

bedroom camera da letto (f.) *(KAH-meh-rah dah LEHT-toh)*

beef manzo (m.) *(MAHN-dzoh)*

beer birra (f.) *(BEER-rah)*

before prima *(PREE-mah)*

begin cominciare *(koh-meen-CHAH-reh)*

beginning inizio (m.) *(ee-NEE-tsyoh)*

behind dietro, indietro *(DYEH-troh, een-DYEH-troh)*

(late) in ritardo *(een ree-TAHR-doh)*

believe credere *(KREH-deh-reh)*

bellboy fattorino (m.) *(faht-toh-REE-noh)*

below sotto *(SOHT-toh)*

belt cintura (f.) *(cheen-TOO-rah)*

beneath sotto *(SOHT-toh)*

beside accanto a *(ahk-KAHN-toh ah)*

best il/la migliore *(eel/lah mee-LYOH-reh)*

better (adj.) migliore *(mee-LYOH-reh)*

(adv.) meglio *(MEH-lyoh)*

between tra, fra *(trah, frah)*

beyond oltre *(OHL-treh)*

big grande *(GRAHN-deh)*

bill conto (m.) *(KOHN-toh)*

birthday compleanno (m.) *(kohm-pleh-AHN-noh)*

bite morso (m.) *(MOHR-soh)*

to bite mordere *(MOHR-deh-reh)*

bitter amaro *(ah-MAH-roh)*

black nero *(NEH-roh)*

blanket coperta (f.) *(koh-PEHR-tah)*

block (city) isolato (m.) *(ee-zoh-LAH-toh)*

blond biondo *(BYOHN-doh)*

blood sangue (m.) *(SAHN-gweh)*

blouse camicetta (f.) *(kah-mee-CHEHT-tah)*

blue blu *(bloo)*

boarding pass carta d'imbarco (f.) *(KAHR-tah deem-BAHR-koh)*

boat barca (f.), battello (m.) *(BAHR-kah, baht-TEHL-loh)*

body corpo (m.) *(KOHR-poh)*

boiled bollito *(bohl-LEE-toh)*

bone osso (m.) *(OHS-soh)*

book libro (m.) *(LEE-broh)*

   book of tickets carnet (m.) *(kahr-NEH)*

   guidebook guida (f.) *(GWEE-dah)*

bookstore libreria (f.) *(lee-breh-REE-ah)*

boot stivale (m.) *(stee-VAH-leh)*

booth cabina (f.) *(kah-BEE-nah)*

border frontiera (f.) *(frohn-TYEH-rah)*

born nato *(NAH-toh)*

borrow prendere a prestito *(PREHN-deh-reh ah PREH-stee-toh)*

bother infastidire, seccare, dare fastidio a *(een-fah-stee-DEE-reh, sehk-KAH-reh, DAHR-eh fah-STEE-dyoh ah)*

   don't bother non si preoccupi *(nohn see preh-OHK-koo-pee)*

bottle bottiglia (f.) *(boht-TEE-lyah)*

box scatola (f.) *(SKAH-toh-lah)*

box office botteghino (m.) *(boht-teh-GHEE-noh)*

boy ragazzo (m.) *(rah-GAHT-tsoh)*

bracelet braccialetto (m.) *(braht-chah-LEHT-toh)*

brain cervello (m.) *(chehr-VEHL-loh)*

brakes freni (m.pl.) *(FREH-nee)*

bread pane (m.) *(PAH-neh)*

break rompere *(ROHM-peh-reh)*

breakdown (car) guasto (m.), panne (f.) *(GWAH-stoh, PAHN-neh)*

breakfast (prima) colazione (f.) *(PREE-mah koh-lah-TSYOH-neh)*

bridge ponte (m.) *(POHN-teh)*

bring portare *(pohr-TAH-reh)*

broiled alla griglia *(AHL-lah GREE-lyah)*

broken rotto *(ROHT-toh)*

brother fratello (m.) *(frah-TEHL-loh)*

brown marrone *(mahr-ROH-neh)*

brush spazzola (f.) *(SPAHT-tsoh-lah)*

building edificio (m.) *(eh-dee-FEE-choh)*

to burn bruciare, scottare *(broo-CHAH-reh, skoht-TAH-reh)*

bus autobus (m.) *(OW-toh-boos)*

   bus stop fermata d'autobus (f.) *(fehr-MAH-tah DOW-toh-boos)*

business affari (m.pl.) *(ahf-FAH-ree)*

busy occupato *(ohk-koo-PAH-toh)*

but ma *(mah)*

butcher shop macelleria (f.) *(mah-chehl-leh-REE-ah)*

butter burro (m.) *(BOOR-roh)*

button bottone (m.) *(boht-TOH-neh)*

buy comprare *(kohm-PRAH-reh)*

by da, con, in, per *(dah, kohn, een, pehr)*

C

cab tassì (m.) *(tah-SEE)*

cake torta (f.), dolce (m.) *(TOHR-tah, DOHL-cheh)*

call chiamare *(kyah-MAH-reh)*

   (by name) chiamarsi *(kyah-MAHR-see)*

   telephone call chiamata (f.) *(kyah-MAH-tah)*

calm calmo, tranquillo *(KAHL-moh, trahn-KWEEL-loh)*

camera macchina fotografica (f.) *(MAHK-kee-nah foh-toh-GRAH-fee-kah)*

camp campeggio (m.) *(kahm-PEHD-joh)*

can
(to be able) potere *(poh-TEH-reh)*

cancel annullare, cancellare *(ahn-nool-LAH-reh, kahn-chehl-LAH-reh)*

car automobile (f.), macchina (f.) *(ow-toh-MOH-bee-leh, MAHK-kee-nah)*
car rental agency autonoleggio (m.) *(ow-toh-noh-LEHD-joh)*

carbonated gassato *(gahs-SAH-toh)*

card (playing) carta (f.) *(KAHR-tah)*

care (caution) attenzione (f.) *(aht-tehn-TSYOH-neh)*

careful attento *(aht-TEHN-toh)*
to be careful fare attenzione *(FAH-reh aht-tehn-TSYOH-neh)*

carry portare *(pohr-TAH-reh)*

carry-on luggage bagaglio a mano (m.) *(bah-GAH-lyoh ah MAH-noh)*

cart carrello (m.) *(kahr-REHL-loh)*

cash contanti (m.pl.) *(kohn-TAHN-tee)*

cash register cassa (f.) *(KAHS-sah)*

to cash incassare *(een-kahs-SAH-reh)*

cashier cassiera(-e) (f., m.) *(kahs-SYEH-rah, -reh)*

castle castello (m.) *(kah-STEHL-loh)*

cat gatto (m.) *(GAHT-toh)*

catch afferrare *(ahf-fehr-RAH-reh)*

cathedral cattedrale (f.) *(kaht-teh-DRAH-leh)*

caution cautela (f.) *(kow-TEH-lah)*

center centro (m.) *(CHEHN-troh)*

certainly certamente *(chehr-tah-MEHN-teh)*

change (money) spiccioli (m.pl.) *(SPEET-choh-lee)*
to change cambiare *(kahm-BYAH-reh)*

chapel cappella (f.) *(kahp-PEHL-lah)*

charge, cover coperto (m.), consumazione (f.) *(koh-PEHR-toh, kohn-soo-mah-TSYOH-neh)*
to charge fare pagare *(FAH-reh pah-GAH-reh)*

cheap a buon mercato, economico *(ah bwohn mehr-KAH-toh, eh-koh-NOH-mee-koh)*

check assegno (m.) *(ahs-SEH-nyoh)*

cheese formaggio (m.) *(fohr-MAHD-joh)*

chicken pollo (m.) *(POHL-loh)*

child bambino(-a) (m., f.) *(bahm-BEE-noh)(-nah)*

chin mento (m.) *(MEHN-toh)*

chocolate cioccolato(-a) (m., f.) *(chohk-koh-LAH-toh)(-tah)*

choose scegliere *(SHEH-lyeh-reh)*

church chiesa (f.) *(KYEH-zah)*

cigarette sigaretta (f.) *(see-gah-REHT-tah)*

cinnamon cannella (f.) *(kahn-NEHL-lah)*

city città (f.) *(cheet-TAH)*

class classe (f.) *(KLAHS-seh)*

clean pulito *(poo-LEE-toh)*
to clean pulire *(poo-LEE-reh)*

climb scalare *(skah-LAH-reh)*

clock orologio (m.) *(oh-roh-LOH-joh)*

close (near) vicino *(vee-CHEE-noh)*

closed chiuso *(KYOO-soh)*
  to close chiudere *(KYOO-deh-reh)*
closet armadio (m.) *(ahr-MAH-dyoh)*
clothes vestiti (m.pl.) *(veh-STEE-tee)*
cloudy nuvoloso *(noo-voh-LOH-zoh)*
clutch (automobile) frizione (f.) *(free-TSYOH-neh)*
coast costa (f.) *(KOH-stah)*
coat cappotto (m.) *(kahp-POHT-tah)*
coffee caffè (m.) *(kahf-FEH)*
  (with milk) caffellatte (m.) *(kahf-fehl-LAHT-teh)*
coin (money) moneta (f.) *(moh-NEH-tah)*
cold (temperature) freddo (m.) *(FREHD-doh)*
  (illness) raffreddore (m.) *(rahf-frehd-DOH-reh)*
cold cuts affettato (m.) *(ahf-feht-TAH-toh)*
color colore (m.) *(koh-LOH-reh)*
comb pettine (m.) *(PEHT-tee-neh)*
come venire *(veh-NEE-reh)*
  to come back ritornare *(ree-tohr-NAH-reh)*
  to come in entrare *(ehn-TRAH-reh)*
comfortable comodo *(KOH-moh-doh)*
company compagnia (f.) *(kohm-pah-NYEE-ah)*
complaint protesta (f.) *(proh-TEH-stah)*
computer computer (m.) *(kohm-PYOO-tehr)*
concert concerto (m.) *(kohn-CHEHR-toh)*
confirm confermare *(kohn-fehr-MAH-reh)*

congratulations congratulazioni (f.pl.) *(kohn-grah-too-lah-TSYOH-nee)*
contact lens lente a contatto (f.) *(LEHN-teh ah kohn-TAHT-toh)*
continue continuare *(kohn-tee-NWAH-reh)*
to cook cucinare *(koo-chee-NAH-reh)*
cookies biscotti (m.pl.) *(bee-SKOHT-tee)*
cool fresco *(FREH-skoh)*
corkscrew cavatappi (m.) *(kah-vah-TAHP-pee)*
corn granoturco (m.), mais (m.) *(grah-noh-TOOR-koh, MAH-ees)*
corner angolo (m.) *(AHN-goh-loh)*
correspondence corrispondenza (f.) *(kohr-ree-spohn-DEHN-tsah)*
cost (amount) costo (m.) *(KOH-stoh)*
  to cost costare *(koh-STAH-reh)*
count contare *(kohn-TAH-reh)*
country (nation) paese (m.) *(pah-EH-zeh)*
countryside campagna (f.) *(kahm-PAH-nyah)*
cousin cugino (m.), cugina (f.) *(koo-JEE-noh, koo-JEE-nah)*
cover (charge) coperto (m.) *(koh-PEHR-toh)*
  covered coperto *(koh-PEHR-toh)*
  to cover coprire *(koh-PREE-reh)*
crazy matto, pazzo *(MAHT-toh, PAHT-tsoh)*
cream crema (f.) *(KREH-mah)*
credit card carta di credito (f.) *(KAHR-tah dee KREH-dee-toh)*
cross attraversare *(aht-trah-vehr-SAH-reh)*

crosswalk passaggio pedonale (m.) *(pahs-SAHD-joh peh-doh-NAH-leh)*

cry piangere *(PYAHN-jeh-reh)*

cucumber cetriolo (m.) *(cheh-tree-OH-loh)*

cup tazza (f.) *(TAHT-tsah)*

currency cambio (m.) *(KAHM-byoh)*

currency exchange ufficio cambio (m.) *(oof-FEE-choh KAHM-byoh)*

customer cliente (m./f.) *(klee-EHN-teh)*

customs dogana (f.) *(doh-GAH-nah)*

cut taglio (m.) *(TAH-lyoh)*

to cut tagliare *(tah-LYAH-reh)*

cycling ciclismo (m.) *(chee-CLEE-zmoh)*

D

daily quotidiano *(kwoh-tee-DYAH-noh)*

dance ballo (m.) *(BAHL-loh)*

to dance ballare *(bahl-LAH-reh)*

danger pericolo (m.) *(peh-REE-koh-loh)*

dangerous pericoloso *(peh-ree-koh-LOH-zoh)*

dark scuro *(SKOO-roh)*

date (calendar) data (f.) *(DAH-tah)*

daughter figlia (f.) *(FEE-lyah)*

day giorno (m.) *(JOHR-noh)*

dead morto *(MOHR-toh)*

dear caro *(KAH-roh)*

death morte (f.) *(MOHR-teh)*

decaffeinated decaffeinato *(deh-kaf-fay-NAH-toh)*

decide decidere *(deh-CHEE-deh-reh)*

declare dichiarare *(dee-kyah-RAH-reh)*

delay ritardo (m.) *(ree-TAHR-doh)*

delicatessen salumeria (f.) *(sah-loo-meh-REE-ah)*

delighted lieto *(LYEH-toh)*

dentist dentista (m./f.) *(dehn-TEE-stah)*

deodorant deodorante (m.) *(deh-oh-doh-RAHN-teh)*

department store grande magazzino (m.) *(GRAHN-deh mah-gahd-DZEE-noh)*

desire desiderio (m.), voglia (f.) *(deh-zee-DEH-ryoh, VOH-lyah)*

desk scrivania (f.) *(skree-vah-NEE-ah)*

dessert dolce (m.) *(DOHL-cheh)*

detour deviazione (f.) *(deh-vyah-TSYOH-neh)*

diamond diamante (m.) *(dyah-MAHN-teh)*

diapers pannolini (m.pl.) *(pahn-noh-LEE-nee)*

dictionary dizionario (m.) *(dee-tsyoh-NAH-ryoh)*

diet dieta (f.) *(DYEH-tah)*

different differente, diverso *(deef-feh-REHN-teh, dee-VEHR-soh)*

difficult difficile *(deef-FEE-chee-leh)*

dine cenare *(cheh-NAH-reh)*

dining room sala da pranzo (f.) *(SAH-lah dah PRAHN-dzoh)*

dinner pranzo (m.), cena (f.) *(PRAHN-dzoh, CHEH-nah)*

direct diretto *(dee-REHT-toh)*

direction direzione (f.) *(dee-reh-TSYOH-neh)*

directory (telephone) elenco telefonico (m.) *(eh-LEHN-koh teh-leh-FOH-nee-koh)*

dirty sporco *(SPOHR-koh)*

discount sconto (m.) *(SKOHN-toh)*

dish piatto (m.) *(PYAHT-toh)*

distance distanza (f.) *(dee-STAHN-tsah)*

do fare *(FAH-reh)*

doctor dottore (m.) *(doht-TOH-reh)*

dog cane (m.) *(KAH-neh)*

dollar dollaro (m.) *(DOHL-lah-roh)*

door porta (f.) *(POHR-tah)*

downstairs dabbasso, giù *(dahb-BAHS-soh, joo)*

downtown centro (m.) *(CHEHN-troh)*

dozen dozzina (f.) *(dohd-DZEE-nah)*

dress vestito (m.) *(veh-STEE-toh)*
   to dress vestirsi (refl.) *(veh-STEER-see)*

drink (beverage) bevanda (f.) *(beh-VAHN-dah)*
   to drink bere *(BEH-reh)*

drive (a car) guidare *(gwee-DAH-reh)*

drugstore farmacia (f.) *(fahr-mah-CHEE-ah)*

dry secco *(SEHK-koh)*
   dry cleaner lavasecco (m.), tintoria (f.) *(lah-vah-SEHK-koh, teen-toh-REE-ah)*

dubbed doppiato *(dohp-PYAH-toh)*

during durante *(doo-RAHN-teh)*

duty-free esente da dogana *(eh-ZEHN-teh dah dah-GAH-nah)*

E

E-mail posta elettrònica (f.) *(POH-stah eh-leh-TROH-nee-kah)*

each ogni *(OH-nyee)*

each one ciascuno, ognuno *(chah-SKOO-noh, oh-NYOO-noh)*

ear orecchio (m.) *(oh-REHK-kyoh)*

early presto *(PREH-stoh)*

earring orecchino (m.) *(oh-rehk-KEE-noh)*

easy facile *(FAH-chee-leh)*

eat mangiare *(mahn-JAH-reh)*

eel anguilla (f.) *(ahn-GWEEL-lah)*

egg uovo (m.s.), uova (f.pl.) *(WOH-voh, WOH-vah)*

eggplant melanzana (f.) *(meh-lahn-DZAH-nah)*

electricity elettricità (f.) *(eh-leht-tree-chee-TAH)*

elevator ascensore (m.) *(ah-shehn-SOH-reh)*

elsewhere altrove *(ahl-TROH-veh)*

emergency emergenza (f.) *(eh-mehr-JEHN-tsah)*

empty vuoto *(voo-OH-toh)*

end fine (f.) *(FEE-neh)*
   to end finire *(fee-NEE-reh)*

engine motore (m.) *(moh-TOH-reh)*

enough abbastanza *(ahb-bah-STAHN-tsah)*

entire intero *(een-TEH-roh)*

entrance entrata (f.) *(ehn-TRAH-tah)*

entry prohibited vietato entrare *(vyeh-TAH-toh ehn-TRAH-reh)*

evening sera (f.) *(SEH-rah)*

every ogni *(OH-nyee)*

everybody ognuno, tutti, ciascuno *(oh-NYOO-noh, TOOT-tee, chah-SKOO-noh)*

everything tutto *(TOOT-toh)*

example esempio (m.) *(eh-ZEHM-pyoh)*

excellent eccellente *(eht-chehl-LEHN-teh)*

exchange cambio (m.) *(KAHM-byoh)*
   exchange office ufficio cambio (m.) *(oof-FEE-choh KAHM-byoh)*
   to exchange cambiare *(kahm-BYAH-reh)*

excursion escursione (f.), gita (f.) *(eh-skoor-ZYOH-neh, JEE-tah)*

excuse scusa (f.) *(SKOO-zah)*
to excuse scusare *(skoo-ZAH-reh)*

exhausted esausto *(eh-ZOW-stoh)*

exit uscita (f.) *(oo-SHEE-tah)*

expensive caro *(KAH-roh)*

express train espresso (m.) *(eh-SPREHS-soh)*

extra extra (m.), supplemento (m.) *(EHK-strah, sooppleh-MEHN-toh)*

eye occhio (m.) *(OHK-kyoh)*

eyeglasses occhiali (m.pl.) *(ohk-KYAH-lee)*
sunglasses occhiali da sole (m.pl.) *(ohk-KYAH-lee dah SOH-leh)*

F

face faccia (f.), viso (m.) *(FAHT-chah, VEE-zoh)*

factory fabbrica (f.) *(FAHB-bree-kah)*

to fall cadere *(kah-DEH-reh)*

false falso *(FAHL-soh)*

familiar with, be essere a conoscenza di *(EHS-seh-reh ah koh-noh-SHEHN-tsah dee)*

family famiglia (f.) *(fah-MEE-lyah)*

far lontano *(lohn-TAH-noh)*

farm fattoria (f.) *(faht-toh-REE-ah)*

fast rapido, veloce *(RAH-pee-doh, veh-LOH-cheh)*

fat grasso *(GRAHS-soh)*

father padre (m.) *(PAH-dreh)*

fax fax (m.) *(FAHKS)*

fear paura (f.) *(pah-OO-rah)*
to fear avere paura di *(ah-VEH-reh pah-OO-rah dee)*

feel sentirsi (refl.) *(sehn-TEER-see)*

fever febbre (f.) *(FEHB-breh)*

few alcuni *(ahl-KOO-nee)*

fill riempire *(ryehm-PEE-reh)*
fill her up! (car) il pieno! *(eel PYEH-noh!)*

film film (m.), pellicola (f.) *(feelm, pehl-LEE-koh-lah)*
(cartridge) pellicola (f.) *(pehl-LEE-koh-lah)*

find trovare *(troh-VAH-reh)*

fine (good quality) bello, fine *(BEHL-loh, FEE-neh)*

fine (penalty) multa (f.) *(MOOL-tah)*

fine arts belle arti (f.pl.) *(BEHL-leh AHR-tee)*

finger dito (m.) *(DEE-toh)*

finish finire *(fee-NEE-reh)*

fire fuoco (m.) *(FWOH-koh)*
(destructive) incendio (m.) *(een-CHEHN-dyoh)*

first primo *(PREE-moh)*

fish pesce (m.) *(PEH-sheh)*

to fit (clothes) andar bene *(ahn-DAHR BEH-neh)*

fix riparare *(ree-pah-RAH-reh)*
fixed price a prezzo fisso *(ah PREHT-tsoh FEES-soh)*

flashlight pila (f.) *(PEE-lah)*

flat piatto, piano *(PYAHT-toh, PYAH-noh)*
flat tire gomma a terra (f.) *(GOHM-mah ah TEHR-rah)*

flavor sapore (m.) *(sah-POH-reh)*

flea market mercato delle pulci (m.) *(mehr-KAH-toh DEHL-leh POOL-chee)*

flight volo (m.) *(VOH-loh)*

floor piano (m.) *(PYAH-noh)*

flour farina (f.) *(fah-REE-nah)*

flower fiore (m.) *(FYOH-reh)*

fly mosca (f.) *(MOH-skah)*
to fly volare *(voh-LAH-reh)*

fog nebbia *(NEHB-byah)*

follow seguire *(seh-GWEE-reh)*

food cibo (m.) *(CHEE-boh)*

foot piede (m.) *(PYEH-deh)*

for per *(pehr)*

forbidden proibito, vietato *(proy-BEE-toh, vyeh-TAH-toh)*

foreign forestiero, straniero *(foh-reh-STYEH-roh, strah-NYEH-roh)*

forest foresta (f.) *(foh-REH-stah)*

forget dimenticare *(dee-mehn-tee-KAH-reh)*

fork forchetta (f.) *(fohr-KEHT-tah)*

format formato (m.) *(fohr-MAH-toh)*

forward avanti *(ah-VAHN-tee)*

fountain fontana (f.) *(fohn-TAH-nah)*

fowl pollame (m.), volatile (m.) *(pohl-LAH-meh, voh-LAH-tee-leh)*

free libero *(LEE-beh-roh)*

fresh fresco *(FREH-skoh)*

Friday venerdì (m.) *(veh-nehr-DEE)*

fried fritto *(FREET-toh)*

friendship amicizia (f.) *(ah-mee-CHEE-tsyah)*

from da *(dah)*

front (position) davanti, di fronte *(dah-VAHN-tee, dee FROHN-teh)*

frozen gelato *(jeh-LAH-toh)*

fruit frutta (f.) *(FROOT-tah)*

full pieno *(PYEH-noh)*

to have fun divertirsi (refl.) *(dee-vehr-TEER-see)*

furnished ammobiliato *(ahm-moh-bee-LYAH-toh)*

furniture mobili (m.pl.) *(MOH-bee-lee)*

G

garage garage (m.) *(gah-RAHZH)*

garden giardino (m.) *(jahr-DEE-noh)*

garlic aglio (m.) *(AH-lyoh)*

gas (fuel) benzina (f.) *(behn-DZEE-nah)*

gas station distributore di benzina (m.) *(dee-stree-boo-TOH-reh dee behn-DZEE-nah)*

gate cancello (m.) *(kahn-CHEHL-loh)*

(airport) uscita (f.) *(oo-SHEE-tah)*

gentleman signore (m.) *(see-NYOH-reh)*

to get (obtain) ottenere *(oht-teh-NEH-reh)*

to get in/on salire *(sah-LEE-reh)*

to get off scendere *(SHEHN-deh-reh)*

to get out uscire *(oo-SHEE-reh)*

to get up alzarsi (refl.) *(ahl-TSAHR-see)*

gift regalo (m.) *(reh-GAH-loh)*

girl ragazza *(rah-GAHT-tsah)*

give dare *(DAH-reh)*

glass (drinking) bicchiere (m.) *(beek-KYEH-reh)*

glove guanto (m.) *(GWAHN-toh)*

go andare *(ahn-DAH-reh)*

to go down scendere *(SHEHN-deh-reh)*

to go up salire *(sah-LEE-reh)*

gold oro (m.) *(OH-roh)*

good buono *(BWOH-noh)*

good-bye arrivederci *(ahr-ree-veh-DEHR-chee)*

grandfather nonno (m.) *(NOHN-noh)*

grandmother nonna (f.) *(NOHN-nah)*

grandson nipote (m.) *(nee-POH-teh)*

grape uva (f.) *(OO-vah)*

grapefruit pompelmo (m.) *(pohm-PEHL-moh)*

grass erba (f.) *(EHR-bah)*
grateful grato *(GRAH-toh)*
grave (burial place) tomba (f.) *(TOHM-bah)*
  (serious) serio *(SEH-ryoh)*
gray grigio *(GREE-joh)*
green verde *(VEHR-deh)*
green beans fagiolini (m.pl.) *(fah-joh-LEE-nee)*
grilled alla griglia *(AHL-lah GREE-lyah)*
grocery drogheria (f.) *(droh-geh-REE-ah)*
ground suolo (m.), terra (f.) *(SWOH-loh, TEHR-rah)*
  ground floor pianterreno (m.) *(pyahn-tehr-REH-noh)*
guest ospite *(OH-spee-teh)*
guide guida (m./f.) *(GWEE-dah)*
guidebook guida (f.) *(GWEE-dah)*

H

hair capelli (m.pl.) *(kah-PEHL-lee)*
  (body) pelo (m.) *(PEH-loh)*
  hair dryer asciugacapelli (m.) *(ah-shoo-gah-kah-PEH-lee)*
hairbrush spazzola (f.) *(SPAHT-tsoh-lah)*
haircut taglio (m.) *(TAH-lyoh)*
hairdresser parrucchiere (m.) *(pahr-rook-KYEH-reh)*
half metà (f.) *(meh-TAH)*
  (adjective) mezzo *(MEHD-dzoh)*
  half-bottle mezza bottiglia (f.) *(MEHD-dzah boht-TEE-lyah)*
hall porter concierge (m.), portiere (m.) *(kohn-SYEHRZH, pohr-TYEH-reh)*
ham prosciutto (m.) *(proh-SHOOT-toh)*
hand mano (f.) *(MAH-noh)*

handbag borsetta (f.) *(bohr-SEHT-tah)*
handmade fatto a mano *(FAHT-toh ah MAH-noh)*
handsome bello, affascinante *(BEHL-loh, ahf-fah-shee-NAHN-teh)*
hanger (clothes) attaccapanni (m.) *(ah-tah-kah-PAH-nee)*
happen accadere, succedere *(ahk-kah-DEH-reh, soot-CHEH-deh-reh)*
happy felice, contento *(feh-LEE-cheh, kohn-TEHN-toh)*
harbor porto (m.) *(POHR-toh)*
hard (difficult) difficile *(deef-FEE-chee-leh)*
  (tough) duro *(DOO-roh)*
have avere *(ah-VEH-reh)*
  to have fun divertirsi (refl.) *(dee-vehr-TEER-see)*
  to have to dovere *(doh-VEH-reh)*
he lui *(LOO-ee)*
head testa (f.) *(TEH-stah)*
  headache mal di testa (m.) *(mahl dee TEH-stah)*
health salute (f.) *(sah-LOO-teh)*
hear sentire *(sehn-TEE-reh)*
heart cuore (m.) *(KWOH-reh)*
heat calore (m.), caldo (m.) *(kah-LOH-reh, KAHL-doh)*
heavy pesante *(peh-ZAHN-teh)*
height altezza (f.) *(ahl-TEHT-tsah)*
hello buongiorno, ciao *(bwohn-JOHR-noh, chow)*
  (on telephone) pronto *(PROHN-toh)*
help aiuto (m.) *(ah-YOO-toh)*
  to help aiutare *(ah-yoo-TAH-reh)*

her, hers (possessive pronoun) il suo/la sua/i suoi/le sue *(eel SOO-oh/lah SOO-ah/ee SWOH-ee/leh SOO-eh)*

herself (pronoun) lei stessa *(lay STEHS-sah)*

herbs erbe (f.pl.) *(EHR-beh)*

here qui *(kwee)*

here is/are ecco *(EHK-koh)*

high alto *(AHL-toh)*

highway autostrada (f.) *(ow-toh-STRAH-dah)*

hill collina (f.) *(kohl-LEE-nah)*

him (pronoun—dir. obj., ind. obj., after prep.) lo/gli/lui *(loh/lyee/LOO-ee)*

himself (pronoun) lui stesso *(LOO-ee STEHS-soh)*

his (possessive pronoun) il suo/la sua/i suoi/le sue *(eel SOO-ah/lah SOO-ah/ee SWOH-ee/leh SOO-eh)*

holiday vacanza (f.) *(vah-KAHN-tsah)*

home casa (f.) *(KAH-zah)*

hope speranza (f.) *(speh-RAHN-tsah)*

hors d'oeuvres antipasto (m.) *(ahn-tee-PAH-stoh)*

horse cavallo (m.) *(kah-VAHL-loh)*

hospital ospedale (m.) *(oh-speh-DAH-leh)*

hostel, youth ostello (m.) *(oh-STEHL-loh)*

hot caldo *(KAHL-doh)*

(piquant) piccante *(peek-KAHN-teh)*

hotel hotel (m.), albergo (m.) *(oh-TEHL, ahl-BEHR-goh)*

hour ora (f.) *(OH-rah)*

house casa (f.) *(KAH-zah)*
  at the house of a casa di, . . . da *(ah KAH-zah dee, . . . dah)*

how? come? *(KOH-meh?)*
  how do you say? come si dice? *(KOH-meh see DEE-cheh?)*
  how many? quanti(-e)? *(KWAHN-tee?)(-teh?)*
  how much? quanto(-a)? *(KWAHN-toh?)(-tah?)*

hundred cento *(CHEHN-toh)*

hungry, be avere fame *(ah-VEH-reh FAH-meh)*

hurry affrettarsi *(ahf-freht-TAHR-see)*

hurt fare male *(FAH-reh MAH-leh)*

husband marito (m.) *(mah-REE-toh)*

I

I io *(EE-oh)*

ice ghiaccio (m.) *(GYAHT-choh)*

ice cream gelato (m.) *(jeh-LAH-toh)*

if se *(seh)*

ill malato *(mah-LAH-toh)*

illness malattia (f.) *(mah-laht-TEE-ah)*

important importante *(eem-pohr-TAHN-teh)*

impossible impossibile *(eem-pohs-SEE-bee-leh)*

in in *(een)*

included compreso, incluso *(kohm-PREH-zoh, een-KLOO-zoh)*

inform informare *(een-fohr-MAH-reh)*

information informazione (f.) *(een-fohr-mah-TSYOH-neh)*

in-laws suoceri (m.pl.), cognati (m.pl.) *(SWOH-cheh-ree, koh-NYAH-tee)*

inn locanda (f.) *(loh-KAHN-dah)*

inside dentro *(DEHN-troh)*

instead of invece di *(een-VEH-cheh dee)*

insure assicurare *(ahs-see-koo-RAH-reh)*

intelligent intelligente *(een-tehl-lee-JEHN-teh)*

interesting interessante *(een-teh-rehs-SAHN-teh)*

  to be interested in interessarsi di (refl.) *(een-teh-rehs-SAHR-see dee)*

internet Internet (m.) *(EEN-tehr-net)*

intersection incrocio (m.) *(een-KROH-choh)*

into dentro a *(DEHN-troh ah)*

introduce presentare *(preh-zehn-TAH-reh)*

invite invitare *(een-vee-TAH-reh)*

is è *(eh)*

island isola (f.) *(EE-zoh-lah)*

Italian italiano(-a) *(ee-tah-LYAH-noh)(-nah)*

Italy Italia (f.) *(ee-TAH-lyah)*

J

jacket giacca (f.) *(JAHK-kah)*

jam (fruit) marmellata (f.) *(mahr-mehl-LAH-tah)*

jar vasetto (m.) *(vah-ZEHT-toh)*

jewelry gioielli (m.pl.) *(joh-YEHL-lee)*

  jewelry store gioielleria (f.) *(joh-yehl-leh-REE-ah)*

job lavoro (m.) *(lah-VOH-roh)*

jogging footing (m.) *(FOO-teeng)* or jogging (m.) *(JOH-geeng)*

journey viaggio (m.) *(VYAHD-joh)*

juice succo (m.), sugo (m.) *(SOOK-koh, SOO-goh)*

K

keep tenere *(teh-NEH-reh)*

key chiave (f.) *(KYAH-veh)*

kilogram chilo (m.) *(KEE-loh)*

kilometer chilometro *(kee-LOH-meh-troh)*

kind (nice) gentile *(jehn-TEE-leh)*

  (type) genere (m.), tipo (m.) *(JEH-neh-reh, TEE-poh)*

kiosk chiosco (m.), edicola (f.) *(KYOH-skoh, eh-DEE-koh-lah)*

kiss bacio (m.) *(BAH-choh)*

  to kiss baciare *(bah-CHAH-reh)*

kitchen cucina (f.) *(koo-CHEE-nah)*

knee ginocchio (m.) *(jee-NOHK-kyoh)*

knife coltello (m.) *(kohl-TEHL-loh)*

knock bussare *(boos-SAH-reh)*

know (a fact, how) sapere *(sah-PEH-reh)*

  (a person, a thing) conoscere *(koh-NOH-sheh-reh)*

L

label etichetta (f.) *(eh-tee-KEHT-tah)*

to lack mancare *(mahn-KAH-reh)*

ladies' room signore (f.pl.), donne (f.pl.) *(see-NYOH-reh, DOHN-neh)*

lady signora (f.) *(see-NYOH-rah)*

lake lago (m.) *(LAH-goh)*

lamp lampada (f.) *(LAHM-pah-dah)*

land terra (f.) *(TEHR-rah)*

language lingua (f.) *(LEEN-gwah)*

large largo *(LAHR-goh)*
last (final) ultimo *(OOL-tee-moh)*
  (preceding) scorso *(SKOHR-soh)*
late tardi *(TAHR-dee)*
to laugh ridere *(REE-deh-reh)*
laundromat lavanderia automatica (f.) *(lah-vahn-deh-REE-ah ow-toh-MAH-tee-kah)*
laundry bucato (m.) *(boo-KAH-toh)*
lawyer avvocato (m.) *(ahv-voh-KAH-toh)*
learn imparare *(eem-pah-RAH-reh)*
at least almeno *(ahl-MEH-noh)*
leather cuoio (m.), pelle (f.) *(KWOH-yoh, PEHL-leh)*
leave (behind) lasciare *(lah-SHAH-reh)*
  (to depart) partire *(pahr-TEE-reh)*
left sinistra *(see-NEE-strah)*
leg gamba (f.) *(GAHM-bah)*
lend prestare *(preh-STAH-reh)*
lens lente (f.) *(LEHN-teh)*
less meno *(MEH-noh)*
lesson lezione (f.) *(leh-TSYOH-neh)*
let lasciare *(lah-SHAH-reh)*
letter lettera (f.) *(LEHT-teh-rah)*
library biblioteca (f.) *(bee-blyoh-TEH-kah)*
license licenza (f.) *(lee-CHEHN-tsah)*
life vita (f.) *(VEE-tah)*
lifeguard bagnino (m.) *(bah-NYEE-noh)*
light (weight) leggero *(lehd-JEH-roh)*
  (brightness) luce (f.) *(LOO-cheh)*
like, as come *(KOH-meh)*
  I'd like vorrei *(vohr-RAY)*
  to like piacere *(pyah-CHEH-reh)*

line (of people) fila (f.), coda (f.) *(FEE-lah, KOH-dah)*
linen lino (m.) *(LEE-noh)*
lip labbro (m.) *(LAHB-broh)*
lipstick rossetto (m.) *(rohs-SEHT-toh)*
liquor liquore (m.) *(lee-KWOH-reh)*
list lista (f.) *(LEE-stah)*
listen ascoltare *(ah-skohl-TAH-reh)*
liter litro (m.) *(LEE-troh)*
little (small) piccolo *(PEEK-koh-loh)*
  a little of un po' di *(oon poh dee)*
live vivere *(VEE-veh-reh)*
living room salotto (m.), soggiorno (m.) *(sah-LOHT-toh, sohd-JOHR-noh)*
local locale *(loh-KAH-leh)*
lock serratura (f.) *(sehr-rah-TOO-rah)*
long lungo *(LOON-goh)*
look at guardare *(gwahr-DAH-reh)*
  look for cercare *(chehr-KAH-reh)*
lose perdere *(PEHR-deh-reh)*
lost-and-found oggetti smarriti (m.pl.) *(ohd-JEHT-tee smahr-REE-tee)*
lotion lozione (f.) *(loh-TSYOH-neh)*
lots of (much) molto *(MOHL-toh)*
  (many) molti *(MOHL-tee)*
love amore (m.) *(ah-MOH-reh)*
  to love amare *(ah-MAH-reh)*
low basso *(BAHS-soh)*
luck fortuna (f.) *(fohr-TOO-nah)*
luggage bagaglio (m.) *(bah-GAH-lyoh)*
lunch pranzo (m.) *(PRAHN-dzoh)*

machine macchina (f.) *(MAHK-kee-nah)*

madam signora (f.) *(see-NYOH-rah)*

magazine rivista (f.) *(ree-VEE-stah)*

maid domestica (f.), colf (f.) *(doh-MEH-stee-kah, kohlf)*

mail posta (f.) *(POH-stah)*
  to mail impostare *(eem-poh-STAH-reh)*

mailbox cassetta della posta (f.) *(kahs-SEHT-tah DEHL-lah POH-stah)*

make fare *(FAH-reh)*

man uomo (m.) *(WOH-moh)*
  men uomini (m.pl.) *(WOH-mee-nee)*

manager direttore (m.), manager (m.) *(dee-reht-TOH-reh, MEH-neh-jehr)*

many molti *(MOHL-tee)*

map (road) carta stradale (f.) *(KAHR-tah strah-DAH-leh)*

market mercato (m.) *(mehr-KAH-toh)*

married sposato *(spoh-ZAH-toh)*

marvelous meraviglioso *(meh-rah-vee-LYOH-zoh)*

match (game) partita (f.) *(pahr-TEE-tah)*
  (light) fiammifero (m.) *(fyahm-MEE-feh-roh)*

matter, it does not non importa *(nohn eem-POHR-tah)*
  what's the matter? cosa c'è? *(KOH-zah cheh?)*

maybe forse *(FOHR-seh)*

me me *(meh)*

meal pasto (m.) *(PAH-stoh)*

mean significare *(see-nyee-fee-KAH-reh)*

meat carne (f.) *(KAHR-neh)*

medicine medicina (f.) *(meh-dee-CHEE-nah)*

meet incontrare *(een-kohn-TRAH-reh)*
  (for the first time) conoscere *(koh-NOH-sheh-reh)*

meeting incontro (m.), riunione (f.) *(een-KOHN-troh, ryoo-NYOH-neh)*

melon melone (m.) *(meh-LOH-neh)*

men's room signori (m.pl.), uomini (m.pl.) *(see-NYOH-ree, WOH-mee-nee)*

menu menu (m.) *(meh-NOO)*

merchant negoziante (m./f.), commerciante (m./f.) *(neh-goh-TSYAHN-teh, kohm-mehr-CHAHN-teh)*

middle (center) mezzo (m.), centro (m.) *(MEHD-dzoh, CHEHN-troh)*

midnight mezzanotte (f.) *(mehd-dzah-NOHT-teh)*

mileage chilometraggio (m.) *(kee-loh-meh-TRAHD-joh)*

milk latte (m.) *(LAHT-teh)*

mineral water acqua minerale (f.) *(AHK-kwah mee-neh-RAH-leh)*

minister ministro (m.) *(mee-NEE-stroh)*

minute minuto (m.) *(mee-NOO-toh)*

mirror specchio (m.) *(SPEHK-kyoh)*

Miss signorina (f.) *(see-nyoh-REE-nah)*

miss (the absence of) mancare *(mahn-KAH-reh)*
  (a train) perdere *(PEHR-deh-reh)*

mistake errore (m.), sbaglio (m.) *(ehr-ROH-reh, ZBAH-lyoh)*

moment momento (m.) *(moh-MEHN-toh)*

money soldi (m.pl.), denaro (m.) *(SOHL-dee, deh-NAH-roh)*

(change) spiccioli (m.pl.) *(SPEET-choh-lee)*

money order vaglia postale (m.) *(VAH-lyah poh-STAH-leh)*

month mese (m.) *(MEH-zeh)*

moon luna (f.) *(LOO-nah)*

more più *(pyoo)*

morning mattina (f.) *(maht-TEE-nah)*

mother madre (f.) *(MAH-dreh)*

mountain montagna (f.) *(mohn-TAH-nyah)*

mouth bocca (f.) *(BOHK-kah)*

movies (movie theater) cinema (m.) *(CHEE-neh-mah)*

Mr. signore (m.) *(see-NYOH-reh)*

Mrs. signora (f.) *(see-NYOH-rah)*

much molto *(MOHL-toh)*

museum museo (m.) *(moo-ZEH-oh)*

mushroom fungo (m.) *(FOON-goh)*

music musica (f.) *(MOO-zee-kah)*

must dovere *(doh-VEH-reh)*

mustard senape (f.) *(SEH-nah-peh)* .

my il mio/la mia/i miei/le mie *(eel MEE-oh/lah MEE-ah/ee MYEH-ee/leh MEE-eh)*

N

nail (finger-, toe-) unghia (f.) *(OON-gyah)*

name nome (m.) *(NOH-meh)*

named, to be chiamarsi (refl.) *(kyah-MAHR-see)*

napkin tovagliolo (m.) *(toh-vah-LYOH-loh)*

narrow stretto *(STREHT-toh)*

nationality nazionalità (f.) *(nah-tsyoh-nah-lee-TAH)*

nature natura (f.) *(nah-TOO-rah)*

near vicino *(vee-CHEE-noh)*

nearly quasi *(KWAH-zee)*

necessary necessario *(neh-chehs-SAH-ryoh)*

neck collo (m.) *(KOHL-loh)*

necklace collana (f.) *(kohl-LAH-nah)*

necktie cravatta (f.) *(krah-VAHT-tah)*

need avere bisogno di *(ah-VEH-reh bee-ZOH-nyoh dee)*

neighbor vicino (m.) *(vee-CHEE-noh)*

neighborhood zona (f.), quartiere (m.) *(DZOH-nah, kwahr-TYEH-reh)*

never mai *(MAH-ee)*

new nuovo *(NWOH-voh)*

newspaper giornale (m.) *(johr-NAH-leh)*

newsstand edicola (f.) *(eh-DEE-koh-lah)*

next (adj.) prossimo *(PROHS-see-moh)*

(adv.) poi, dopo *(poy, DOH-poh)*

nice carino, gentile, simpatico *(kah-REE-noh, jehn-TEE-leh, seem-PAH-tee-koh)*

night notte (f.) *(NOHT-teh)*

nightclub locale notturno (m.) *(loh-KAH-leh noht-TOOR-noh)*

no no *(noh)*

noise rumore (m.) *(roo-MOH-reh)*

none nessuno *(nehs-SOO-noh)*

noon mezzogiorno (m.) *(mehd-dzoh-JOHR-noh)*

north nord (m.) *(nohrd)*

nose naso (m.) *(NAH-zoh)*

no-smoking section sezione non fumatori (f.) *(seh-TSYOH-neh nohn foo-mah-TOH-ree)*

not non *(nohn)*
  not at all affatto, per niente *(ahf-FAHT-toh, pehr NYEHN-teh)*

nothing niente *(NYEHN-teh)*

notice (announcement) avviso (m.) *(ahv-VEE-zoh)*
  to notice notare *(noh-TAH-reh)*

novel (book) romanzo (m.) *(roh-MAHN-dzoh)*

now ora, adesso *(OH-rah, ah-DEHS-soh)*

number numero (m.) *(NOO-meh-roh)*

nurse infermiera (f.), nurse (f.) *(een-fehr-MYEH-rah, nehrs)*

nut noce (f.) *(NOH-cheh)*

O

obliged to, be essere grato *(EHS-seh-reh GRAH-toh)*

obtain ottenere *(oht-teh-NEH-reh)*

occupied occupato *(ohk-koo-PAH-toh)*

ocean oceano (m.) *(oh-CHEH-ah-noh)*

odd dispari *(DEE-spah-ree)*

of di *(dee)*
  of course naturalmente *(nah-too-rahl-MEHN-teh)*

office ufficio (m.) *(oof-FEE-choh)*

often spesso *(SPEHS-soh)*

oil olio (m.) *(OH-lyoh)*

okay, it's va bene, d'accordo *(vah BEH-neh, dahk-KOHR-doh)*

old vecchio *(VEHK-kyoh)*

on su *(soo)*

once (one time) una volta *(OO-nah VOHL-tah)*
  at once subito *(SOO-bee-toh)*

one uno *(OO-noh)*

only solamente, soltanto *(soh-lah-MEHN-teh, sohl-TAHN-toh)*

open aperto *(ah-PEHR-toh)*
  to open aprire *(ah-PREE-reh)*

operator (phone) centralinista (m./f.) *(chen-trah-lee-NEE-stah)*

opportunity occasione (f.), opportunità *(ohk-kah-ZYOH-neh, ohp-pohr-too-nee-TAH)*

opposite contrario, opposto *(kohn-TRAH-ryoh, ohp-POH-stoh)*
  (across from) di fronte a *(dee FROHN-teh ah)*

or o *(oh)*

orange arancia (f.) *(ah-RAHN-chah)*

order ordine (m.) *(OHR-dee-neh)*
  to order ordinare *(ohr-dee-NAH-reh)*

ordinary ordinario, comune *(ohr-dee-NAH-ryoh, koh-MOO-neh)*

oregano origano (m.) *(oh-REE-gah-noh)*

other altro *(AHL-troh)*

our; ours il nostro/la nostra/i nostri/le nostre *(eel NOH-stroh/lah NOH-strah/ee NOH-stree/leh NOH-streh)*

out fuori, all'aperto *(FWOH-ree, ahl-lah-PEHR-toh)*

outside fuori *(FWOH-ree)*

oven forno (m.) *(FOHR-noh)*

over sopra *(SOH-prah)*
  it's over è finito *(eh fee-NEE-toh)*

overcoat cappotto (m.), soprabito (m.) *(kahp-POHT-toh, soh-PRAH-bee-toh)*

overnight (to stay) passare la notte *(pahs-SAH-reh lah NOHT-teh)*

owe dovere, essere debitore *(doh-VEH-reh, EHS-seh-reh deh-bee-TOH-reh)*

own possedere *(pohs-seh-DEH-reh)*

owner proprietario (m.) *(proh-pryeh-TAH-ryoh)*

P

pack (luggage) fare le valigie *(FAH-reh leh vah-LEE-jeh)*

package pacco (m.) *(PAHK-koh)*

page pagina (f.) *(PAH-jee-nah)*

pain dolore (m.) *(doh-LOH-reh)*

paint vernice (f.) *(vehr-NEE-cheh)*

painting pittura (f.), quadro (m.) *(peet-TOO-rah, KWAH-droh)*

pair paio (m.) *(PAH-yoh)*

palace palazzo (m.) *(pah-LAHT-tsoh)*

pants pantaloni (m.pl.) *(pahn-tah-LOH-nee)*

paper carta (f.) *(KAHR-tah)*

park parco (m.) *(PAHR-koh)*

parking parcheggio (m.) *(pahr-KEHD-joh)*

parsley prezzemolo (m.) *(preht-TSEH-moh-loh)*

part parte (f.) *(PAHR-teh)* **(separate)** dividere, separare *(dee-VEE-deh-reh, seh-pah-RAH-reh)*

to pass passare *(pahs-SAH-reh)*

passage passaggio (m.) *(pahs-SAHD-joh)*

passenger passeggero (m.) *(pahs-sehd-JEH-roh)*

passport passaporto (m.) *(pahs-sah-POHR-toh)*

past passato (m.) *(pahs-SAH-toh)*

pastry paste (f.pl.) *(PAH-steh)* **(shop)** pasticceria (f.) *(pah-steet-cheh-REE-ah)*

pay pagare *(pah-GAH-reh)*

pedestrian pedone (m.) *(peh-DOH-neh)*

pen penna (f.) *(PEHN-nah)*

pencil matita (f.) *(mah-TEE-tah)*

people gente (f.) *(JEHN-teh)*

pepper pepe (m.) *(PEH-peh)*

perfect perfetto *(pehr-FEHT-toh)*

performance rappresentazione (f.) *(rahp-preh-zehn-tah-TSYOH-neh)*

perfume profumo (m.) *(proh-FOO-moh)*

perhaps forse *(FOHR-seh)*

period periodo (m.) *(peh-REE-oh-doh)*

permit permesso (m.) *(pehr-MEHS-soh)* **to permit** permettere *(pehr-MEHT-teh-reh)*

person persona (f.) *(pehr-SOH-nah)*

photograph fotografia (f.) *(foh-toh-grah-FEE-ah)*

picnic picnic (m.), scampagnata (f.) *(peek-NEEK, skahm-pah-NYAH-tah)*

picture (art) quadro (m.) *(KWAH-droh)*

pie torta (f.) *(TOHR-tah)*

piece pezzo (m.) *(PEHT-tsoh)*

pill pillola (f.) *(PEEL-loh-lah)*

pillow cuscino (m.) *(koo-SHEE-noh)*

229

pity!, what a che peccato! *(keh pehk-KAH-toh!)*

place posto (m.) *(POH-stoh)*
to place mettere, posare *(MEHT-teh-reh, poh-ZAH-reh)*

plate piatto (m.) *(PYAHT-toh)*

platform binario (m.), piattaforma (f.) *(bee-NAH-ryoh, pyaht-tah-FOHR-mah)*

play dramma (m.) *(DRAH-mah)*
to play (game) giocare *(joh-KAH-reh)*
to play (instrument) suonare *(swoh-NAH-reh)*
to play (role) recitare *(reh-chee-TAH-reh)*

playground campo (m.) *(KAHM-poh)*

please per piacere, per favore *(pehr pyah-CHEH-reh, pehr fah-VOH-reh)*

pleasure piacere (m.) *(pyah-CHEH-reh)*

pocket tasca (f.) *(TAH-skah)*

pocketbook portafoglio (m.) *(pohr-tah-FOH-lyoh)*

point punto (m.) *(POON-toh)*

police polizia (f.) *(poh-lee-TSEE-ah)*
(station) posto di polizia (f.) *(POH-stoh dee poh-lee-TSEE-ah)*

policeman poliziotto (m.) *(poh-lee-TSYOHT-toh)*

polite cortese, gentile *(kohr-TEH-zeh, jehn-TEE-leh)*

pool piscina (f.) *(pee-SHEE-nah)*

poor povero *(POH-veh-roh)*

pork porco (m.), maiale (m.) *(POHR-koh, mah-YAH-leh)*

port porto (m.) *(POHR-toh)*

porter portabagagli (m.) *(pohr-tah-bah-GAH-lyee)*

possess possedere *(pohs-seh-DEH-reh)*

possible possibile *(pohs-SEE-bee-leh)*

postage affrancatura (f.) *(ahf-frahn-kah-TOO-rah)*

post office ufficio postale (m.) *(oof-FEE-choh poh-STAH-leh)*

postcard cartolina (f.) *(kahr-toh-LEE-nah)*

practical pratico *(PRAH-tee-koh)*

prefer preferire *(preh-feh-REE-reh)*

pregnant incinta *(een-CHEEN-tah)*

prepare preparare *(preh-pah-RAH-reh)*

prescription ricetta (f.) *(ree-CHEHT-tah)*

present regalo (m.) *(reh-GAH-loh)*
to present presentare *(preh-zehn-TAH-reh)*

pretty carino *(kah-REE-noh)*

price prezzo (m.) *(PREHT-tsoh)*

priest prete (m.), sacerdote (m.) *(PREH-teh, sah-chehr-DOH-teh)*

print (photo) copia (f.) *(KOH-pyah)*

private privato *(pree-VAH-toh)*

profession professione (f.), lavoro (m.) *(proh-fehs-SYOH-neh, lah-VOH-roh)*

prohibit proibire *(proh-ee-BEE-reh)*

promise promettere *(proh-MEHT-teh-reh)*

protect proteggere *(proh-TEHD-jeh-reh)*

public pubblico *(POOB-blee-koh)*

purchase acquisto (m.) *(ahk-KWEE-stoh)*

purple viola *(VYOH-lah)*

push spingere *(SPEEN-jeh-reh)*

put mettere *(MEHT-teh-reh)*

Q

quality qualità (f.) *(kwah-lee-TAH)*

quarter quarto (m.) *(KWAHR-toh)*

question domanda (f.) *(doh-MAHN-dah)*

quick veloce *(veh-LOH-cheh)*

quiet silenzioso *(see-lehn-TSYOH-zoh)*

quite abbastanza *(ahb-bah-STAHN-tsah)*

R

radio radio (f.) *(RAH-dyoh)*

railroad ferrovia (f.) *(fehr-roh-VEE-ah)*

  railroad crossing passaggio a livello (m.) *(pahs-SAHD-joh ah lee-VEHL-loh)*

  railroad station stazione ferroviaria (f.) *(stah-TSYOH-neh fehr-roh-VYAH-ryah)*

rain pioggia (f.) *(PYOHD-jah)*

  it's raining piove *(PYOH-veh)*

raincoat impermeabile (m.) *(eem-pehr-meh-AH-bee-leh)*

rapid rapido, veloce *(RAH-pee-doh, veh-LOH-cheh)*

rare (meat) al sangue *(ahl SAHN-gweh)*

raspberry lampone (m.) *(lahm-POH-neh)*

rather piuttosto *(pyoot-TOH-stoh)*

raw vegetables verdura cruda (f.) *(vehr-DOO-rah KROO-dah)*

razor rasoio (m.) *(rah-ZOH-yoh)*

razor blade lametta (f.) *(lah-MEHT-tah)*

read leggere *(LEHD-jeh-reh)*

ready pronto *(PROHN-toh)*

real vero *(VEH-roh)*

really veramente *(veh-rah-MEHN-teh)*

reason ragione (f.) *(rah-JOH-neh)*

reasonable ragionevole *(rah-joh-NEH-voh-leh)*

receipt ricevuta (f.) *(ree-cheh-VOO-tah)*

receive ricevere *(ree-CHEH-veh-reh)*

recent recente *(reh-CHEHN-teh)*

recommend raccomandare *(rahk-koh-mahn-DAH-reh)*

red rosso *(ROHS-soh)*

reduction riduzione (f.) *(ree-doo-TSYOH-neh)*

refund rimborso (m.) *(reem-BOHR-soh)*

refuse rifiutare *(ree-fyoo-TAH-reh)*

regards saluti (m.pl.) *(sah-LOO-tee)*

register (check) registrare *(reh-jee-STRAH-reh)*

regret rimpiangere *(reem-PYAHN-jeh-reh)*

regular regolare *(reh-goh-LAH-reh)*

remain rimanere *(ree-mah-NEH-reh)*

remember ricordare *(ree-kohr-DAH-reh)*

to rent (car) noleggiare *(noh-lehd-JAH-reh)*

to rent (house) affittare *(ahf-feet-TAH-reh)*

repair riparare *(ree-pah-RAH-reh)*

repeat ripetere *(ree-PEH-teh-reh)*

reservation prenotazione (f.) *(preh-noh-tah-TSYOH-neh)*

reserve prenotare *(preh-noh-TAH-reh)*

231

reserved seat posto riservato (m.) *(POH-stoh ree-zehr-VAH-toh)*

responsible responsabile *(reh-spohn-SAH-bee-leh)*

rest riposo (m.) *(ree-POH-zoh)*

to rest riposare *(ree-poh-ZAH-roh)*

restroom toelette (f.) *(toh-eh-LEHT)*

restaurant ristorante (m.) *(ree-stoh-RAHN-teh)*

result risultato (m.) *(ree-zool-TAH-toh)*

return (give back) restituire *(reh-stee-too-EE-reh)*

(go back) ritornare *(ree-tohr-NAH-reh)*

rice riso (m.) *(REE-zoh)*

rich ricco *(REEK-koh)*

ride giro (m.) *(JEE-roh)*

right (direction) destra *(DEH-strah)*

all right d'accordo *(dahk-KOHR-doh)*

right now subito *(SOO-bee-toh)*

to be right avere ragione *(ah-VEH-reh rah-JOH-neh)*

ring anello (m.) *(ah-NEHL-loh)*

river fiume (m.) *(FYOO-meh)*

road strada (f.) *(STRAH-dah)*

(highway) autostrada (f.) *(ow-toh-STRAH-dah)*

road map carta stradale (f.) *(KAHR-tah strah-DAH-leh)*

roast arrosto (m.) *(ahr-ROH-stoh)*

roll (bread) panino (m.) *(pah-NEE-noh)*

(film) rullino (m.) *(rool-LEE-noh)*

roof tetto (m.) *(TEHT-toh)*

room camera (f.), stanza (f.) *(KAH-meh-rah, STAHN-tsah)*

(bedroom) camera da letto (f.) *(KAH meh-rah dah LEHT-toh)*

room service servizio in camera (m.) *(sehr-VEE-tsyoh een KAH-meh-rah)*

room with all meals pensione completa (f.) *(pehn-SYOH-neh kohm-PLEH-tah)*

round-trip viaggio d'andata e ritorno (m.) *(VYAHD-joh dahn-DAH-tah eh ree-TOHR-noh)*

row (theater) fila (f.) *(FEE-lah)*

rubber gomma (f.) *(GOHM-mah)*

rug tappeto (m.) *(tahp-PEH-toh)*

ruins rovine (f. pl.) *(roh-VEE-neh)*

rule regola (f.) *(REH-goh-lah)*

run correre *(KOH-reh-reh)*

S

sad triste *(TREE-steh)*

safe cassaforte (f.) *(kahs-sah-FOHR-teh)*

(adj.) sicuro *(see-KOO-roh)*

sale vendita (f.) *(VEHN-dee-tah)*

salesman commesso (m.) *(kohm-MEHS-soh)*

salt sale (m.) *(SAH-leh)*

same stesso *(STEHS-soh)*

sand sabbia (f.) *(SAHB-byah)*

sandals sandali (m.pl.) *(SAHN-dah-lee)*

sandwich panino (m.), sandwich (m.) *(pah-NEE-noh, SEHND-weech)*

sanitary napkins assorbenti igienici (m.pl.) *(ahs-sohr-BEHN-tee ee-JEH-nee-chee)*

sauce salsa (f.) *(SAHL-sah)*

sausage salsiccia (f.) *(sahl-SEET-chah)*

say dire *(DEE-reh)*

scarf (wool) sciarpa (f.) *(SHAR-pah)*

(silk) foulard (m.) *(foo-LAHR)*

schedule orario (m.) *(oh-RAH-ryoh)*

school scuola (f.) *(SKWOH-lah)*

scissors forbici (f.pl.) *(FOHR-bee-chee)*

sculpture scultura (f.) *(skool-TOO-rah)*

sea mare (m.) *(MAH-reh)*

seafood pesce (m.), frutti di mare (m.pl.) *(PEH-sheh, FROOT-tee dee MAH-reh)*

season stagione (f.) *(stah-JOH-neh)*

seat posto (m.) *(POH-stoh)*

to seat sedersi (refl.) *(seh-DEHR-see)*

second secondo *(seh-KOHN-doh)*

section sezione (f.), zona (f.) *(seh-TSYOH-neh, DZOH-nah)*

see vedere *(veh-DEH-reh)*

seem sembrare *(sehm-BRAH-reh)*

sell vendere *(VEHN-deh-reh)*

send mandare *(mahn-DAH-reh)*

senior citizens anziani (m.pl.) *(ahn-TSYAH-nee)*

sentence (grammatical) frase (f.) *(FRAH-zeh)*

serious serio *(SEH-ryoh)*

serve servire *(sehr-VEE-reh)*

service servizio (m.) *(sehr-VEE-tsyoh)*

shampoo sciampo (m.) *(SHAHM-poh)*

share dividere *(dee-VEE-deh-reh)*

shave farsi la barba (refl.), radersi (refl.) *(FAHR-see lah BAHR-bah, RAH-dehr-see)*

she lei *(lay)*

sheet (bed) lenzuolo (m.) *(lehn-TSWOH-loh)*

ship nave (f.) *(NAH-veh)*

shirt camicia (f.) *(kah-MEE-chah)*

shoe scarpa (f.) *(SKAHR-pah)*

shoe size misura (f.) *(mee-ZOO-rah)*

shopping, go (grocery) andare a fare la spesa *(ahn-DAH-reh ah FAH-reh lah SPEH-zah)*

(general) andare a fare compere *(ahn-DAH-reh ah FAH-reh KOHM-peh-reh)*

shopping center centro commerciale (m.) *(CHEHN-troh kom-mehr-CHAH-leh)*

short corto, basso *(KOHR-toh, BAHS-soh)*

shoulder spalla (f.) *(SPAHL-lah)*

show (art) mostra (f.) *(MOH-strah)*

(performance) spettacolo (m.) *(speht-TAH-koh-loh)*

shower doccia (f.) *(DOHT-chah)*

sick malato *(mah-LAH-toh)*

sickness malattia (f.) *(mah-laht-TEE-ah)*

side lato (m.) *(LAH-toh)*

sidewalk marciapiede (m.) *(mahr-chah-PYEH-deh)*

sign (traffic) segnale (m.) *(seh-NYAH-leh)*

to sign firmare *(feer-MAH-reh)*

silk seta (f.) *(SEH-tah)*

silver argento (m.) *(ahr-JEHN-toh)*

since da *(dah)*

since when? da quando? *(dah KWAHN-doh?)*

sing cantare *(kahn-TAH-reh)*

single (unmarried, man) celibe, single *(CHEH-lee-beh, SEEN-gol)*

(woman) nubile *(NOO-bee-leh)*

sister sorella (f.) *(soh-REHL-lah)*

sit down sedersi (refl.) *(seh-DEHR-see)*

site posizione (f.) *(poh-zee-TSYOH-neh)*

size misura (f.), taglia (f.) *(mee-ZOO-rah, TAH-lyah)*

skating rink pista di pattinaggio (f.) *(PEE-stah dee paht-tee-NAHD-joh)*

ski sci (m.) *(shee)*
to ski sciare *(shee-AH-reh)*

skin pelle (f.) *(PEHL-leh)*

skirt gonna (f.) *(GOHN-nah)*

sky cielo (m.) *(CHEH-loh)*

sleep dormire *(dohr-MEE-reh)*

sleeping berth cuccetta (f.) *(koot-CHEHT-tah)*

sleeping car vagone letto (m.) *(vah-GOH-neh LEHT-toh)*

sleepy, to be avere sonno *(ah-VEH-reh SOHN-noh)*

slice fetta (f.) *(FEHT-tah)*

slide (photo) diapositiva (f.) *(dyah-poh-zee-TEE-vah)*

slippery scivoloso *(shee-voh-LOH-zoh)*

slow lento *(LEHN-toh)*

slow down rallentare *(rahl-lehn-TAH-reh)*

slowly lentamente *(lehn-tah-MEHN-teh)*

small piccolo *(PEEK-koh-loh)*
to smoke fumare *(foo-MAH-reh)*

smoked affumicato *(ahf-foo-mee-KAH-toh)*

snack bar tavola calda (f.), snack bar (m.) *(TAH-voh-lah KAHL-dah, "snack bar")*

snow neve (f.) *(NEH-veh)*
to snow nevicare *(neh-vee-KAH-reh)*

so così *(koh-ZEE)*

so many tanti(-e) *(TAHN-tee)(-teh)*

so much tanto(-a) *(TAHN-toh)(-tah)*

soap sapone (m.), saponetta (f.) *(sah-POH-neh, sah-poh-NEHT-tah)*

soccer calcio (m.) *(KAHL-choh)*

socks calzini (m.pl.) *(kahl-TSEE-nee)*

soft soffice *(SOHF-fee-cheh)*

some qualche *(KWAHL-keh)*

someone qualcuno *(kwahl-KOO-noh)*

something qualcosa *(kwahl-KOH-zah)*

sometimes a volte, qualche volta *(ah VOHL-teh, KWAHL-keh VOHL-tah)*

somewhere da qualche parte *(dah KWAHL-keh PAHR-teh)*

son figlio (m.) *(FEE-lyoh)*

song canzone (f.) *(kahn-TSOH-neh)*

soon presto *(PREH-stoh)*

sore throat mal di gola (m.) *(mahl dee GOH-lah)*

sorry, to be dispiacere *(dee-spyah-CHEH-reh)*
I'm sorry mi dispiace *(mee dee-SPYAH-cheh)*

soup zuppa (f.), minestra in brodo (f.) *(TSOOP-pah, mee-NEH-strah een BROH-doh)*

south sud (m.) *(sood)*

souvenir souvenir (m.), ricordo (m.) *(soo-veh-NEER, ree-KOHR-doh)*

speak parlare *(pahr-LAH-reh)*

specialty specialità (f.) *(speh-chah-lee-TAH)*

speed velocità (f.) *(veh-loh-chee-TAH)*

spend (money) spendere *(SPEHN-deh-reh)*
(time) passare *(pahs-SAH-reh)*

spice spezie (f.pl.) *(SPEH-tsyeh)*

spicy (hot) piccante *(peek-KAHN-teh)*

spoon cucchiaio (m.) *(kook-KYAH-yoh)*

spring (season) primavera (f.) *(pree-mah-VEH-rah)*

square (town) piazza (f.) *(PYAHT-tsah)*

stadium stadio (m.) *(STAH-dyoh)*

stairs scale (f.pl.) *(SKAH-leh)*

stamp (postage) francobollo (m.) *(frahn-koh-BOHL-loh)*

start cominciare *(koh-meen-CHAH-reh)*

station stazione (f.) *(stah-TSYOH-neh)*

stationery carta da lettere (f.) *(KAHR-tah dah LEHT-teh-reh)*

stationery store cartoleria (f.) *(kahr-toh-leh-REE-ah)*

statue statua (f.) *(STAH-twah)*

stay soggiorno (m.) *(sohd-JOHR-noh)*
  to stay rimanere *(ree-mah-NEH-reh)*

steal rubare *(roo-BAH-reh)*

steward(-ess) assistente di volo (m./f.) *(ahs-see-STEHN-teh dee VOH-loh)*

still (again) ancora *(ahn-KOH-rah)*

stock exchange borsa (f.) *(BOHR-sah)*

stockings calze (f.pl.) *(KAHL-tseh)*

stomach stomaco (m.) *(STOH-mah-koh)*

strong forte *(FOHR-teh)*

subway metropolitana (f.) *(meh-troh-poh-lee-TAH-nah)*

sudden improvviso *(eem-prohv-VEE-zoh)*

suede camoscio (m.) *(kah-MOH-shoh)*

sugar zucchero (m.) *(TSOOK-keh-roh)*

suit abito (m.) completo (m.) *(AH-bee-toh, kohm-PLEH-toh)*

suitcase valigia (f.) *(vah-LEE-jah)*

summer estate (f.) *(eh-STAH-teh)*

sun sole (m.) *(SOH-leh)*

sunglasses occhiali da sole (m.pl.) *(ohk-KYAH-lee dah SOH-leh)*

sunny soleggiato *(soh-lehd-JAH-toh)*

suntan lotion abbronzante (m.) *(ahb-brohn-DZAHN-teh)*

supermarket supermercato (m.) *(soo-pehr-mehr-KAH-toh)*

supper cena (f.) *(CHEH-nah)*

sure sicuro *(see-KOO-roh)*

sweater pullover (m.) *(pool-LOH-vehr)*

sweet dolce *(DOHL-cheh)*

swim nuotare *(nwoh-TAH-reh)*

swimming pool piscina (f.) *(pee-SHEE-nah)*

switch (electric) interruttore (m.) *(een-tehr-root-TOH-reh)*

T

table tavola (f.), tavolo (m.) *(TAH-voh-lah, TAH-voh-loh)*

tailor sarto (m.) *(SAHR-toh)*

take prendere *(PREHN-deh-reh)*
  (carry) portare *(pohr-TAH-reh)*

taste assaggiare *(ahs-sahd-JAH-reh)*

tavern taverna (f.) *(tah-VEHR-nah)*

tax tassa (f.) *(TAHS-sah)*

taxi taxi (m.) *(TAHK-see)*

tea tè (m.) *(teh)*

teach insegnare *(een-seh-NYAH-reh)*

telegram telegramma (m.) *(teh-leh-GRAHM-mah)*

telephone telefono (m.) *(teh-LEH-foh-noh)*

tell dire *(DEE-reh)*

teller (window) sportello (m.) *(spohr-TEHL-loh)*

tennis tennis (m.) *(TEHN-nees)*

terrace terrazza (f.) *(tehr-RAHT-tsah)*

thank ringraziare *(reen-grah-TSYAH-reh)*

thank you grazie *(GRAH-tsyeh)*

that quello *(KWEHL-loh)*

(thing) ciò *(choh)*

(which) che *(keh)*

the il, lo, la, i, gli, le *(eel, loh, lah, ee, lyee, leh)*

theater teatro (m.) *(teh-AH-troh)*

their il/la/i/le loro *(eel/lah/ee/leh LOH-roh)*

them loro *(LOH-roh)*

then allora *(ahl-LOH-rah)*

there là *(lah)*

there is c'è *(cheh)*

there are ci sono *(chee SOH-noh)*

therefore quindi *(KWEEN-dee)*

these questi *(KWEH-stee)*

they loro *(LOH-roh)*

thick spesso, denso *(SPEHS-soh, DEHN-soh)*

thief ladro *(LAH-droh)*

thin magro *(MAH-groh)*

thing cosa (f.) *(KOH-zah)*

think pensare *(pehn-SAH-reh)*

thirsty, to be aver sete *(ah-VEHR SEH-teh)*

this questo *(KWEH-stoh)*

those quelli *(KWEHL-lee)*

through attraverso *(aht-trah-VEHR-soh)*

ticket biglietto (m.) *(bee-LYEHT-toh)*

ticket window biglietteria (f.) *(bee-lyeh-teh-REE-ah)*

tie (neck-) cravatta (f.) *(krah-VAHT-tah)*

time tempo (m.) *(TEHM-poh)*

tip mancia (f.) *(MAHN-chah)*

tired, to be essere stanco *(EHS-seh-reh STAHN-koh)*

tissues fazzolettini di carta (m.pl.), kleenex (m.pl.) *(faht-tsoh-leht-TEE-nee dee KAHR-tah, KLEE-nehks)*

to a *(ah)*

toast (bread) pane tostato (m.), toast (m.) *(PAH-neh toh-STAH-toh, tohst)*

(drink) brindisi (m.) *(BREEN-dee-zee)*

tobacco tobacco (m.) *(toh-BAHK-koh)*

today oggi *(OHD-jee)*

together insieme *(een-SYEH-meh)*

toilet toilette (f.) *(twah-LEHT)*

toilet paper carta igienica (f.) *(KAHR-tah ee-JEH-nee-kah)*

token gettone (m.) *(jeht-TOH-neh)*

toll pedaggio (m.) *(peh-DAHD-joh)*

tomato pomodoro (m.) *(poh-moh-DOH-roh)*

tomorrow domani *(doh-MAH-nee)*

tongue lingua (f.) *(LEEN-gwah)*

too anche *(AHN-keh)*

too much troppo *(TROHP-poh)*

tooth dente (m.) *(DEHN-teh)*

toothbrush spazzolino da denti (m.) *(spaht-tsoh-LEE-noh dah DEHN-tee)*

toothpaste dentifricio (m.) *(dehn-tee-FREE-choh)*

touch toccare *(tohk-KAH-reh)*

to touch up ritoccare *(ree-tohk-KAH-reh)*

tour giro (m.), gita (f.) *(JEE-roh, JEE-tah)*

tourist turista (m./f.) *(too-REE-stah)*

toward verso *(VEHR-soh)*

towel asciugamano (m.) *(ah-shoo-gah-MAH-noh)*

town città (f.) *(cheet-TAH)*

traffic light semaforo (m.) *(seh-MAH-foh-roh)*

train treno (m.) *(TREH-noh)*

translate tradurre *(trah-DOOR-reh)*

to travel viaggiare *(vyahd-JAH-reh)*

travel agency agenzia viaggi (f.) *(ah-jehn-TSEE-ah VYAHD-jee)*

traveler's check travellers cheques (m.pl.) *(TREH-vehl-ler check)*

tree albero (m.) *(AHL-beh-roh)*

trip viaggio (m.) *(VYAHD-joh)*

trouble disturbo (m.) *(dee-STOOR-boh)*

trout trota (f.) *(TROH-tah)*

truck camion (m.) *(KAH-myohn)*

true vero *(VEH-roh)*

truth verità (f.) *(veh-ree-TAH)*

try provare *(proh-VAH-reh)*

turn girare, voltare *(jee-RAH-reh, vohl-TAH-reh)*

TV set televisore (m.) *(teh-leh-vee-ZOH-reh)*

type tipo (m.), genere (m.) *(TEE-poh, JEH-neh-reh)*

typical tipico *(TEE-pee-koh)*

U

ugly brutto *(BROOT-toh)*

umbrella ombrello (m.) *(ohm-BREHL-loh)*

unbelievable incredibile *(een-kreh-DEE-bee-leh)*

uncle zio (m.) *(TSEE-oh)*

uncomfortable scomodo *(SKOH-moh-doh)*

under sotto *(SOHT-toh)*

underpants mutande (f.pl.) *(moo-TAHN-deh)*

understand capire *(kah-PEE-reh)*

underwear biancheria intima (f.) *(byahn-keh-REE-ah EEN-tee-mah)*

unhappy scontento *(skohn-TEHN-toh)*

unique unico *(OO-nee-koh)*

United States Stati Uniti (m.pl.) *(STAH-tee oo-NEE-tee)*

university università (f.) *(oo-nee-vehr-see-TAH)*

until fino a *(FEE-noh ah)*

up, upstairs sù *(soo)*

upon sopra *(SOH-prah)*

urgent urgente *(oor-JEHN-teh)*

us noi *(noy)*

use usare *(oo-ZAH-reh)*

useful utile *(OO-tee-leh)*

useless inutile *(ee-NOO-tee-leh)*

usher maschera (f.) *(MAH-skeh-rah)*

V

vacation vacanza (f.) *(vah-KAHN-tsah)*

valley valle (f.) *(VAHL-leh)*

value valore (m.) *(vah-LOH-reh)*

veal vitello (m.) *(vee-TEHL-loh)*

vegetables legumi (m.pl.), verdura (f.) *(leh-GOO-mee, vehr-DOO-rah)*

very molto *(MOHL-toh)*

view vista (f.) *(VEE-stah)*

villa villa (f.) *(VEEL-lah)*

village paese (m.) *(pah-EH-zeh)*

vinegar aceto (m.) *(ah-CHEH-toh)*

vineyard vigna (f.) *(VEE-nyah)*

to visit visitare *(vee-zee-TAH-reh)*

W

waist (size) cintura (f.), vita (f.) *(cheen-TOO-rah, VEE-tah)*

wait attesa (f.) *(aht-TEH-zah)*
  to wait for aspettare *(ah-speht-TAH-reh)*

waiter cameriere (m.) *(kah-meh-RYEH-reh)*

waiting room sala d'attesa, . . . d'aspetto (f.) *(SAH-lah daht-TEH-zah, . . . dah-SPEHT-toh)*

waitress cameriera (f.) *(kah-meh-RYEH-rah)*

wake up svegliarsi (refl.) *(zveh-LYAHR-see)*

walk passeggiata (f.) *(pahs-sehd-JAH-tah)*
  to walk camminare *(kahm-mee-NAH-reh)*

wall muro (m.), parete (f.) *(MOO-roh, pah-REH-teh)*

wallet portafoglio (m.) *(pohr-tah-FOH-lyoh)*

want volere *(voh-LEH-reh)*

war guerra (f.) *(GWEHR-rah)*

warm caldo *(KAHL-doh)*

wash lavare *(lah-VAH-reh)*
  (oneself) lavarsi (refl.) *(lah-VAHR-see)*

watch orologio (m.) *(oh-roh-LOH-joh)*
  to watch guardare, osservare *(gwahr-DAH-reh, ohs-sehr-VAH-reh)*

water acqua (f.) *(AHK-kwah)*

way (manner) maniera (f.), modo (m.) *(mah-NYEH-rah, MOH-doh)*

we noi *(noy)*

wear indossare, portare *(een-dohs-SAH-reh, pohr-TAH-reh)*

weather tempo (m.) *(TEHM-poh)*
  (forecast) previsioni del tempo (f.pl.) *(preh-vee-ZYOH-nee dehl TEHM-poh)*

wedding matrimonio (m.) *(mah-tree-MOH-nyoh)*

week settimana (f.) *(seht-tee-MAH-nah)*

weight peso (m.) *(PEH-zoh)*

welcome benvenuto *(behn-veh-NOO-toh)*
  you're welcome prego *(PREH-goh)*

well bene *(BEH-neh)*
  (then) allora, dunque *(ahl-LOH-rah, DOON-kweh)*

well-done (meat) ben cotto *(behn KOHT-toh)*

west ovest (m.) *(OH-vehst)*

wet bagnato *(bah-NYAH-toh)*

what? che cosa? *(keh KOH-zah?)*

when? quando? *(KWAHN-doh?)*

where? dove? *(DOH-veh?)*

which? quale? *(KWAH-leh?)*

white bianco *(BYAHN-koh)*

who che *(keh)*
  who? chi? *(kee?)*

whole intero *(een-TEH-roh)*

why? perché? *(pehr-KEH?)*

wide ampio *(AHM-pyoh)*

wife moglie (f.) *(MOH-lyeh)*

wild selvaggio *(sehl-VAHD-joh)*

win vincere *(VEEN-cheh-reh)*

window finestra (f.) *(fee-NEH-strah)*

wine vino (m.) *(VEE-noh)*

winter inverno (m.) *(een-VEHR-noh)*

wish desiderio (m.) *(deh-zee-DEH-ryoh)*

with con *(kohn)*
without senza *(SEHN-tsah)*
woman donna (f.) *(DOHN-nah)*
wonderful meraviglioso *(meh-rah-vee-LYOH-zoh)*
wood legno (m.) *(LEH-nyoh)*
wool lana (f.) *(LAH-nah)*
word parola (f.) *(pah-ROH-lah)*
work lavoro (m.) *(lah-VOH-roh)*
   to work lavorare *(lah-voh-RAH-reh)*
world mondo (m.) *(MOHN-doh)*
worse peggio *(PEHD-joh)*
worst peggiore *(pehd-JOH-reh)*
worth, be valere *(vah-LEH-reh)*
write scrivere *(SKREE-veh-reh)*
wrong, be aver torto *(ah-VEHR TOHR-toh)*

X

X ray raggi x (m.pl.), radiografia (f.) *(RAHD-jee eeks, rah-dyoh-grah-FEE-ah)*

Y

year anno (m.) *(AHN-noh)*
yellow giallo *(JAHL-loh)*
yes sì *(see)*
yesterday ieri *(YEH-ree)*

yet ancora *(ahn-KOH-rah)*
yogurt yogurt (m.) *(YOH-goort)*
you (familiar sing.) tu/te/ti *(too/teh/tee)*
   (familiar pl.) voi/vi *(voy/vee)*
   (polite sing.) Lei/La/Le *(lay/lah/leh)*
   (polite pl.) Loro *(LOH-roh)*
young giovane *(JOH-vah-neh)*
younger (age) minore *(mee-NOH-reh)*
your (fam. s.) il tuo/la tua/i tuoi/le tue *(eel TOO-oh/lah TOO-ah/ee TWOH-ee/leh TOO-eh)*
   (fam. pl.) il vostro/la vostra/i vostri/le vostre *(eel VOH-stroh/lah VOH-strah/ee VOH-stree/leh VOH-streh)*
   (pol. s.) il Suo/la Sua/i Suoi/le Sue *(eel SOO-oh/lah SOO-ah/ee SWOH-ee/leh SOO-eh)*
   (pol. pl.) il/la/i/le Loro *(eel/lah/ee/leh LOH-roh)*
youth hostel ostello per la gioventù (m.) *(oh-STEHL-loh pehr lah joh-vehn-TOO)*

Z

zero zero *(DZEH-roh)*
zipper lampo (f.) *(LAHM-poh)*
zoo zoo (m.) *(DZOH)*

ITALIAN-ENGLISH DICTIONARY

See usage note under English-Italian Dictionary.

A

a *(ah)* to, at, in, by

abbastanza *(ahb-bah-STAHN-tsah)* enough

abbigliamento (m.) *(ahb-bee-lyah-MEHN-toh)* clothes, clothing

abbronzarsi (refl.) *(ahb-brohn-DZAHR-see)* to get tanned

abbronzato *(ahb-brohn-DZAH-toh)* tanned

abito (m.) *(AH-bee-toh)* man's suit

abito da sera (m.) *(AH-bee-toh dah SEH-rah)* evening suit; formal

accadere *(ahk-kah-DEH-reh)* to happen

accendere *(aht-CHEHN-deh-reh)* to light, to turn/switch on

accendino (m.) *(ah-chen-DEE-noh)* lighter

accomodare *(ahk-koh-moh-DAH-reh)* to repair

accordo (m.) *(ahk-KOHR-doh)* agreement

accorgersi (refl.) *(ahk-KOHR-jehr-see)* to notice, to realize

acqua (f.) *(AHK-kwah)* water
acqua minerale *(. . . mee-neh-RAH-leh)* mineral water
acqua potabile *(. . . poh-TAH-bee-leh)* drinking water

acquistare *(ahk-kwee-STAH-reh)* to buy, to purchase

adagio *(ah-DAH-joh)* slowly

adesso *(ah-DEHS-soh)* now

aereo (m.) *(ah-EH-reh-oh)* airplane

aeroporto (m.) *(ah-eh-roh-POHR-toh)* airport

affare (m.) *(ahf-FAH-reh)* matter, business, bargain

affettato (m.) *(ahf-feht-TAH-toh)* cold cuts

affitto (m.) *(ahf-FEET-toh)* rent

affrancatura (f.) *(ahf-frahn-kah-TOO-rah)* postage

affrettarsi *(ahf-freht-TAHR-see)* to hurry up

agenzia (f.) *(ah-jehn-TSEE-ah)* agency
agenzia viaggi *(. . . VYAHD-jee)* travel agency

aggiustare *(ahd-joo-STAH-reh)* to repair, to adjust

aglio (m.) *(AH-lyoh)* garlic

aiutare *(ah-yoo-TAH-reh)* to help

aiuto (m.) *(ah-YOO-toh)* help

albergo (m.) *(ahl-BEHR-goh)* hotel

albero (m.) *(AHL-beh-roh)* tree

alcuno *(ahl-KOO-noh)* some, a few

alimentari (m.pl.) *(ah-lee-mehn-TAH-ree)* groceries

allegro *(ahl-LEH-groh)* merry, cheerful

allora *(ahl-LOH-rah)* then

alt *(ahlt)* stop

altezza (f.) *(ahl-TEHT-tsah)* height

alto *(AHL-toh)* high

altrettanto *(ahl-treht-TAHN-toh)* the same

altro *(AHL-troh)* other

alzarsi (refl.) *(ahl-TSAHR-see)* to get up

amare *(ah-MAH-reh)* to love

ambasciata (f.) *(ahm-bah-SHAH-tah)* embassy

americano(-a) *(ah-meh-ree-KAH-noh)(-nah)* American

amico (m.) *(ah-MEE-koh)* friend

ammobiliato *(ahm-moh-bee-LYAH-toh)* furnished

ampio *(AHM-pyoh)* wide

anche *(AHN-keh)* also, too

ancora *(ahn-KOH-rah)* still, yet

andare *(ahn-DAH-reh)* to go
andarsene *(ahn-DAHR-seh-neh)* to go away, to leave

anello (m.) *(ah-NEHL-loh)* ring

angolo (m.) *(AHN-goh-loh)* corner

anno (m.) *(AHN-noh)* year

annullare *(ahn-nool-LAH-reh)* to annul, to cancel

antico *(ahn-TEE-koh)* old

antipasto (m.) *(ahn-tee-PAH-stoh)* appetizer, hors d'oeuvre

antipatico *(ahn-tee-PAH-tee-koh)* unpleasant, disagreeable

aperto *(ah-PEHR-toh)* open
all'aperto *(ahl-lah-PEHR-toh)* in the open (air)

appartamento (m.) *(ahp-pahr-tah-MEHN-toh)* apartment

apprendere *(ahp-PREHN-deh-reh)* to learn

appuntamento (m.) *(ahp-poon-tah-MEHN-toh)* date, meeting

arancia (f.) *(ah-RAHN-chah)* orange

argento (m.) *(ahr-JEHN-toh)* silver

aria (f.) *(AH-ryah)* air

armadio (m.) *(ahr-MAH-dyoh)* closet

arrivare *(ahr-ree-VAH-reh)* to arrive

arrivederci *(ahr-ree-veh-DEHR-chee)* good-bye

arrivo (m.) *(ahr-REE-voh)* arrival

arte (f.) *(AHR-teh)* art

ascensore (m.) *(ah-shehn-SOH-reh)* elevator

asciugamano (m.) *(ah-shoo-gah-MAH-noh)* towel
asciutto *(ah-SHOOT-toh)* dry, dried

ascoltare *(ah-skohl-TAH-reh)* to listen

aspettare *(ah-speht-TAH-reh)* to wait
aspettarsi (refl.) *(ah-speht-TAHR-see)* to expect

aspetto (m.) *(ah-SPEHT-toh)* look, waiting
sala d'aspetto (f.) *(SAH-lah dah-SPEHT-toh)* waiting room

aspirina (f.) *(ah-spee-REE-nah)* aspirin

assaggiare *(ahs-sahd-JAH-reh)* to taste

assegno (m.) *(ahs-SEH-nyoh)* check

assicurazione (f.) *(ahs-see-koo-rah-TSYOH-neh)* insurance (policy)

attenzione (f.) *(aht-ten-TSYOH-neh)* attention
fare attenzione *(FAH-reh . . .)* to pay attention

atterrare *(aht-tehr-RAH-reh)* to land

attorno *(aht-TOHR-noh)* around

attraversare *(aht-trah-vehr-SAH-reh)* to cross

attraverso *(aht-trah-VEHR-soh)* across, through

augurare *(ow-goo-RAH-reh)* to wish

auguri! *(ow-GOO-ree!)* best wishes!

autista (m.) *(ow-TEE-stah)* driver

autobus (m.) *(OW-toh-boos)*
bus
automobile (f.) *(ow-toh-MOH-bee-leh)* car
autostrada (f.) *(ow-toh-STRAH-dah)* highway
autunno (m.) *(ow-TOON-noh)*
autumn, fall
avanti *(ah-VAHN-tee)* ahead
avere *(ah-VEH-reh)* to have
avvocato (m.) *(ahv-voh-KAH-toh)*
lawyer

B

bacio (m.) *(BAH-choh)* kiss
bagaglio (m.) *(bah-GAH-lyoh)*
luggage
　fare i bagagli *(FAH-reh ee bah-GAH-lyee)* to pack
bagnarsi (refl.) *(bah-NYAHR-see)*
to bathe
bagnato *(bah-NYAH-toh)* wet
bagno (m.) *(BAH-nyoh)* bath
ballare *(bahl-LAH-reh)* to
dance
bambinaia (f.) *(bahm-bee-NAH-yah)* babysitter, nanny
bambino (m.) *(bahm-BEE-noh)*
child
banca (f.) *(BAHN-kah)* bank
banconota (f.) *(bahn-koh-NOH-tah)* banknote
barbiere (m.) *(bahr-BYEH-reh)*
barber
barca (f.) *(BAHR-kah)* boat
basilico (m.) *(bah-ZEE-lee-koh)*
basel
basso *(BAHS-soh)* low, short
basta! *(BAH-stah!)* enough!
bello *(BEHL-loh)* beautiful,
handsome, lovely
benché *(ben-KEH)* although
bene *(BEH-neh)* well
bere *(BEH-reh)* to drink
bevanda (f.) *(beh-VAHN-dah)*
drink

biancheria (f.) *(byahn-keh-REE-ah)* linen
　biancheria intima (f.)
　(. . . EEN-tee-mah)
　underwear
bianco *(BYAHN-koh)* white
biblioteca (f.) *(bee-blyoh-TEH-kah)* library
bicchiere (m.) *(beek-KYEH-reh)*
drinking glass
bicicletta (f.) *(bee-chee-KLEHT-tah)* bicycle
bigliettaio (m.) *(bee-lyeht-TAH-yoh)* conductor
biglietteria (f.) *(bee-lyeht-teh-REE-oh)* ticket office, box
office
biglietto (m.) *(bee-LYEHT-toh)*
ticket
binario (m.) *(bee-NAH-ryoh)*
track, platform
biondo *(BYOHN-doh)* blond,
fair
birra (f.) *(BEER-rah)* beer
bisogno (m.) *(bee-ZOH-nyoh)*
need
avere bisogno di *(ah-VEH-reh bee-SOH-nyoh dee)* to need
blu *(bloo)* blue
bocca (f.) *(BOHK-kah)* mouth
bollito *(bohl-LEE-toh)* boiled
borsa (f.) *(BOHR-sah)* bag
borsetta (f.) *(bohr-SEHT-tah)*
handbag
bosco (m.) *(BOH-skoh)* woods
bottega (f.) *(boht-TEH-gah)*
shop
bottiglia (f.) *(boht-TEE-lyah)*
bottle
braccio (m.) *(BRAHT-choh)* arm
bravo *(BRAH-voh)* good,
shout of approval
breve *(BREH-veh)* short
brillante *(breel-LAHN-teh)*
sparkling, bright, brilliant
brindisi (m.) *(BREEN-dee-zee)*
toast (to one's health)

bruciare *(broo-CHAH-reh)* to burn
  bruciarsi (refl.) *(broo-CHAHR-see)* to burn oneself
bruno *(BROO-noh)* brown
brutto *(BROOT-toh)* ugly
buio (m.) *(BOO-yoh)* dark
buonanotte (buona notte) (f.) *(bwoh-nah-NOHT-teh)* good night
buonasera (buona sera) (f.) *(bwoh-nah-SEH-rah)* good evening
buongiorno (buon giorno) (m.) *(bwohn-JOHR-noh)* good morning, good day
buono *(BWOH-noh)* good
burro (m.) *(BOOR-roh)* butter
busta (f.) *(BOO-stah)* envelope

C

cabina (f.) *(kah-BEE-nah)* booth
caffè (m.) *(kahf-FEH)* coffee
calcio (m.) *(KAHL-choh)* kick, soccer
caldo *(KAHL-doh)* warm
calma (f.) *(KAHL-mah)* calm
calore (m.) *(kah-LOH-reh)* heat
calza (f.) *(KAHL-tsah)* stocking
calzatura (f.) *(kahl-tsah-TOO-rah)* footwear, shoe
calzino (m.) *(kahl-TSEE-noh)* sock
calzoleria (f.) *(kahl-tsoh-leh-REE-ah)* shoe store
calzoni (m.pl.) *(kahl-TSOH-nee)* pants
cambiare *(kahm-BYAH-reh)* to change
cambio (m.) *(KAHM-byoh)* change, auto clutch
camera (da letto) (f.) *(KAH-meh-rah dah LEHT-toh)* bedroom

cameriera (f.) *(kah-meh-RYEH-rah)* waitress, maid
cameriere (m.) *(kah-meh-RYEH-reh)* waiter
camicetta (f.) *(kah-mee-CHEHT-tah)* blouse
camicia (f.) *(kah-MEE-chah)* shirt
camion (m.) *(KAH-myohn)* truck
camminare *(kahm-mee-NAH-reh)* to walk
campagna (f.) *(kahm-PAH-nyah)* country, countryside
campana (f.) *(kahm-PAH-nah)* bell
campanile (m.) *(kahm-pah-NEE-leh)* bell tower
campo (m.) *(KAHM-poh)* field
cane (m.) *(KAH-neh)* dog
cantare *(kahn-TAH-reh)* to sing
cantina (f.) *(kahn-TEE-nah)* wine cellar
canzone (f.) *(kahn-TSOH-neh)* song
capelli (m.pl.) *(kah-PEHL-lee)* hair
capire *(kah-PEE-reh)* to understand
capitare *(kah-pee-TAH-reh)* to happen
capo (m.) *(KAH-poh)* head
cappello (m.) *(kahp-PEHL-loh)* hat
cappotto (m.) *(kahp-POHT-toh)* coat
carne (f.) *(KAHR-neh)* meat
caro *(KAH-roh)* dear, expensive
carta (f.) *(KAHR-tah)* paper
cartella (f.) *(kahr-TEHL-lah)* briefcase
cartoleria (f.) *(kahr-toh-leh-REE-ah)* stationery store
cartolina (f.) *(kahr-toh-LEE-nah)* postcard
casa (f.) *(KAH-zah)* house, home

casalingo *(kah-zah-LEEN-goh)* homemade

caso (m.) *(KAH-zoh)* chance, case

cassa (f.) *(KAHS-sah)* case, box

cassetta (f.) *(kahs-SEHT-tah)* box, audio-videocassette

cassetto (m.) *(kahs-SEHT-toh)* drawer

cassiere (m.) *(kahs-SYEH-reh)* cashier

castano *(kah-STAH-noh)* brown (hair)

castello (m.) *(kah-STEHL-loh)* castle

cattivo *(kaht-TEE-voh)* bad

cavallo (m.) *(kah-VAHL-loh)* horse

caviglia (f.) *(kah-VEE-lyah)* ankle

celebre *(CHEH-leh-breh)* famous

cena (f.) *(CHEH-nah)* dinner, supper

cenare *(cheh-NAH-reh)* to have dinner/supper

centrale *(chehn-TRAH-leh)* central

centralinista (m./f.) *(chehn-trah-lee-NEE-stah)* operator

centralino (m.) *(chehn-trah-LEE-noh)* switchboard

centro (m.) *(CHEHN-troh)* center

cercare *(chehr-KAH-reh)* to look for

certamente *(chehr-tah-MEHN-teh)* certainly

certo *(CHEHR-toh)* certain(ly)

che *(keh)* (who, that, which, whom, what

chi *(kee)* (he who, she who, whoever, anyone who, someone who, who, whom, which

chiamare *(kyah-MAH-reh)* to call

chiamarsi (refl.) *(kyah-MAHR-see)* to call oneself

chiaro *(KYAH-roh)* clear

chiave (f.) *(KYAH-veh)* key

chiedere *(KYEH-deh-reh)* to ask

chiesa (f.) *(KYEH-zah)* church

chiudere *(KYOO-deh-reh)* to close

chiudere a chiave *(. . . ah KYAH-veh)* to lock

chiuso *(KYOO-zoh)* closed

ciao *(chow)* hello, good-bye (familiar)

cibo (m.) *(CHEE-boh)* food

cielo (m.) *(CHEH-loh)* sky

cin cin *(cheen cheen)* cheers

cinema (m.) *(CHEE-neh-mah)* cinema, movies, movie theatre

cintura (f.) *(cheen-TOO-rah)* belt

cintura di sicurezza *(. . . dee see-koo-REHT-tsah)* safety belt

cioccolata(-o) (f.,m.) *(chohk-koh-LAH-tah)(-toh)* chocolate

cipolla (f.) *(chee-POHL-lah)* onion

circa *(CHEER-kah)* about, around

città (f.) *(cheet-TAH)* city

cittadino (m.) *(cheet-tah-DEE-noh)* citizen

cliente (m.) *(klee-EHN-teh)* customer

coda (f.) *(KOH-dah)* line

fare la coda *(FAH-reh lah . . .)* to stand on line

cognato (m.) *(koh-NYAH-toh)* brother-in-law

cognome (m.) *(koh-NYOH-meh)* surname, family name

colazione (f.) *(koh-lah-TSYOH-neh)* breakfast, lunch

collana (f.) *(kohl-LAH-nah)* necklace

collo (m.) *(KOHL-loh)* neck

colore (m.) *(koh-LOH-reh)* color

coltello (m.) *(kohl-TEHL-loh)* knife

come *(KOH-meh)* as, how

cominciare *(koh-meen-CHAH-reh)* to begin, to start

commedia (f.) *(kohm-MEH-dyah)* comedy, play

commessa(-o) (f., m.) *(kohm-MEHS-sah)(-soh)* shop assistant

commissariato (di polizia) (m.) *(kohm-mees-sah-RYAH-toh dee poh-lee-TSEE-ah)* police station

commissione (f.) *(kom-mees-SYOH-neh)* errand

comodo *(KOH-moh-doh)* convenient, comfortable

compagnia (f.) *(kohm-pah-NYEE-ah)* company

compartimento (m.) *(kohm-pahr-tee-MEHN-toh)* compartment

compera (f.) *(KOHM-peh-rah)* purchase

compleanno (m.) *(kohm-pleh-AHN-noh)* birthday

completo *(kohm-PLEH-toh)* full

comprare *(kohm-PRAH-reh)* to buy

comprendere *(kohm-PREHN-deh-reh)* to understand

compreso *(kohm-PREH-zoh)* included

computer (m.) *(kohm-PYOO-tehr)* computer

con *(kohn)* with, by

concerto (m.) *(kohn-CHEHR-toh)* concert

conducente (m.) *(kohn-doo-CHEHN-teh)* driver

conferenza (f.) *(kohn-feh-REHN-tsah)* lecture, conference

confermare *(kohn-fehr-MAH-reh)* to confirm

confortevole *(kohn-fohr-TEH-voh-leh)* comfortable

confusione (f.) *(kohn-foo-ZYOH-neh)* noise

congratulazioni (f.pl.) *(kohn-grah-too-lah-TSYOH-nee)* congratulations

conoscere *(koh-NOH-sheh-reh)* to know, to meet

consegna (f.) *(kohn-SEH-nyah)* delivery

considerare *(kohn-see-deh-RAH-reh)* to consider, to think

consolato (m.) *(kohn-soh-LAH-toh)* consulate

contare *(kohn-TAH-reh)* to count

contento *(kohn-TEHN-toh)* happy, satisfied, glad

continuare *(kohn-tee-NWAH-reh)* to continue

conto (m.) *(KOHN-toh)* bill, check (restaurant, hotel)

contro *(KOHN-troh)* against

controllo (m.) *(kohn-TROHL-loh)* check, inspection, control

conveniente *(kohn-veh-NYEHN-teh)* convenient

coperta (f.) *(koh-PEHR-tah)* blanket, bedspread

coperto *(koh-PEHR-toh)* covered

corda (f.) *(KOHR-dah)* rope

corpo (m.) *(KOHR-poh)* body

correre *(KOHR-reh-reh)* to run

corsia (f.) *(kohr-SEE-ah)* lane (highway)

cortese *(kohr-TEH-zeh)* kind, polite

cortesia (f.) *(kohr-teh-ZEE-ah)* kindness, politeness

corto *(KOHR-toh)* short

cosa (f.) *(KOH-zah)* thing
  che cosa? *(keh . . . ?)* what?

così *(koh-ZEE)* thus, this way

costare *(koh-STAH-reh)* to cost

costo (m.) *(KOH-stoh)* cost

costume (m.) *(koh-STOO-meh)* custom, habit
  costume da bagno (m.) *(. . . dah BAH-nyoh)* bathing suit

cotone (m.) *(koh-TOH-neh)* cotton

cotto *(KOHT-toh)* cooked, done

cravatta (f.) *(krah-VAHT-tah)* necktie

credere *(KREH-deh-reh)* to believe, to think

crema (f.) *(KREH-mah)* cream

crescere *(KREH-sheh-reh)* to grow, to rise

crudo *(KROO-doh)* raw

cuccetta (f.) *(koot-CHEHT-tah)* berth, couchette

cucchiaino (m.) *(kook-kyah-EE-noh)* teaspoon

cucchiaio (m.) *(kook-KYAH-yoh)* spoon

cucina (f.) *(koo-CHEE-nah)* kitchen, cooking, cuisine, food

cucinare *(koo-chee-NAH-reh)* to cook

cuffia (f.) *(KOOF-fyah)* cap, headphones (radio/TV)

cuocere *(KWOH-cheh-reh)* to cook

cuoio (m.) *(KWOH-yoh)* leather

cuore (m.) *(KWOH-reh)* heart

cura (f.) *(KOO-rah)* care

cuscino (m.) *(koo-SHEE-noh)* cushion, pillow

D

da *(dah)* from, to, at, for, since

danno (m.) *(DAHN-noh)* damage, harm

dare *(DAH-reh)* to give

data (f.) *(DAH-tah)* date

davanti *(dah-VAHN-tee)* in front of, before

dazio (m.) *(DAH-tsyoh)* duty

debole *(DEH-boh-leh)* weak

decaffeinato *(deh-kahf-fay-NAH-toh)* decaffeinated

decidere *(deh-CHEE-deh-reh)* to decide

decisione (f.) *(deh-chee-ZYOH-neh)* decision

decollare *(deh-kohl-LAH-reh)* to take off

denaro (m.) *(deh-NAH-roh)* money

dente (m.) *(DEHN-teh)* tooth

dentifricio (m.) *(dehn-tee-FREE-choh)* toothpaste

dentista (m./f.) *(dehn-TEE-stah)* dentist

dentro *(DEHN-troh)* inside

deposito (m.) *(deh-POH-zee-toh)* deposit
  deposito bagagli (m.) *(. . . bah-GAH-lyee)* baggage checkroom

desiderare *(deh-zee-deh-RAH-reh)* to wish

destinazione (f.) *(deh-stee-nah-TSYOH-neh)* destination

destra (f.) *(DEH-strah)* right

di *(dee)* of

dieta (f.) *(DYEH-tah)* diet

dietro *(DYEH-troh)* behind

difficile *(deef-FEE-chee-leh)* difficult

difficoltà (f.) *(deef-fee-kohl-TAH)* difficulty

dimagrire *(dee-mah-GREE-reh)* to lose weight

dimenticare *(dee-mehn-tee-KAH-reh)* to forget

dire *(DEE-reh)* to say, to tell

direttore (m.) *(dee-reht-TOH-reh)* manager, director

diritto/dritto *(dee-REET-toh)* straight

diritto (m.) right (legal, moral)

discoteca (f.) *(dee-skoh-TEH-kah)* disco

disdire *(dee-ZDEE-reh)* to cancel, to discontinue

dispiacere *(dee-spyah-CHEH-reh)* to be sorry, to regret
  mi dispiace *(mee dee-SPYAH-cheh)* I am sorry
distanza (f.) *(dee-STAHN-tsah)* distance
distare *(dee-STAH-reh)* to be far
  quanto dista? *(KWAHN-toh DEE-stah?)* how far is it?
disturbare *(dee-stoor-BAH-reh)* to disturb, to bother
dito (m.) *(DEE-toh)* finger
diventare *(dee-vehn-TAH-reh)* to become
diverso *(dee-VEHR-soh)* different
divertimento (m.) *(dee-vehr-tee-MEHN-toh)* amusement
divertirsi (refl.) *(dee-vehr-TEER-see)* to have a good time
dividere *(dee-VEE-deh-reh)* to divide
divorziato *(dee-vohr-TSYAH-toh)* divorced
dizionario (m.) *(dee-tsyoh-NAH-ryoh)* dictionary
dogana (f.) *(doh-GAH-nah)* customs
  passare la dogana *(pahs-SAH-reh la . . .)* to go through customs
dolce *(DOHL-cheh)* sweet
  dolce (m.) cake, pie, pastry
dollaro (m.) *(DOHL-lah-roh)* dollar
dolore (m.) *(doh-LOH-reh)* pain
domanda (f.) *(doh-MAHN-dah)* question
domandare *(doh-mahn-DAH-reh)* to ask
domani *(doh-MAH-nee)* tomorrow
donna (f.) *(DOHN-nah)* woman
dono (m.) *(DOH-noh)* gift

dopo *(DOH-poh)* after
dopodomani *(doh-poh-doh-MAH-nee)* the day after tomorrow
dormire *(dohr-MEE-reh)* to sleep
dottore (m.) *(doht-TOH-reh)* doctor
dove *(DOH-veh)* where
dovere *(doh-VEH-reh)* must, to have to
dozzina (f.) *(dohd-DZEE-nah)* dozen
drogheria (f.) *(droh-geh-REE-ah)* grocery store
durare *(doo-RAH-reh)* to last
durata (f.) *(doo-RAH-tah)* length
duro *(DOO-roh)* hard

E

e *(eh)* and
eccellente *(eht-chehl-LEHN-teh)* excellent
ecco *(EHK-koh)* here
edicola (f.) *(eh-DEE-koh-lah)* newsstand
edificio (m.) *(eh-dee-FEE-choh)* building
elegante *(eh-leh-GAHN-teh)* elegant
elenco (m.) *(eh-LEHN-koh)* list
  elenco telefonico *(. . . teh-leh-FOH-nee-koh)* telephone book
elettrico *(eh-LEHT-tree-koh)* electric
entrambi *(ehn-TRAHM-bee)* both
entrare *(ehn-TRAH-reh)* to enter
entrata (f.) *(ehn-TRAH-tah)* entrance
entro *(EHN-troh)* within
epoca (f.) *(EH-poh-kah)* epoch, era

era (f.) *(EHR-bah)* grass
errore (m.) *(ehr-ROH-reh)* mistake, error
esatto *(eh-ZAHT-toh)* exact
esaurito *(eh-zow-REE-toh)* out of stock, sold out
escursione (f.) *(eh-skoor-ZYOH-neh)* excursion, trip
esempio (m.) *(eh-ZEHM-pyoh)* example, instance
   per esempio *(pehr . . .)* for instance
esente *(eh-ZEHN-teh)* exempt, free
   esente da imposta *(. . . dah eem-POH-stah)* duty-free
espresso *(eh-SPREHS-soh)* express, espresso coffee
essere *(EHS-seh-reh)* to be
   c'è *(cheh)* there is
   ci sono *(chee SOH-noh)* there are
estate (f.) *(eh-STAH-teh)* summer
esterno *(eh-STEHR-noh)* exterior, outside
estero *(EH-steh-roh)* foreign
estraneo (m.) *(eh-STRAH-neh-oh)* stranger
età (f.) *(eh-TAH)* age
etichetta (f.) *(eh-tee-KEHT-tah)* label
etto (m.) *(EHT-toh)* one hundred grams
evitare *(eh-vee-TAH-reh)* to avoid
evviva! *(ehv-VEE-vah!)* hooray!

F

fa *(fah)* ago
fabbricazione (f.) *(fahb-bree-kah-TSYOH-neh)* manufacture, make
facchino (m.) *(fahk-KEE-noh)* porter

faccia (f.) *(FAHT-chah)* face
fàcile *(FAH-chee-leh)* easy
fame (f.) *(FAH-meh)* hunger
famiglia (f.) *(fah-MEE-lyah)* family
famoso *(fah-MOH-zoh)* famous
fantastico *(fahn-TAH-stee-koh)* fantastic
fare *(FAH-reh)* to do, to make
farmacia (f.) *(fahr-mah-CHEE-ah)* drugstore, pharmacy
fari anteriori (m.pl.) *(FAH-ree ahn-teh-RYOH-ree)* headlights
fari posteriori *(. . . poh-steh-RYOH-ree)* taillights
fascia (f.) *(FAH-shah)* band
fastidio (m.) *(fah-STEE-dyoh)* trouble, annoyance
fatto *(FAHT-toh)* made, (m.) a fact
   fatto a mano *(. . . ah MAH-noh)* handmade
fattorino (m.) *(faht-toh-REE-noh)* errand boy
favoloso *(fah-voh-LOH-zoh)* fabulous
favore (m.) *(fah-VOH-reh)* favor
   per favore *(pehr . . .)* please
fax (m.) *(FAHKS)* fax
febbre (f.) *(FEHB-breh)* fever, temperature
felice *(feh-LEE-cheh)* happy
femmina (f.) *(FEHM-mee-nah)* female
ferita (f.) *(feh-REE-tah)* wound, injury
fermare *(fehr-MAH-reh)* to stop (something)
   fermarsi (refl.) *(fehr-MAHR-see)* to stop
fermo *(FEHR-moh)* still, stationary
ferro (m.) *(FEHR-roh)* iron

ferrovia (f.) *(fehr-roh-VEE-ah)* railway

festa (f.) *(FEH-stah)* holiday, party

festivo *(feh-STEE-voh)* Sunday
giorno festivo *(JOHR-noh . . .)* Sunday, public holiday

fetta (f.) *(FEHT-tah)* slice

fiammifero (m.) *(fyahm-MEE-feh-roh)* match

fianco (m.) *(FYAHN-koh)* side

figlia (f.) *(FEE-lyah)* daughter

figlio (m.) *(FEE-lyoh)* son

fila (f.) *(FEE-lah)* row, line

film (m.) *(feelm)* film, movie

filo (m.) *(FEE-loh)* thread

fine (f.) *(FEE-neh)* end

finestra (f.) *(fee-NEH-strah)* window

finestrino (m.) *(fee-neh-STREE-noh)* window (vehicle)

finire *(fee-NEE-reh)* to finish, to end
finito *(fee-NEE-toh)* finished

fino (a) *(FEE-noh ah)* till, until, up to

finto *(FEEN-toh)* false

fiore (m.) *(FYOH-reh)* flower

firma (f.) *(FEER-mah)* signature

fiume (m.) *(FYOO-meh)* river

fontana (f.) *(fohn-TAH-nah)* fountain

forbici (f.pl.) *(FOHR-bee-chee)* scissors

forchetta (f.) *(fohr-KEHT-tah)* fork

formaggio (m.) *(fohr-MAHD-joh)* cheese

fornaio (m.) *(fohr-NAH-yoh)* baker

forno (m.) *(FOHR-noh)* oven

forse *(FOHR-seh)* perhaps

forte *(FOHR-teh)* strong

fortuna (f.) *(fohr-TOO-nah)* luck

forza (f.) *(FOHR-tsah)* strength

fotografare *(foh-toh-grah-FAH-reh)* to photograph

fotografia (f.) *(foh-toh-grah-FEE-ah)* photograph, picture

foulard (m.) *(foo-LAHR)* (silk) scarf

fra *(frah)* between, among; in (time)

fragile *(FRAH-jee-leh)* fragile

fragola (f.) *(FRAH-goh-lah)* strawberry

francobollo (m.) *(frahn-koh-BOHL-loh)* stamp

frase (f.) *(FRAH-zeh)* sentence

fratello (m.) *(frah-TEHL-loh)* brother

freddo *(FREHD-doh)* cold

freno (m.) *(FREH-noh)* brake

fresco *(FREH-skoh)* fresh

fretta (f.) *(FREHT-tah)* haste, hurry

friggere *(FREED-jeh-reh)* to fry

frigorifero (m.) *(free-goh-REE-feh-roh)* refrigerator

fronte (f.) *(FROHN-teh)* forehead, front
di fronte a *(dee . . . ah)* in front of

frutta (f.) *(FROOT-tah)* fruit

frutti di mare (m.pl.) *(FROOT-tee dee MAH-reh)* seafood

fumare *(foo-MAH-reh)* to smoke

fumo (m.) *(FOO-moh)* smoke

fungo (m.) *(FOON-goh)* mushroom

fuoco (m.) *(FWOH-koh)* fire

fuori *(FWOH-ree)* out, outside, outdoors

furto (m.) *(FOOR-toh)* theft

futuro (m.) *(foo-TOO-roh)* future

G

gabinetto (m.) *(gah-bee-NEHT-toh)* lavatory, toilet

galleria (f.) *(gahl-leh-REE-ah)* tunnel (road), (art) gallery, balcony (theater)

gas (m.) *(gahs)* gas

gassare *(gahs-SAH-reh)* to carbonate

gatto (m.) *(GAHT-toh)* cat

gelateria (f.) *(jeh-lah-teh-REE-ah)* ice-cream parlor

gelato (m.) *(jeh-LAH-toh)* ice cream

genere (m.) *(JEH-neh-reh)* kind, sort

gentile *(jehn-TEE-leh)* kind

genuino *(jeh-noo-EE-noh)* genuine

gerente (m.) *(jeh-REHN-teh)* manager (store)

gettare *(jeht-TAH-reh)* to throw

gettone (m.) *(jeht-TOH-neh)* token

ghiacciato *(gyaht-CHAH-toh)* frozen

già *(jah)* already

giacca (f.) *(JAHK-kah)* coat, jacket

giallo *(JAHL-loh)* yellow

giardino (m.) *(jahr-DEE-noh)* garden

ginocchio (m.) *(jee-NOHK-kyoh)* knee

giocare *(joh-KAH-reh)* to play

gioielleria (f.) *(joh-yehl-leh-REE-ah)* jewelry store

giornale (m.) *(johr-NAH-leh)* newspaper

giorno (m.) *(JOHR-noh)* day

giovane *(JOH-vah-neh)* young

giovedì (m.) *(joh-veh-DEE)* Thursday

girare *(jee-RAH-reh)* to turn, to tour

giro (m.) *(JEE-roh)* turn, stroll, short walk
fare un giro *(FAH-reh oon . . .)* to go for a walk

gita (f.) *(JEE-tah)* trip, excursion

giù *(joo)* down

giungere *(JOON-jeh-reh)* to arrive, to reach

giusto *(JOO-stoh)* right

godere *(goh-DEH-reh)* to enjoy

gola (f.) *(GOH-lah)* throat
mal di gola *(mahl dee . . .)* sore throat

goloso *(goh-LOH-zoh)* greedy

gomma (f.) *(GOHM-mah)* rubber, gum

gonfiare *(gohn-FYAH-reh)* to swell

gonna (f.) *(GOHN-nah)* skirt

governo (m.) *(goh-VEHR-noh)* government

grande *(GRAHN-deh)* big, great

grano (m.) *(GRAH-noh)* grain (wheat, corn)

grasso *(GRAHS-soh)* fat

gridare *(gree-DAH-reh)* to shout

griglia (f.) *(GREE-lyah)* grill

grosso *(GROHS-soh)* big, large

gruccia (f.) *(GROOT-chah)* (clothes) hanger

guanto (m.) *(GWAHN-toh)* glove

guardare *(gwahr-DAH-reh)* to look at

guasto (m.) *(GWAH-stoh)* damage, breakdown

guida (f.) *(GWEE-dah)* guide, drive

guidare *(gwee-DAH-reh)* to drive, to lead

gustare *(goo-STAH-reh)* to taste

gusto (m.) *(GOO-stoh)* taste

H

hostess (f.) *(OH-stehs)* hostess, stewardess

hotel (m.) *(oh-TEHL)* hotel

I

idea (f.) *(ee-DEH-ah)* idea

idioma (m.) *(ee-DYOH-mah)* idiom, language

ieri *(YEH-ree)* yesterday
  ieri l'altro *(. . . LAHL-troh)* the day before yesterday

illuminato *(eel-loo-mee-NAH-toh)* lit up

imbarcarsi (refl.) *(eem-bahr-KAHR-see)* to embark, to sail

imparare *(eem-pah-RAH-reh)* to learn

impermeabile (m.) *(eem-pehr-meh-AH-bee-leh)* raincoat

impiegare *(eem-pyeh-GAH-reh)* to employ, to use

importante *(eem-pohr-TAHN-teh)* important

importanza (f.) *(eem-pohr-TAHN-tsah)* importance

importo (m.) *(eem-POHR-toh)* amount

impossibile *(eem-pohs-SEE-bee-leh)* impossible

imposta (f.) *(eem-POH-stah)* tax, duty

improvviso *(eem-prohv-VEE-zoh)* sudden
  all'improvviso *(ahl-leem-prohv-VEE-zoh)* suddenly

in *(een)* in, at, to, on, by

incantevole *(een-kahn-TEH-voh-leh)* charming, wonderful

incendio (m.) *(een-CHEHN-dyoh)* fire

incidente (m.) *(een-chee-DEHN-teh)* accident

incontrare *(een-kohn-TRAH-reh)* to meet

incontro (m.) *(een-KOHN-troh)* meeting

incrocio (m.) *(een-KROH-choh)* crossing, crossroads

indicare *(een-dee-KAH-reh)* to show, to point at

indietro *(een-DYEH-troh)* back, backwards, behind

indigestione (f.) *(een-dee-jeh-STYOH-neh)* indigestion

indirizzo (m.) *(een-dee-REET-tsoh)* address

infatti *(een-FAHT-tee)* in fact, as a matter of fact

infermiere(-a) (m.,f.) *(een-fehr-MYEH-reh)(-rah)* nurse

informare *(een-fohr-MAH-reh)* to inform

informazione (f.) *(een-fohr-mah-TSYOH-neh)* information

inglese *(een-GLEH-zeh)* English

ingrandire *(een-grahn-DEE-reh)* to enlarge

ingrassare(-rsi) (refl.) *(een-grahs-SAH-reh)(-SAHR-see)* to gain/put on weight

ingresso (m.) *(een-GREHS-soh)* entry, entrance, admission

inizio (m.) *(ee-NEE-tsyoh)* beginning

inoltre *(ee-NOHL-treh)* besides

insalata (f.) *(een-sah-LAH-tah)* salad

insegnante (m./f.) *(een-seh-NYAHN-teh)* teacher

insegnare *(een-seh-NYAH-reh)* to teach

insieme *(een-SYEH-meh)* together

insipido *(een-SEE-pee-doh)* tasteless

interessante *(een-teh-rehs-SAHN-teh)* interesting

interessare *(een-teh-rehs-SAH-reh)* to interest

interessarsi di (refl.) *(een-teh-rehs-SAHR-see dee)* to be interested in

intero *(een-TEH-roh)* whole, all

invece *(een-VEH-cheh)* on the contrary, instead

inverno (m.) *(een-VEHR-noh)* winter

inviare *(een-VYAH-reh)* to send, to forward

invitare *(een-vee-TAH-reh)* to invite

io *(EE-oh)* I

isola (f.) *(EE-zoh-lah)* island

Italia (f.) *(ee-TAH-lyah)* Italy

italiano(-a) *(ee-tah-LYAH-noh)(-nah)* Italian

L

là *(lah)* there

labbro (m.) *(LAHB-broh)* lip

ladro (m.) *(LAH-droh)* thief, burglar

laggiù *(lahd-JOO)* down there

lago (m.) *(LAH-goh)* lake

lampada (f.) *(LAHM-pah-dah)* lamp

lampo (m.) *(LAHM-poh)* lightning

lana (f.) *(LAH-nah)* wool

lanciare *(lahn-CHAH-reh)* to throw

largo *(LAHR-goh)* wide

lasciapassare (m.) *(lah-shah-pahs-SAH-reh)* pass

lasciare *(lah-SHAH-reh)* to leave, to let

lato (m.) *(LAH-toh)* side

latte (m.) *(LAHT-teh)* milk

lattina (f.) *(laht-TEE-nah)* can (soft drinks, beer)

lattuga (f.) *(laht-TOO-gah)* lettuce

lavanderia (f.) *(lah-vahn-deh-REE-ah)* laundry

lavandino (m.) *(lah-vahn-DEE-noh)* sink

lavare *(lah-VAH-reh)* to wash

lavasecco (m.) *(lah-vah-SEHK-koh)* dry cleaner

lavorare *(lah-voh-RAH-reh)* to work

lavoro (m.) *(lah-VOH-roh)* work

legge (f.) *(LEHD-jeh)* law

leggere *(LEHD-jeh-reh)* to read

leggero *(lehd-JEH-roh)* light

legno (m.) *(LEH-nyoh)* wood *(legume (m.) (leh-GOO-meh)* vegetable

lei *(lay)* she, her

lentamente *(lehn-tah-MEHN-teh)* slowly

lento *(LEHN-toh)* slow

lenzuolo (m.) *(lehn-TSWOH-loh)* bedsheet

lettera (f.) *(LEHT-teh-rah)* letter

letto (m.) *(LEHT-toh)* bed

  letto matrimoniale *(. . . mah-tree-moh-NYAH-leh)* double bed

  letti gemelli *(LEHT-tee jeh-MEHL-lee)* twin beds

lezione (f.) *(leh-TSYOH-neh)* lesson

lì *(lee)* there

libero *(LEE-beh-roh)* free

libreria (f.) *(lee-breh-REE-ah)* bookstore

libro (m.) *(LEE-broh)* book

lieto *(LYEH-toh)* happy, glad

limite (m.) *(LEE-mee-teh)* limit

  limite di velocità *(. . . dee veh-loh-chee-TAH)* speed limit

limonata (f.) *(lee-moh-NAH-tah)* lemonade

limone (m.) *(lee-MOH-neh)* lemon

linea (f.) *(LEE-neh-ah)* line

lingua (f.) *(LEEN-gwah)* tongue, language

linguaggio (m.) *(leen-GWAHD-joh)* language

lino (m.) *(LEE-noh)* linen

liscio *(LEE-shoh)* smooth

lista (f.) *(LEE-stah)* list
  lista dei vini *(. . . day VEE-nee)* wine list
litro (m.) *(LEE-troh)* liter
locale *(loh-KAH-leh)* local
  locale (m.) room
  locale notturno (m.) *(. . . noht-TOOR-noh)* nightclub
lontano *(lohn-TAH-noh)* far
loro *(LOH-roh)* they, them
luce (f.) *(LOO-cheh)* light
  accendere la luce *(aht-CHEHN-deh-reh lah . . .)* to put/turn the light on
  spegnere la luce *(SPEH-nyeh-reh lah . . .)* to put/turn the light off
lui *(LOO-ee)* he, him
luminoso *(loo-mee-NOH-zoh)* bright
luna (f.) *(LOO-nah)* moon
lungo *(LOON-goh)* long
luogo (m.) *(LWOH-goh)* place
lusso (m.) *(LOOS-soh)* luxury

M

ma *(mah)* but
macchiato *(mahk-KYAH-toh)* stained, spotted
macchina (f.) *(MAHK-kee-nah)* car, automobile, machine
macelleria (f.) *(mah-chehl-leh-REE-ah)* butcher's shop
madre (f.) *(MAH-dreh)* mother
maggiore *(mahd-JOH-reh)* older, the oldest (age)
maglietta (f.) *(mah-LYEHT-tah)* T-shirt
magnifico *(mah-NYEE-fee-koh)* magnificent
magro *(MAH-groh)* thin
mai *(mahy)* never
maiale (m.) *(mah-YAH-leh)* pig, pork
mais (m.) *(MAH-ees)* corn

malato *(mah-LAH-toh)* ill
malattia (f.) *(mah-laht-TEE-ah)* illness
male (m.) *(MAH-leh)* pain
mal di testa *(. . . dee TEH-stah)* headache
maleducato *(mah-leh-doo-KAH-toh)* rude
mamma (f.) *(MAHM-mah)* mom
mancare *(mahn-KAH-reh)* to lack, to miss
mancia (f.) *(MAHN-chah)* tip
  dare la mancia *(DAH-reh lah . . .)* to tip
mandare *(mahn-DAH-reh)* to send
mangiare *(mahn-JAH-reh)* to eat
maniera (f.) *(mah-NYEH-rah)* manner, fashion, way
mano (f.) *(MAH-noh)* hand
mantenere *(mahn-teh-NEH-reh)* to keep
manzo (m.) *(MAHN-dzoh)* beef
mappa (f.) *(MAHP-pah)* map
marciapiede (m.) *(mahr-chah-PYEH-deh)* sidewalk
mare (m.) *(MAH-reh)* sea
marito (m.) *(mah-REE-toh)* husband
marmo (m.) *(MAHR-moh)* marble
marrone *(mahr-ROH-neh)* brown
maschio (m.) *(MAH-skyoh)* male
massimo *(MAHS-see-moh)* greatest, maximum
materasso (m.) *(mah-teh-RAHS-soh)* mattress
matita (f.) *(mah-TEE-tah)* pencil
matrimonio (m.) *(mah-tree-MOH-nyoh)* marriage
mattina(-o) (m.,f.) *(maht-TEE-nah)(-noh)* morning

matto *(MAHT-toh)* mad, crazy

medicina (f.) *(meh-dee-CHEE-nah)* medicine

medico (m.) *(MEH-dee-koh)* doctor

meglio *(MEH-lyoh)* better

mela (f.) *(MEH-lah)* apple

memoria (f.) *(meh-MOH-ryah)* memory

meno *(MEH-noh)* less

mente (f.) *(MEHN-teh)* mind
  venire in mente *(veh-NEE-reh een . . .)* to remember, to come to mind

mentre *(MEHN-treh)* while

meraviglioso *(meh-rah-vee-LYOH-zoh)* wonderful

mercato (m.) *(mehr-KAH-toh)* market
  a buon mercato *(ah bwohn . . .)* cheap, low-priced

meridionale *(meh-ree-dyoh-NAH-leh)* southern

mescolare *(meh-skoh-LAH-reh)* to mix

mese (m.) *(MEH-zeh)* month

messa (f.) *(MEHS-sah)* (Catholic) mass

messaggio (m.) *(mehs-SAHD-joh)* message

metà (f.) *(meh-TAH)* half

metro (m.) *(MEH-troh)* meter

metropolitana (f.) *(meh-troh-poh-lee-TAH-nah)* subway

mettere *(MEHT-teh-reh)* to put, to put on, to wear

mezzanotte (f.) *(mehd-dzah-NOHT-teh)* midnight

mezzo *(MEHD-dzoh)* half

mezzogiorno (m.) *(mehd-dzoh-JOHR-noh)* noon

miele (m.) *(MYEH-leh)* honey

migliore *(mee-LYOH-reh)* better, the best

minestra in brodo (f.) *(mee-NEH-strah een BROH-doh)* soup

minimo *(MEE-nee-moh)* minimum, slightest, smallest

minore *(mee-NOH-reh)* younger, the youngest (age)

minuto (m.) *(mee-NOO-toh)* minute

misura (f.) *(mee-ZOO-rah)* measure, size

mobile (m.) *(MOH-bee-leh)* piece of furniture

moda (f.) *(MOH-dah)* fashion

modo (m.) *(MOH-doh)* way

moglie (f.) *(MOH-lyeh)* wife

molle *(MOHL-leh)* soft

molto *(MOHL-toh)* much, very

momento (m.) *(moh-MEHN-toh)* moment

mondo (m.) *(MOHN-doh)* world

moneta (f.) *(moh-NEH-tah)* coin

montagna (f.); monte (m.) *(mohn-TAH-nyah; MOHN-teh)* mountain

monumento (m.) *(moh-noo-MEHN-toh)* monument

morbido *(MOHR-bee-doh)* soft

morire *(moh-REE-reh)* to die

morto *(MOHR-toh)* dead

morso (m.) *(MOHR-soh)* bite

morte (f.) *(MOHR-teh)* death

mostra (f.) *(MOH-strah)* show, exhibition

mostrare *(moh-STRAH-reh)* to show

motocicletta (f.) *(moh-toh-chee-KLEHT-tah)* motorcycle

motore (m.) *(moh-TOH-reh)* motor

motorino (m.) *(moh-toh-REE-noh)* moped

motoscafo (m.) *(moh-toh-SKAH-foh)* motorboat

multa (f.) *(MOOL-tah)* fine, ticket

muoversi (refl.) *(MWOH-vehr-see)* to move
  muoviti! *(MWOH-vee-tee!)* hurry up!

muro (m.) *(MOO-roh)* wall

museo (m.) *(moo-ZEH-oh)* museum

musica (f.) *(MOO-zee-kah)* music

mutande (f.pl.) *(moo-TAHN-deh)* underpants

N

nascere *(NAH-sheh-reh)* to be born

  nato *(NAH-toh)* born

naso (m.) *(NAH-zoh)* nose

nativo *(nah-TEE-voh)* native

natura (f.) *(nah-TOO-rah)* nature

naturale *(nah-too-RAH-leh)* natural

naturalmente *(nah-too-rahl-MEHN-teh)* naturally

nausea (f.) *(NOW-zeh-ah)* nausea

nave (f.) *(NAH-veh)* ship

nazionale *(nah-tsyoh-NAH-leh)* national

necessario *(neh-chehs-SAH-ryoh)* necessary

necessità (f.) *(neh-chehs-see-TAH)* necessity, need

negativa (f.) *(neh-gah-TEE-vah)* negative (film)

negozio (m.) *(neh-GOH-tsyoh)* shop, store

nero *(NEH-roh)* black

nervoso *(nehr-VOH-zoh)* nervous

nessuno *(nehs-SOO-noh)* nobody, no one

neve (f.) *(NEH-veh)* snow

nevicare *(neh-vee-KAH-reh)* to snow

niente *(NYEHN-teh)* nothing

nipote (m./f.) *(nee-POH-teh)* nephew, niece, grandson, granddaughter

no *(noh)* no

noi *(noy)* we, us

noia (f.) *(NOH-yah)* boredom

noleggiare *(noh-lehd-JAH-reh)* to hire, to rent

nome (m.) *(NOH-meh)* name

non *(nohn)* not

nonna (f.) *(NOHN-nah)* grandmother

nonno (m.) *(NOHN-noh)* grandfather

nord (m.) *(nohrd)* north

normale *(nohr-MAH-leh)* normal

nostro *(NOH-stroh)* our, ours

nota (f.) *(NOH-tah)* note

notare *(noh-TAH-reh)* to note, to notice

notizia (f.) *(noh-TEE-tsyah)* news

noto *(NOH-toh)* well-known

notte (f.) *(NOHT-teh)* night

nozze (f.pl.) *(NOHT-tseh)* wedding

nube (f.) *(NOO-beh)* cloud

nubile *(NOO-bee-leh)* unmarried, single (woman)

nudo *(NOO-doh)* naked

numero (m.) *(NOO-meh-roh)* number

nuotare *(nwoh-TAH-reh)* to swim

nuovo *(NWOH-voh)* new

nuvoloso *(noo-voh-LOH-zoh)* cloudy

O

o *(oh)* or

obbligo (m.) *(OHB-blee-goh)* obligation

occasione (f.) *(ohk-kah-ZYOH-neh)* occasion, opportunity, bargain

occhiali (m.pl.) *(ohk-KYAH-lee)* eyeglasses

  occhiali da sole *(. . . dah SOH-leh)* sunglasses

occhio (m.) *(OHK-kyoh)* eye

occidentale *(oht-chee-dehn-TAH-leh)* western

occorrere *(ohk-KOHR-reh-reh)* to want, to need

occupare *(ohk-koo-PAH-reh)* to occupy

occupato *(ohk-koo-PAH-toh)* taken, busy

oculista *(m./f.)* *(oh-koo-LEE-stah)* eye doctor

odio *(m.)* *(OH-dyoh)* hate

odore *(m.)* *(oh-DOH-reh)* smell, scent

odori *(m.pl.)* *(oh-DOH-ree)* herbs

offerta *(f.)* *(ohf-FEHR-tah)* offer

offrire *(ohf-FREE-reh)* to offer
offerto *(ohf-FEHR-toh)* offered

oggi *(OHD-jee)* today

ogni *(OH-nyee)* every, each

ognuno *(oh-NYOO-noh)* everybody, everyone

olio *(m.)* *(OH-lyoh)* oil

oliva *(f.)* *(oh-LEE-vah)* olive

oltre *(OHL-treh)* beyond

ombra *(f.)* *(OHM-brah)* shade, shadow

ombrello *(m.)* *(ohm-BREHL-loh)* umbrella

onesto *(oh-NEH-stoh)* honest

opera *(f.)* *(OH-peh-rah)* work, opera

operaio *(m.)* *(oh-peh-RAH-yoh)* worker, workman

operare *(oh-peh-RAH-reh)* to operate

opinione *(f.)* *(oh-pee-NYOH-neh)* opinion

opposto *(ohp-POH-stoh)* opposite

oppure *(ohp-POO-reh)* or, otherwise

ora *(f.)* *(OH-rah)* hour

ora *(adv.)* now

orario *(m.)* *(oh-RAH-ryoh)* timetable, schedule
essere in orario *(EHS-seh-reh een . . .)* to be on time

orchestra *(f.)* *(ohr-KEH-strah)* orchestra

ordinare *(ohr-dee-NAH-reh)* to order

ordinario *(ohr-dee-NAH-ryoh)* ordinary, common

ordine *(m.)* *(OHR-dee-neh)* order

orecchino *(m.)* *(oh-rehk-KEE-noh)* earring

orecchio *(m.)* *(oh-REHK-kyoh)* ear

orientale *(oh-ryehn-TAH-leh)* eastern, oriental

orientarsi *(refl.)* *(oh-ryehn-TAHR-see)* to find one's way

originale *(oh-ree-jee-NAH-leh)* original

origine *(f.)* *(oh-REE-jee-neh)* origin, beginning

ormai *(ohr-MAHY)* by

ornare *(ohr-NAH-reh)* to adorn, to decorate

oro *(m.)* *(OH-roh)* gold

orologeria *(f.)* *(oh-roh-loh-jeh-REE-ah)* watchmaker's shop

orologio *(m.)* *(oh-roh-LOH-joh)* watch, klock
orologio da polso *(. . . dah POHL-soh)* wristwatch

orribile *(ohr-REE-bee-leh)* horrible

orso *(m.)* *(OHR-soh)* bear

oscurità *(f.)* *(oh-skoo-ree-TAH)* darkness

ospedale *(m.)* *(oh-speh-DAH-leh)* hospital

ospite *(m./f.)* *(OH-spee-teh)* guest

osservare *(ohs-sehr-VAH-reh)* to observe

ostello *(m.)* *(oh-STEHL-loh)* youth hostel

osteria *(f.)* *(oh-steh-REE-ah)* tavern

ottico *(m.)* *(OHT-tee-koh)* optician

ottimo *(OHT-tee-moh)* very good, excellent

ovest (m.) *(OH-vehst)* west

P

pacchetto (m.) *(pahk-KEHT-toh)* pack, packet

pacco (m.) *(PAHK-koh)* parcel

padre (m.) *(PAH-dreh)* father

padrone (m.) *(pah-DROH-neh)* master, landlord, owner

paesaggio (m.) *(pah-eh-ZAHD-joh)* landscape

paese (m.) *(pah-EH-zeh)* country, land

pagare *(pah-GAH-reh)* to pay

pagina (f.) *(PAH-jee-nah)* page

paio (m.) *(PAH-yoh)* pair, couple

palazzo (m.) *(pah-LAHT-tsoh)* palace, building

palco (m.) *(PAHL-koh)* box

palestra (f.) *(pah-LEH-strah)* gym

palla (f.) *(PAHL-lah)* ball

pallido *(PAHL-lee-doh)* pale

pallone (m.) *(pahl-LOH-neh)* ball

pancetta (f.) *(pahn-CHEHT-tah)* bacon

pane (m.) *(PAH-neh)* bread

panificio (m.) *(pah-nee-FEE-choh)* bakery

panino (m.) *(pah-NEE-noh)* roll (bread)

panna (f.) *(PAHN-nah)* heavy cream

panne, in (f.) *(een-PAHN-neh)* breakdown (car)

pannolino (m.) *(pahn-noh-LEE-noh)* diaper

pantaloni (m.pl.) *(pahn-tah-LOH-nee)* trousers, pants

Papa (m.) *(PAH-pah)* pope

parabrezza (m.) *(pah-rah-BREHD-dzah)* windshield

paradiso (m.) *(pah-rah-DEE-zoh)* paradise

paragone (m.) *(pah-rah-GOH-neh)* comparison

parcheggio (m.) *(pahr-KEHD-joh)* parking lot

parchimetro (m.) *(pahr-KEE-meh-troh)* parking meter

parco (m.) *(PAHR-koh)* park

parere *(pah-REH-reh)* to seem, to look, to appear

parete (f.) *(pah-REH-teh)* wall

parlare *(pahr-LAH-reh)* to speak, to talk

parola (f.) *(pah-ROH-lah)* word

parte (f.) *(PAHR-teh)* part

partenza (f.) *(pahr-TEHN-tsah)* departure

particolare *(pahr-tee-koh-LAH-reh)* particular, special

partire *(pahr-TEE-reh)* to leave

partita (f.) *(pahr-TEE-tah)* game, match

Pasqua (f.) *(PAH-skwah)* Easter

passaggio (m.) *(pahs-SAHD-joh)* passage, passing, passageway

passare *(pahs-SAH-reh)* to pass

passato *(pahs-SAH-toh)* past

passeggiata (f.) *(pahs-sehd-JAH-tah)* walk, stroll

  fare una passeggiata *(FAH-reh OO-nah . . .)* to go for a walk

pasta (f.) *(PAH-stah)* dough, pasta, pastry

pasticceria (f.) *(pah-steet-cheh-REE-ah)* pastry shop

pasticcino (m.) *(pah-steet-CHEE-noh)* pastry, cookie

pasto (m.) *(PAH-stoh)* meal

patente (f.) *(pah-TEHN-teh)* license

patria (f.) *(PAH-tryah)* country

patto (m.) *(PAHT-toh)* pact, agreement

pattumiera (f.) *(paht-too-MYEH-rah)* garbage can

paura (f.) *(pah-OO-rah)* fear

pavimento (m.) *(pah-vee-MEHN-toh)* floor

pazienza (f.) *(pah-TSYEHN-tsah)* patience

pazzo *(PAHT-tsoh)* mad, crazy

peccato (m.) *(pehk-KAH-toh)* sin
che peccato! *(keh . . . !)* what a pity!

pedaggio (m.) *(peh-DAHD-joh)* toll

pedone (m.) *(peh-DOH-neh)* pedestrian

peggio, peggiore *(PEHD-joh, pehd-JOH-reh)* worse, the worst

pelle (f.) *(PEHL-leh)* skin, complexion

pelliccia (f.) *(pehl-LEET-chah)* fur

pellicola (f.) *(pehl-LEE-koh-lah)* film

pelo (m.) *(PEH-loh)* hair (body)

pensare *(pehn-SAH-reh)* to think

pensiero (m.) *(pehn-SYEH-roh)* thought

pensione (f.) *(pehn-SYOH-neh)* pension, boarding house
pensione completa *(. . . kohm-PLEH-tah)* full board

pepe (m.) *(PEH-peh)* pepper

per *(pehr)* for

perché *(pehr-KEH)* because, why

percorso (m.) *(pehr-KOHR-soh)* run, distance, way

perdere *(PEHR-deh-reh)* to lose
perduto, perso *(pehr-DOO-toh, PEHR-soh)* lost

perdita (f.) *(PEHR-dee-tah)* loss

perdonare *(pehr-doh-NAH-reh)* to forgive

perfetto *(pehr-FEHT-toh)* perfect

pericoloso *(peh-ree-koh-LOH-zoh)* dangerous

periferia (f.) *(peh-ree-feh-REE-ah)* suburbs

permanenza (f.) *(pehr-mah-NEHN-tsah)* stay, sojourn

permesso (m.) *(pehr-MEHS-soh)* permission

permettere *(pehr-MEHT-teh-reh)* to allow, to let, to permit

persona (f.) *(pehr-SOH-nah)* person

personale *(pehr-soh-NAH-leh)* personal

pesante *(peh-ZAHN-teh)* heavy

pesca (f.) *(PEH-skah)* peach, fishing

pesce (m.) *(PEH-sheh)* fish

peso (m.) *(PEH-zoh)* weight

pettine (m.) *(PEHT-tee-neh)* comb

petto (m.) *(PEHT-toh)* breast, chest

pezzo (m.) *(PEHT-tsoh)* piece

phon (m.) *(fohn)* hair dryer

piacere *(pyah-CHEH-reh)* to like
mi piace/piacciono *(mee PYAH-cheh/PYAHT-choh-noh)* I like
piacere (m.) pleasure

piangere *(PYAHN-jeh-reh)* to cry, to weep

piano *(PYAH-noh)* flat, even

piano (m.) floor, plan

pianta (f.) *(PYAHN-tah)* plant

piatto *(PYAHT-toh)* flat
piatto (m.) plate

piazza (f.) *(PYAHT-tsah)* square

piccante *(peek-KAHN-teh)* sharp, spicy, hot

piccolo *(PEEK-koh-loh)* small

piede (m.) *(PYEH-deh)* foot

  a piedi *(ah PYEH-dee)* on foot

pieno *(PYEH-noh)* full

pietanza (f.) *(pyeh-TAHN-tsah)* main course, dish

pietra (f.) *(PYEH-trah)* stone

pila (f.) *(PEE-lah)* battery

pioggia (f.) *(PYOHD-jah)* rain

piovere *(PYOH-veh-reh)* to rain

  piove *(PYOH-veh)* it's raining

pittura (f.) *(peet-TOO-rah)* painting

più *(pyoo)* more, the most

piuttosto *(pyoot-TOH-stoh)* rather

platea (f.) *(plah-TEH-ah)* orchestra (theater)

pneumatico (m.) *(pneh-oo-MAH-tee-koh)* tire

po'; poco *(poh, POH-koh)* little

  un po'; un poco *(oon . . .)* a little (of), some

poi *(poy)* then, afterwards, later

politica (f.) *(poh-LEE-tee-kah)* politics

polizia (f.) *(poh-lee-TSEE-ah)* police

pollo (m.) *(POHL-loh)* chicken

polmone (m.) *(pohl-MOH-neh)* lung

pomeriggio (m.) *(poh-meh-REED-joh)* afternoon

pomodoro (m.) *(poh-moh-DOH-roh)* tomato

ponte (m.) *(POHN-teh)* bridge

popolo (m.) *(POH-poh-loh)* people

porta (f.) *(POHR-tah)* door

portabagagli (m.) *(pohr-tah-bah-GAH-lyee)* porter, luggage rack (train, car)

portafoglio (m.) *(pohr-tah-FOH-lyoh)* wallet

portare *(pohr-TAH-reh)* to bring, to carry, to wear

portata (f.) *(pohr-TAH-tah)* course (meal)

porto (m.) *(POHR-toh)* harbor

posizione (f.) *(poh-zee-TSYOH-neh)* position

possibile *(pohs-SEE-bee-leh)* possible

posta (f.) *(POH-stah)* mail

  posta aerea *(. . . ah-EH-reh-ah)* airmail

posta elettronica (f.) *(POH-stah eh-leh-TROH-nee-kah)* e-mail

posteggio (m.) *(poh-STEHD-joh)* parking lot/space

  posteggio taxi *(. . . TAHK-see)* taxi stand

posto (m.) *(POH-stoh)* place, job, position

potere *(poh-TEH-reh)* can, to be able

potere (m.) power

povero *(POH-veh-roh)* poor

pranzo (m.) *(PRAHN-dzoh)* lunch

preciso *(preh-CHEE-zoh)* precise

preferire *(preh-feh-REE-reh)* to prefer

pregare *(preh-GAH-reh)* to pray

premio (m.) *(PREH-myoh)* prize

prendere *(PREHN-deh-reh)* to take

prenotazione (f.) *(preh-noh-tah-TSYOH-neh)* booking, reservation

preoccuparsi (refl.) *(preh-ohk-koo-PAHR-see)* to worry

  non si preoccupi *(nohn see preh-OHK-koo-pee)* don't worry (formal)

preparare *(preh-pah-RAH-reh)* to prepare

presentare *(preh-zehn-TAH-reh)* to present, to introduce

pressione (f.) *(prehs-SYOH-neh)* pressure

prestare *(preh-STAH-reh)* to lend

presto *(PREH-stoh)* soon

prezzo (m.) *(PREHT-tsoh)* price

prima *(PREE-mah)* before

primavera (f.) *(pree-mah-VEH-rah)* spring

primo *(PREE-moh)* first

probabile *(proh-BAH-bee-leh)* probable, likely

procedere *(proh-CHEH-deh-reh)* to proceed

procurare *(proh-koo-RAH-reh)* to get

produrre *(proh-DOOR-reh)* to produce

professione (f.) *(proh-fehs-SYOH-neh)* profession

professore (m.) *(proh-fehs-SOH-reh)* professor, teacher

profondo *(proh-FOHN-doh)* deep

profumo (m.) *(proh-FOO-moh)* perfume, scent

proibito *(proh-ee-BEE-toh)* forbidden

promessa (f.) *(proh-MEHS-sah)* promise

promettere *(proh-MEHT-teh-reh)* to promise

pronto *(PROHN-toh)* ready, hello (phone)

pronuncia (f.) *(proh-NOON-chah)* pronunciation

pronunciare *(proh-noon-CHAH-reh)* to pronounce

proprietà (f.) *(proh-pryeh-TAH)* property

proprietario (m.) *(proh-pryeh-TAH-ryoh)* owner

prossimo *(PROHS-see-moh)* next

protestante *(proh-teh-STAHN-teh)* Protestant

protezione (f.) *(proh-teh-TSYOH-neh)* protection

pugno (m.) *(POO-nyoh)* fist

pulire *(poo-LEE-reh)* to clean

pulito *(poo-LEE-toh)* clean

punto (m.) *(POON-toh)* point, moment

puntuale *(poon-TWAH-leh)* punctual

puntura (f.) *(poon-TOO-rah)* injection, shot, sting

puro *(POO-roh)* pure

puzzare *(poot-TSAH-reh)* to stink, to smell bad

Q

qua *(kwah)* here

quadro (m.) *(KWAH-droh)* picture, painting

qualche *(KWAHL-keh)* some, a few

qualcosa *(kwahl-KOH-zah)* something

qualcuno *(kwahl-KOO-noh)* someone

quale *(KWAH-leh)* which, what

qualità (f.) *(kwah-lee-TAH)* quality

qualsiasi; qualunque *(kwahl-SEE-ah-see, kwah-LOON-kweh)* any, whatever

quando *(KWAHN-doh)* when

quantità (f.) *(kwahn-tee-TAH)* quantity

quanto *(KWAHN-toh)* how much, how many, as many as

quartiere (m.) *(kwahr-TYEH-reh)* neighborhood, section

quasi *(KWAH-zee)* almost

quello *(KWEHL-loh)* that

questione (f.) *(kweh-STYOH-neh)* matter

questo *(KWEH-stoh)* this

qui *(kwee)* here

quiete (f.) *(kwee-EH-teh)* calm

quieto *(kwee-EH-toh)* quiet, calm

quindi *(KWEEN-dee)* therefore

quotidiano *(kwoh-tee-DYAH-noh)* daily

quotidiano (m.) daily newspaper

R

raccomandare *(rahk-koh-mahn-DAH-reh)* to recommend

racconto (m.) *(rahk-KOHN-toh)* story, tale

radersi (refl.) *(RAH-dehr-see)* to shave

radio (f.) *(RAH-dyoh)* radio

radiografia (f.) *(rah-dyoh-grah-FEE-ah)* X-ray

raffreddore (m.) *(rahf-frehd-DOH-reh)* cold

ragazza (f.) *(rah-GAHT-tsah)* girl

ragazzo (m.) *(rah-GAHT-tsoh)* boy

raggiungere *(rahd-JOON-jeh-reh)* to reach, to arrive

ragione (f.) *(rah-JOH-neh)* reason
   aver ragione *(ah-VEHR . . .)* to be right

ragù (m.) *(rah-GOO)* meat sauce

rallentare *(rahl-lehn-TAH-reh)* to slow down

rapido *(RAH-pee-doh)* swift, quick

raro *(RAH-roh)* rare

rasarsi (refl.) *(rah-ZAHR-see)* to shave

rasoio (m.) *(rah-ZOH-yoh)* razor

razza (f.) *(RAHT-tsah)* race

re (m.) *(reh)* king

reale *(reh-AH-leh)* real, royal

realizzare *(reh-ah-leed-DZAH-reh)* to carry out, to achieve

recente *(reh-CHEHN-teh)* recent

recitare *(reh-chee-TAH-reh)* to act, to play

regalo (m.) *(reh-GAH-loh)* present, gift

reggia (f.) *(REHD-jah)* royal palace

reggipetto; reggiseno (m.) *(rehd-jee-PEHT-toh, rehd-jee-SEH-noh)* bra

regina (f.) *(reh-JEE-nah)* queen

regista (m./f.) *(reh-JEE-stah)* director (movie)

registrare *(reh-jee-STRAH-reh)* to record, to register

regola (f.) *(REH-goh-lah)* rule

regolare *(reh-goh-LAH-reh)* to adjust, to regulate

rendere *(REHN-deh-reh)* to give back, to return

reparto (m.) *(reh-PAHR-toh)* department

residenza (f.) *(reh-zee-DEHN-tsah)* residence

respirare *(reh-spee-RAH-reh)* to breathe

respiro (m.) *(reh-SPEE-roh)* breath

resto (m.) *(REH-stoh)* change (money)

rialzo (m.) *(ree-AHL-tsoh)* rise, increase

ribasso (m.) *(ree-BAHS-soh)* fall, drop

ricambio (m.) *(ree-KAHM-byoh)* replacement

ricchezza (f.) *(reek-KEHT-tsah)* wealth

riccio (m.) *(REET-choh)* curl, curly

ricco *(REEK-koh)* rich

ricetta (f.) *(ree-CHEHT-tah)* recipe, prescription

ricevere *(ree-CHEH-veh-reh)* to receive

ricevuta (f.) *(ree-cheh-VOO-tah)* receipt

ricevimento (m.) *(reh-chee-vee-MEN-toh)* reception

richiedere *(ree-KYEH-deh-reh)* to ask for

richiesta (f.) *(ree-KYEH-stah)* request

riconoscere *(ree-koh-NOH-sheh-reh)* to recognize

ricordare *(ree-kohr-DAH-reh)* to remember

ricordo (m.) *(ree-KOHR-doh)* recollection, souvenir

ridere *(REE-deh-reh)* to laugh

ridotto *(ree-DOHT-toh)* reduced, discounted

riduzione (f.) *(ree-doo-TSYOH-neh)* reduction, discount

rientrare *(ryehn-TRAH-reh)* to reenter, to go back

rifare *(ree-FAH-reh)* to do/make again, to re-make, to make (a bed)

riga (f.) *(REE-gah)* line

riguardo (m.) *(ree-GWAHR-doh)* regard, care, respect

rilassarsi (refl.) *(ree-lahs-SAHR-see)* to relax

rimanere *(ree-mah-NEH-reh)* to stay, to remain, to be left

rimborsare *(reem-bohr-SAH-reh)* to refund

rimborso (m.) *(reem-BOHR-soh)* refund

rimescolare *(ree-meh-skoh-LAH-reh)* to mix, to stir

rinfresco (m.) *(reen-FREH-skoh)* refreshments

ringraziamento (m.) *(reen-grah-tsyah-MEHN-toh)* thanks

ringraziare *(reen-grah-TSYAH-reh)* to thank

ripetere *(ree-PEH-teh-reh)* to repeat

riposare *(ree-poh-ZAH-reh)* to rest, to sleep

riscaldamento (m.) *(ree-skahl-dah-MEHN-toh)* heating

riscaldare *(ree-skahl-DAH-reh)* to warm up, to heat

riscuotere *(ree-SKWOH-teh-reh)* to cash, to collect

riso (m.) *(REE-zoh)* rice, laugh, laughter

risparmiare *(ree-spahr-MYAH-reh)* to save

rispetto (m.) *(ree-SPEHT-toh)* respect

rispondere *(ree-SPOHN-deh-reh)* to answer

risposta (f.) *(ree-SPOH-stah)* answer, reply

ristorante (m.) *(ree-stoh-RAHN-teh)* restaurant

ritardo (m.) *(ree-TAHR-doh)* delay

essere in ritardo *(EHS-seh-reh een . . .)* to be late

ritornare *(ree-tohr-NAH-reh)* to return, to come back

ritratto (m.) *(ree-TRAHT-toh)* portrait

riuscire *(ryoo-SHEE-reh)* to succeed

rivista (f.) *(ree-VEE-stah)* magazine

rivolgere; rivolgersi (refl.) *(ree-VOHL-jeh-reh; ree-VOHL-jehr-see)* to turn around, to revolve; to address oneself

roba (f.) *(ROH-bah)* stuff

romanzo (m.) *(roh-MAHN-dzoh)* novel

rompere *(ROHM-peh-reh)* to break

rotto *(ROHT-toh)* broken

rosa *(ROH-zah)* pink

rosa (f.) rose

rosso *(ROHS-soh)* red

rovina (f.) *(roh-VEE-nah)* ruin

rovinare *(roh-vee-NAH-reh)* to ruin, to spoil
　rovinato *(roh-vee-NAH-toh)* ruined
rubrica (f.) *(roo-BREE-kah)* address book
rullino (m.) *(rool-LEE-noh)* roll of film
rumore (m.) *(roo-MOH-reh)* noise
rumoroso *(roo-moh-ROH-zoh)* noisy
ruota (f.) *(RWOH-tah)* wheel

S

sabbia (f.) *(SAHB-byah)* sand
sacchetto (m.) *(sahk-KEHT-toh)* small bag
sala (f.) *(SAH-lah)* room
sale (m.) *(SAH-leh)* salt
salire *(sah-LEE-reh)* to get on/into, to go up
salone (m.) *(sah-LOH-neh)* parlor, hall
salotto (m.) *(sah-LOHT-toh)* living room
salsa (f.) *(SAHL-sah)* sauce
saltare *(sahl-TAH-reh)* to jump
salutare *(sah-loo-TAH-reh)* to greet
salute (f.) *(sah-LOO-teh)* health
　salute! to your health! cheers!
saluto (m.) *(sah-LOO-toh)* greeting
salvietta (f.) *(sahl-VYEHT-tah)* (table) napkin, towel
sangue (m.) *(SAHN-gweh)* blood
sano *(SAH-noh)* healthy
sapere *(sah-PEH-reh)* to know
saponetta (f.) *(sah-poh-NEHT-tah)* soap
sapore (m.) *(sah-POH-reh)* taste

sbagliare *(zbah-LYAH-reh)* to make a mistake
sbaglio (m.) *(ZBAH-lyoh)* mistake, error
sbarcare *(zbahr-KAH-reh)* to land
sbrigarsi (refl.) *(zbree-GAHR-see)* to hurry up
　sbrigati! *(ZBREE-gah-tee)* hurry up! (familiar)
scala (f.) *(SKAH-lah)* staircase, stairs
scalare *(skah-LAH-reh)* to climb up
scalo (m.) *(SKAH-loh)* stop (airline)
scambio (m.) *(SKAHM-byoh)* exchange
scantinato (m.) *(skahn-tee-NAH-toh)* basement
scarpa (f.) *(SKAHR-pah)* shoe
scatola (f.) *(SKAH-toh-lah)* box
scegliere *(SHEH-lyeh-reh)* to choose
scelta (f.) *(SHEHL-tah)* choice
scendere *(SHEHN-deh-reh)* to go down, to get off
scherzo (m.) *(SKEHR-tsoh)* joke
schiena (f.) *(SKYEH-nah)* back
sci (m.pl.) *(shee)* ski
sciampo *(SHAHM-poh)* shampoo
sciare *(shee-AH-reh)* to ski
sciarpa (f.) *(SHAHR-pah)* scarf
sciogliere *(SHOH-lyeh-reh)* to loosen, to undo, to melt
sciovia (f.) *(shee-oh-VEE-ah)* ski lift
scivolare *(shee-voh-LAH-reh)* to slide, to slip
scomodo *(SKOH-moh-doh)* uncomfortable
scomparire *(skohm-pah-REE-reh)* to disappear
scompartimento (m.) *(skohm-pahr-tee-MEHN-toh)* compartment

sconto (m.) *(SKOHN-toh)* discount

scontrino (m.) *(skohn-TREE-noh)* ticket, receipt

scontro (m.) *(SKOHN-troh)* clash, collision

scoprire *(skoh-PREE-reh)* to discover

scordare *(skohr-DAH-reh)* to forget

scorrere *(SKOHR-reh-reh)* to run, to flow

scorso *(SKOHR-soh)* last, past

scortese *(skohr-TEH-zeh)* rude, impolite

scottare *(skoht-TAH-reh)* to burn, to scald

scottatura (f.) *(skoht-tah-TOO-rah)* burn, sunburn

stracotto *(strah-KOH-toh)* overdone (of pasta)

scrittura (f.) *(skreet-TOO-rah)* writing

scrivere *(SKREE-veh-reh)* to write

scultura (f.) *(skool-TOO-rah)* sculpture

scuola (f.) *(SKWOH-lah)* school

scuro *(SKOO-roh)* dark

scusare *(skoo-ZAH-reh)* to excuse, to forgive

scusi! *(SKOO-zee!)* sorry!

scusarsi (refl.) *(skoo-ZAHR-see)* to apologize

se *(seh)* if

seccare *(sehk-KAH-reh)* to dry, to annoy, to bother

non mi seccare! *(nohn mee . . . !)* don't bother me!

secco *(SEHK-koh)* dry; skinny, thin

secolo (m.) *(SEH-koh-loh)* century

secondo (m.) *(seh-KOHN-doh)* second

secondo (prep.) according to

sedere *(seh-DEH-reh)* to sit down

sedia (f.) *(SEH-dyah)* chair

seggiola (f.) *(sehd-JOH-lah)* chair

segnale (m.) *(seh-NYAH-leh)* signal, sign

segnare *(seh-NYAH-reh)* to mark, to score

segno (m.) *(SEH-nyoh)* sign, mark

seguire *(seh-GWEE-reh)* to follow

semaforo (m.) *(seh-MAH-foh-roh)* traffic light

semplice *(SEHM-plee-cheh)* simple

sempre *(SEHM-preh)* always

senso (m.) *(SEHN-soh)* sense, meaning

sentire *(sehn-TEE-reh)* to hear, to feel

senza *(SEHN-tsah)* without

sera (f.); serata (f.) *(SEH-rah; seh-RAH-tah)* evening

serio *(SEH-ryoh)* serious

serratura (f.) *(sehr-rah-TOO-rah)* lock

servire *(sehr-VEE-reh)* to serve

servizio (m.) *(sehr-VEE-tsyoh)* service

seta (f.) *(SEH-tah)* silk

sete (f.) *(SEH-teh)* thirst

settentrione (m.) *(seht-tehn-TRYOH-neh)* north

settimana (f.) *(seht-tee-MAH-nah)* week

sezione (f.) *(seh-TSYOH-neh)* section, department

sfortuna (f.) *(sfohr-TOO-nah)* bad luck

sforzo (m.) *(SFOHR-tsoh)* effort

sguardo (m.) *(SGWAHR-doh)* look, glance

sì *(see)* yes

sicuro *(see-KOO-roh)* sure, certain

siesta (f.) *(SYEH-stah)* or **sonnellino (m.)** *(sohn-nehl-LEE-noh)* nap

significare *(see-nyee-fee-KAH-reh)* to mean

signora (f.) *(see-NYOH-rah)* lady, woman, madam

signore (m.) *(see-NYOH-reh)* gentleman, man, sir

signorina (f.) *(see-nyoh-REE-nah)* young lady, miss

silenzio (m.) *(see-LEHN-tsyoh)* silence

simile *(SEE-mee-leh)* like, similar, alike

simpatico *(seem-PAH-tee-koh)* likeable, pleasant

sindaco (m.) *(SEEN-dah-koh)* mayor

sinfonia (f.) *(seen-foh-NEE-ah)* symphony

sinistra (f.) *(see-NEE-strah)* left

sistema (m.) *(see-STEH-mah)* system

situazione (f.) *(see-twah-TSYOH-neh)* situation

slacciare *(zlaht-CHAH-reh)* to undo, to untie, to unbutton

slip (m.) *(zleep)* bathing suit, briefs

smalto (m.) *(ZMAHL-toh)* enamel, nail polish

smarrire *(zmahr-REE-reh)* to lose

smettere *(ZMEHT-teh-reh)* to stop

smoking (m.) *(ZMOH-keen)* tuxedo

snello *(ZNEHL-loh)* slim, slender

soccorso (m.) *(sohk-KOHR-soh)* help, aid
   pronto soccorso *(PROHN-toh . . .)* first aid

società (f.) *(soh-cheh-TAH)* society, company

soddisfare *(sohd-dee-SFAH-reh)* to satisfy, to please

sodo *(SOH-doh)* firm, hard

soffitto (m.) *(sohf-FEET-toh)* ceiling

soffrire *(sohf-FREE-reh)* to suffer

soggiorno (m.) *(sohd-JOHR-noh)* stay
   azienda di soggiorno (f.) *(ah-DZYEHN-dah dee . . .)* local tourist office

sogno (m.) *(SOH-nyoh)* dream

solaio (m.) *(soh-LAH-yoh)* attic

soldi (m.pl.) *(SOHL-dee)* money

sole (m.) *(SOH-leh)* sun

solito *(SOH-lee-toh)* usual, customary
   di solito *(dee . . .)* usually

solo; solamente; soltanto *(SOH-loh; soh-lah-MEHN-teh; sohl-TAHN-toh)* only (adv.)
   solo alone

somma (f.) *(SOHM-mah)* sum, addition

sonno (m.) *(SOHN-noh)* sleep

sopra *(SOH-prah)* on, upon, above

soprabito (m.) *(soh-PRAH-bee-toh)* overcoat

soprattutto *(soh-praht-TOOT-toh)* above all

sorella (f.) *(soh-REHL-lah)* sister

sorgere *(SOHR-jeh-reh)* to rise, to stand

sorpassare *(sohr-pahs-SAH-reh)* to go beyond, to exceed

sorridere *(sohr-REE-deh-reh)* to smile

sosta (f.) *(SOH-stah)* stop
   divieto di sosta *(dee-VYEH-toh dee . . .)* no parking

sottile *(soht-TEE-leh)* thin

sotto *(SOHT-toh)* under, below

sovraffollato *(soh-vrahf-fohl-LAH-toh)* crowded, packed

spalla (f.) *(SPAHL-lah)* shoulder

spaventare *(spah-vehn-TAH-reh)* to frighten, to scare

spazzatura (f.) *(spaht-tsah-TOO-rah)* garbage

spazzola (f.) *(SPAHT-tsoh-lah)* brush

specchio (m.) *(SPEHK-kyoh)* mirror

speciale *(speh-CHAH-leh)* special

specialità (m.) *(speh-chah-lee-TAH)* specialty

specie (f.) *(SPEH-cheh)* kind, sort

spedire *(speh-DEE-reh)* to send

spegnere *(SPEH-nyeh-reh)* to extinguish, to put out, to switch off

spendere *(SPEHN-deh-reh)* to spend

spesa (f.) *(SPEH-zah)* expense, shopping

spettatore (m.) *(speh-tah-TOH-reh)* spectator

spezie (f.pl.) *(SPEH-tsyeh)* spices

spiccioli (m.pl.) *(SPEET-choh-lee)* small change (money)

spiegare *(spyeh-GAH-reh)* to explain

spilla (f.) *(SPEEL-lah)* pin

spina (f.) *(SPEE-nah)* plug
spina intermedia *(. . . een-tehr-MEH-dyah)* adapter

spingere *(SPEEN-jeh-reh)* to push

splendido *(SPLEHN-dee-doh)* splendid, wonderful

spogliarsi (refl.) *(spoh-LYAHR-see)* to get undressed

sporco *(SPOHR-koh)* dirty

sporgersi (refl.) *(SPOHR-jehr-see)* to lean out of

sportello (m.) *(spohr-TEHL-loh)* teller (bank)

sposa (f.) *(SPOH-zah)* bride

sposarsi (refl.) *(spoh-ZAHR-see)* to get married

sposo (m.) *(SPOH-zoh)* bridegroom

sprecare *(spreh-KAH-reh)* to waste

spuntino (m.) *(spoon-TEE-noh)* snack

squadra (f.) *(SKWAH-drah)* team

stadio (m.) *(STAH-dyoh)* stadium

stagione (f.) *(stah-JOH-neh)* season

stamattina (f.) *(stah-maht-TEE-nah)* this morning

stanco *(STAHN-koh)* tired

stanotte (f.) *(stah-NOHT-teh)* tonight

stanza (f.) *(STAHN-tsah)* room

stare *(STAH-reh)* to stay, to remain, to be (health)

stasera (f.) *(stah-SEH-rah)* this evening

stato (m.) *(STAH-toh)* state, condition

statua (f.) *(STAH-twah)* statue

stazione (f.) *(stah-TSYOH-neh)* station

stella (f.) *(STEHL-lah)* star

stesso *(STEHS-soh)* same, self

stile (m.) *(STEE-leh)* style

stirare *(stee-RAH-reh)* to iron

stivale (m.) *(stee-VAH-leh)* boot

stoffa (f.) *(STOHF-fah)* fabric, material

stomaco (m.) *(STOH-mah-koh)* stomach

storia (f.) *(STOH-ryah)* history, story

storto *(STOHR-toh)* crooked

strada (f.) *(STRAH-dah)* road, street, way

strano *(STRAH-noh)* strange

strappare *(strahp-PAH-reh)* to tear up

stringere *(STREEN-jeh-reh)* to tighten, to fasten

studente (m.); studentessa (f.) *(stoo-DEHN-teh; stoo-dehn-TEHS-sah)* student

studiare *(stoo-DYAH-reh)* to study

su *(soo)* on, upon, over, about

subacqueo *(soo-BAHK-kweh-oh)* underwater

subito *(SOO-bee-toh)* at once, immediately

succedere *(soot-CHEH-deh-reh)* to succeed, to happen

successo (m.) *(soot-CHEHS-soh)* success

succo (m.) *(SOOK-koh)* juice

sud (m.) *(sood)* south

sufficiente *(soof-fee-CHEHN-teh)* sufficient

suggestivo *(sood-jeh-STEE-voh)* impressive, evocative

superbo *(soo-PEHR-boh)* haughty, superb, excellent

superiore *(soo-peh-RYOH-reh)* superior

supermercato (m.) *(soo-pehr-mehr-KAH-toh)* supermarket

supporre *(soop-POHR-reh)* to assume, to suppose

surgelato *(soor-jeh-LAH-toh)* frozen (food)

sveglia (f.) *(ZVEH-lyah)* alarm clock

svegliarsi (refl.) *(zveh-LYAHR-see)* to wake up

svelto *(ZVEHL-toh)* quick

svoltare *(zvohl-TAH-reh)* to turn

svoltare a destra *(. . . ah DEH-strah)* to turn right

T

tabaccheria (f.) *(tah-bahk-keh-REE-ah)* tobacco shop

taglia (f.) *(TAH-lyah)* size

tagliare *(tah-LYAH-reh)* to cut

tagliatelle (f.pl.) *(tah-lyah-TEHL-leh)* flat noodles

taglio (m.) *(TAH-lyoh)* cutting, cut

tallone (m.) *(tahl-LOH-neh)* heel

talvolta *(tahl-VOHL-tah)* sometimes

tamponare *(tahm-poh-NAH-reh)* to collide (car)

tanto *(TAHN-toh)* so, so much

tanti *(TAHN-tee)* so many

tappeto (m.) *(tahp-PEH-toh)* carpet

tappo (m.) *(TAHP-poh)* cork

tardi *(TAHR-dee)* late
  a più tardi *(ah pyoo . . .)* see you later

targa (f.) *(TAHR-gah)* license plate

tariffa (f.) *(tah-REEF-fah)* rate

tartina (f.) *(tahr-TEE-nah)* small sandwich

tartufo (m.) *(tahr-TOO-foh)* truffle

tasca (f.) *(TAH-skah)* pocket

tassa (f.) *(TAHS-sah)* tax

tassista (m.) *(tahs-SEE-stah)* taxi driver

taverna (f.) *(tah-VEHR-nah)* inn

tavola(-o) (f./m.) *(TAH-voh-lah) (-loh)* table
  tavola calda/fredda *(. . . KAHL-dah/FREHD-dah)* snack bar

taxi (m.) *(TAHK-see)* taxi, cab

tazza (f.) *(TAHT-tsah)* cup

tazzina (f.) *(taht-TSEE-nah)* demitasse, small cup

tè (m.) *(teh)* tea

teatro (m.) *(teh-AH-troh)* theater

tela (f.) *(TEH-lah)* cloth

telefonare *(teh-leh-foh-NAH-reh)* to telephone

telefonico (adj.) *(teh-leh-FOH-nee-koh)* telephone
 cabina telefonica *(kah-BEE-nah . . .)* telephone booth
 elenco telefonico (m.) *(eh-LEHN-koh . . .)* telephone book

telefono (m.) *(teh-LEH-foh-noh)* telephone

telegramma (m.) *(teh-leh-GRAHM-mah)* telegram

televisione (f.) *(teh-leh-vee-ZYOH-neh)* television

televisore (m.) *(teh-leh-vee-ZOH-reh)* television set

temere *(teh-MEH-reh)* to fear

temperatura (f.) *(tehm-peh-rah-TOO-rah)* temperature

tempesta (f.) *(tehm-PEH-stah)* tempest, storm

tempo (m.) *(TEHM-poh)* time, weather

tenere *(teh-NEH-reh)* to keep, to hold

tennis (m.) *(TEHN-nees)* tennis

terme (f.pl.) *(TEHR-meh)* thermal baths

terminare *(tehr-mee-NAH-reh)* to end, to finish

termometro (m.) *(tehr-MOH-meh-troh)* thermometer

termosifone (m.) *(tehr-moh-see-FOH-neh)* radiator

terra (f.) *(TEHR-rah)* earth, soil, ground

terrazza(-o) (f./m.) *(tehr-RAHT-tsah)(-tsoh)* terrace

terreno (m.) *(tehr-REH-noh)* ground

terribile *(tehr-REE-bee-leh)* terrible

teso *(TEH-zoh)* tight

tesoro (m.) *(teh-ZOH-roh)* treasure

tesoro! darling! honey!

tessera (f.) *(TEHS-seh-rah)* card (membership)

tessuto (m.) *(tehs-SOO-toh)* fabric, material

testa (f.) *(TEH-stah)* head

testardo *(teh-STAHR-doh)* stubborn

tetto (m.) *(TEHT-toh)* roof

timbro (m.) *(TEEM-broh)* stamp

tinello (m.) *(tee-NEHL-loh)* dining room (informal)

tinta (f.) *(TEEN-tah)* dye, color

tintarella (f.) *(teen-tah-REHL-lah)* suntan

tintoria (f.) *(teen-toh-REE-ah)* dry cleaner

tipico *(TEE-pee-koh)* typical

tipo (m.) *(TEE-poh)* type, guy
 che bel tipo! *(keh behl . . . !)* what a nice guy!

tirare *(tee-RAH-reh)* to pull, to draw

titolo (m.) *(TEE-toh-loh)* title

toccare *(tohk-KAH-reh)* to touch

togliere *(TOH-lyeh-reh)* to take away, to take off

toilette (f.) *(twah-LEHT)* toilet, bathroom, lavatory

tondo *(TOHN-doh)* round

tonno (m.) *(TOHN-noh)* tunafish

tornare *(tohr-NAH-reh)* to return

torre (f.) *(TOHR-reh)* tower

torta (f.) *(TOHR-tah)* cake

tossire *(tohs-SEE-reh)* to cough

totale *(toh-TAH-leh)* total

tovaglia (f.) *(toh-VAH-lyah)* tablecloth

tovagliolo (m.) *(toh-vah-LYOH-loh)* napkin

tradurre *(trah-DOOR-reh)* to translate

traffico (m.) *(TRAHF-fee-koh)* traffic

traghetto (m.) *(trah-GEHT-toh)* ferryboat

tram (m.) *(trahm)* streetcar

tramezzino (m.) *(trah-mehd-DZEE-noh)* sandwich

tranquillo *(trahn-KWEEL-loh)* quiet, calm

traslocare *(trah-zloh-KAH-reh)* to move

trasmissione (f.) *(trah-zmees-SYOH-neh)* transmission, program, broadcast

trasparente *(trah-spah-REHN-teh)* transparent

trasportare *(trah-spohr-TAH-reh)* to carry, to convey

trattamento (m.) *(traht-tah-MEHN-toh)* treatment, service

trattoria (f.) *(traht-toh-REE-ah)* restaurant

traversa (f.) *(trah-VEHR-sah)* crossroad

treno (m.) *(TREH-noh)* train

tribunale (m.) *(tree-boo-NAH-leh)* court

triste *(TREE-steh)* sad

tristezza (f.) *(tree-STEHT-tsah)* sadness

troppo *(TROH-poh)* too much

troppi *(TROHP-pee)* too many

trovare *(troh-VAH-reh)* to find

trucco (m.) *(TROOK-koh)* makeup

tuo *(TOO-oh)* your, yours

tuono (m.) *(TWOH-noh)* thunder

turismo (m.) *(too-REE-smoh)* tourism

turista (m./f.) *(too-REE-stah)* tourist

turistico *(too-REE-stee-koh)* tourist, touristic

turno (m.) *(TOOR-noh)* turn

tutto *(TOOT-toh)* all, every, everything

U

ubbidire *(oob-bee-DEE-reh)* to obey

ubriacarsi (refl.) *(oo-bryah-KAHR-see)* to get drunk

ubriaco *(oo-bree-AH-koh)* drunk

uccello (m.) *(oot-CHEHL-loh)* bird

ufficio (m.) *(oof-FEE-choh)* office

ufficio cambio *(. . . KAHM-byoh)* currency exchange office

ultimo *(OOL-tee-moh)* last, latest

umido *(OO-mee-doh)* damp, humid

umore (m.) *(oo-MOH-reh)* humor, mood

unghia (f.) *(OON-gyah)* nail (finger-/toe-)

unico *(OO-nee-koh)* unique, only

università (f.) *(oo-nee-vehr-see-TAH)* university

uno *(OO-noh)* one, a, an

uomo (m.) *(WOH-moh)* man

uomini (m.pl.) *(WOH-mee-nee)* men

uovo (m.) *(WOH-voh)* egg

uova (f.pl.) *(WOH-vah)* eggs

urbano *(oor-BAH-noh)* city, local

urlare *(oor-LAH-reh)* to shout, to yell

usare *(oo-ZAH-reh)* to use

uscio (m.) *(OO-shoh)* door

uscire *(oo-SHEE-reh)* to go out

uscita (f.) *(oo-SHEE-tah)* exit, way out

uso (m.) *(OO-zoh)* use

utensile (m.) *(oo-TEHN-see-leh)* tool

utile *(OO-tee-leh)* useful, helpful

uva (f.) *(OO-vah)* grapes

V

vacanza (f.) *(vah-KAHN-tsah)* holiday

vaglia (m.) *(VAH-lyah)* money order

vagone (m.) *(vah-GOH-neh)* car (train)

vagone letto *(. . . LEHT-toh)* sleeping car

valere *(vah-LEH-reh)* to be worth

valido *(VAH-lee-doh)* valid, worth

valigia (f.) *(vah-LEE-jah)* suitcase

valle (f.) *(VAHL-leh)* valley

valore (m.) *(vah-LOH-reh)* value

valuta (f.) *(vah-LOO-tah)* currency, money

vantaggio (m.) *(vahn-TAHD-joh)* advantage, profit

vaporetto (m.) *(vah-poh-REHT-toh)* steamboat/ferry

varietà (m.) *(vah-ryeh-TAH)* variety; music hall

vario *(VAH-ryoh)* various, different

vaso (m.) *(VAH-zoh)* vase

vasto *(VAH-stoh)* vast, wide

vecchio *(VEHK-kyoh)* old, ancient

vedere *(veh-DEH-reh)* to see

veduto, visto *(veh-DOO-toh, VEE-stoh)* seen

veduta (f.) *(veh-DOO-tah)* view

vegetable (m.) *(veh-jeh-TAH-leh)* vegetable

vela (f.) *(VEH-lah)* sail

veleno (m.) *(veh-LEH-noh)* poison

veloce *(veh-LOH-cheh)* quick, fast

velocità (f.) *(veh-loh-chee-TAH)* speed

limite di velocità (m.) *(LEE-mee-teh dee . . .)* speed limit

vendere *(VEHN-deh-reh)* to sell

vendita (f.) *(VEHN-dee-tah)* sale

venditore (m.) *(vehn-dee-TOH-reh)* seller, vendor

venire *(veh-NEE-reh)* to come

ventilatore (m.) *(vehn-tee-lah-TOH-reh)* fan

vento (m.) *(VEHN-toh)* wind

veramente *(veh-rah-MEHN-teh)* really, truly

verde *(VEHR-deh)* green

verdura (f.) *(vehr-DOO-rah)* vegetables

vergogna (f.) *(vehr-GOH-nyah)* shame

verità (f.) *(veh-ree-TAH)* truth

vernice (f.) *(vehr-NEE-cheh)* paint/varnish

vero *(VEH-roh)* true, real

versare *(vehr-SAH-reh)* to deposit, to pour, to spill

verso *(VEHR-soh)* toward

veste (f.) *(VEH-steh)* dress, clothes, garments

vestire *(veh-STEE-reh)* to dress, to wear

vestito (m.) *(veh-STEE-toh)* dress, outfit

vetrata (f.) *(veh-TRAH-tah)* glass window

vetrina (f.) *(veh-TREE-nah)* window (shop), showcase

vetro (m.) *(VEH-troh)* glass

via (f.) *(VEE-ah)* street, way, path

viaggiare *(vyahd-JAH-reh)* to travel

viaggio (m.) *(VYAHD-joh)* travel, journey

vicino *(vee-CHEE-noh)* near, close

vicolo (m.) *(VEE-koh-loh)* alley, lane

vietare *(vyeh-TAH-reh)* to forbid
vietato *(vyeh-TAH-toh)* forbidden

vigile (m.) *(VEE-jee-leh)* cop
vigile del fuoco *(... dehl FWOH-koh)* firefighter

vigna (f.); vigneto (m.) *(VEE-nyah; vee-NYEH-toh)* vine-yard

villa (f.) *(VEEL-lah)* villa

villaggio (m.) *(veel-LAHD-joh)* village

villeggiatura (f.) *(veel-lehd-jah-TOO-rah)* holiday, vacation

vincere *(VEEN-cheh-reh)* to win
vinto *(VEEN-toh)* won

vino (m.) *(VEE-noh)* wine

visita (f.) *(VEE-zee-tah)* visit
visitare *(vee-zee-TAH-reh)* to visit

viso (m.) *(VEE-zoh)* face

vista (f.) *(VEE-stah)* sight

vita (f.) *(VEE-tah)* life, waist

vitello (m.) *(vee-TEHL-loh)* veal

viva! *(VEE-vah!)* hurrah!

vivere *(VEE-veh-reh)* to live
vissuto *(vees-SOO-toh)* lived

vivo *(VEE-voh)* alive

vocabolario (m.) *(voh-kah-boh-LAH-ryoh)* dictionary

voce (f.) *(VOH-cheh)* voice

voglia (f.) *(VOH-lyah)* wish, desire

volante (m.) *(voh-LAHN-teh)* steering wheel

volare *(voh-LAH-reh)* to fly

volere *(voh-LEH-reh)* to want, to wish, to desire

volo (m.) *(VOH-loh)* flight

volta (f.) *(VOHL-tah)* time
due volte *(DOO-eh VOHL-teh)* twice

voltare *(vohl-TAH-reh)* to turn

vuoto *(VWOH-toh)* empty

W

water-closet (m.) *(WOH-tah CLOH-zeht)* toilet, lavatory

Y

yogurt (m.) *(YOH-goort)* yogurt

Z

zabaglione (m.) *(dzah-bah-LYOH-neh)* egg cream dessert

zaino (m.) *(DZAH-ee-noh)* backpack

zero (m.) *(DZEH-roh)* zero

zia (f.) *(TSEE-ah)* aunt

zio (m.) *(TSEE-oh)* uncle

zitto *(TSEET-toh)* silent

zolletta (f.) *(dzohl-LEHT-tah)* lump (sugar)

zona (f.) *(DZOH-nah)* zone

zoo (m.) *(DZOH-oh)* zoo

zucchero (m.) *(TSOOK-keh-roh)* sugar

zuppa (f.) *(TSOOP-pah)* soup